Industrial Societies

Industrial Societies

Crisis and Division in Western Capitalism and State Socialism

Edited by

Richard Scase

London
UNWIN HYMAN
Boston   Sydney   Wellington

Published by the Academic Division of
Unwin Hyman Ltd
15/17 Broadwick Street, London W1V 1FP, UK

Unwin Hyman Inc.,
8 Winchester Place, Winchester, Mass. 01890, USA

Allen & Unwin (Australia) Ltd,
8 Napier Street, North Sydney, NSW 2060, Australia

Allen & Unwin (New Zealand) Ltd in association with
the Port Nicholson Press Ltd,
Compusales Building, 75 Ghuznee Street, Wellington 1, New Zealand

First published in 1989

British Library Cataloguing in Publication Data

Industrial societies: crisis and division in Western capitalism and state
socialism.
  1. Industrial society
  I. Scase, Richard
  303.4

  ISBN 0-04-301302-3
  ISBN 0-04-301303-1 pbk

Library of Congress Cataloging in Publication Data

 Industrial societies: crisis and division in Western capitalism and state
socialism/edited by Richard Scase.
    p.   cm.
  Includes index.
  ISBN 0-04-301302-3 (alk. paper). —
  ISBN 0-04-301303-1 (pbk.: alk. paper)
    1. Capitalism. 2. Socialism. 3. Business cycles. 4. Industry-Social
aspects. 5. Social conflict. I. Scase, Richard.
  HB501.I579   1989
  335—dc19   88-31368 CIP

Typeset in 10/11½ point Palatino by Fotographics (Bedford) Ltd
and printed in Great Britain by Billing & Sons, London and Worcester

Contents

Notes on Contributors

Sheila Allen is Professor of Sociology, University of Bradford. She has researched and published extensively in the areas of gender, race and ethnic relations, and work and employment. She is currently researching into women in business enterprise.

Frank Bechhofer is Professor of Social Research and Director of the Research Centre for Social Sciences at Edinburgh University. He has a long-standing interest in the *petite bourgeoisie* and the self-employed. His current research is as part of the Edinburgh team working on the ESRC Social Change and Economic Life initiative. He has published extensively in the fields of class and stratification, Scottish society, social movements, and research methods and methodology. Publications include (with J. H. Goldthorpe *et al.*) *The Affluent Worker* (1969) and *The Petite Bourgeoisie* (1981).

Howard Davis is Senior Lecturer in Sociology at the University of Kent at Canterbury. His publications include *Beyond Class Images* (1980) and, with Richard Scase, *Western Capitalism and State Socialism* (1985). He is also the editor of *Ethics and Defence* (1986). He has a long-standing association with the Glasgow University Media Group and his current research is on changes in the media and the public sphere in both Western and Eastern European countries.

Brian Elliott is currently an Associate Professor in the Department of Sociology at the University of British Columbia, Canada. He was educated at Edinburgh University, where he was a senior lecturer until 1987. His research includes work on small shopkeepers, middle-class movements and the rise of the New Right in Britain and Canada. He has co-edited (with Frank Bechhofer) *The Petite Bourgeoisie: Comparative Studies of the Uneasy Stratum* (1981) and written numerous articles.

John Gardner, until his death, was a Senior Lecturer in Government at the University of Manchester. He wrote numerous articles on Chinese politics and is author of *Chinese Politics and the Succession to Mao* (1982). He died in May 1988 while this book was in production.

Krishan Kumar is Professor of Social Thought at the University of Kent at Canterbury. Has been a BBC talks producer, a Visiting Fellow at Harvard University, and a Visiting Professor of Sociology at the

University of Colorado at Boulder. He is author of *Prophecy and Progress: The Sociology of Industrial and Post-Industrial Society* (1978) and *Utopia and Anti-Utopia in Modern Times* (1987); and editor of *Revolution: The Theory and Practice of a European Idea* (1971) and (with A. Ellis) *Dilemmas of Liberal Democracies* (1983).

David Lane is Professor of Sociology at the University of Birmingham. He studied at Birmingham and Oxford Universities and has taught at the Universities of Essex and Cambridge. He is the author of many books on the Soviet Union, Eastern Europe, and socialism, including *State and Politics in the USSR* (1985), *Soviet Economy and Society* (1985), and *Soviet Labour and the Ethic of Communism* (1987); and editor of *Elites and Political Power in the USSR* (1988).

David McCrone is Senior Lecturer in Sociology at Edinburgh. He has carried out research on landlords, middle-class movements, and the social structure of modern Scotland. He is a co-director of the Social Change and Economic Life initiative on Kirkcaldy. His publications include (with Brian Elliott) *The City: Patterns of Domination and Conflict* (1982) and he is co-editor of the *Scottish Government Yearbook*.

Robert Moore is Professor of Sociology in the University of Aberdeen. He has written widely in the fields of race relations and the sociology of religion. His more recent work includes *The Social Impact of Oil* (1982) and a theoretical Afterword to Lewis *et al.*, *Women, Work and Family in the British, Canadian and Norwegian Offshore Oilfields* (1988). He is currently writing an undergraduate introduction into the problem of racism in Britain.

R. E. Pahl is part-time Research Professor in Sociology at the University of Kent at Canterbury and a Visiting Professor at the University of Essex. His most recent publications include *Divisions of Labour* (1984) and an edited volume *On Work* (1988). In 1989 he completed ten years' work as a sociologist on the University Grants Committee's Social Studies Sub-Committee.

Graeme Salaman is Senior Lecturer in Sociology at the Open University, responsible for courses in the sociology of work and organizations. He is currently researching the impact of mechanized coal-cutting systems in the Indian coal industry and the application of computers to organizational structure through computer-integrated manufacture. His recent publications include (with Craig Littler) *Class at Work* (1984) and *Working* (1986).

Richard Scase is Professor of Sociology at the University of Kent at Canterbury. He is the author of *Social Democracy in Capitalist Society* (1977) and co-author (with Robert Goffee) of *The Entrepreneurial Middle Class* (1982), *Women in Charge* (1985), *The Real World of the*

Small Business Owner (1987), and *Reluctant Managers* (1989); and (with Howard Davis) of *Western Capitalism and State Socialism* (1985). He has edited four volumes and written numerous papers for academic and non-academic books and journals.

Introduction

This book is intended as a sequel to *Industrial Society: Class, Cleavage and Control* which I edited for the British Sociological Association in 1977. The earlier volume, prepared from papers presented at the Association's annual conference attempted to adopt a comparative perspective and, within this, to focus upon some of the more general, large-scale processes of social change. Accordingly, it included discussions of broader developments as these were occurring within both Western capitalist and East European state socialist countries. In that book, issues to do with the nature of *industrialism, convergence*, and *mode of production*, were central to many of the arguments. Indeed, the nature of industrialism was of particular interest to sociologists in the early 1970s, as theoretical discussions and more empirically grounded analyses attempted to determine the extent to which *industrial society* (or societies) *per se*, possessed structural and ideological features which transcended nationally specific historical, cultural and political differences (Kumar, 1978). The conclusions of many of these debates often reflected various ideological perspectives, but were often described during the decade as simply 'Marxist' or 'non-Marxist'.[1] Those of the former often rejected theories of *industrialism* on the grounds that these failed to recognize the fundamental importance of *mode of production* and that although there may be close similarities within the structural and institutional features of East European state socialist and Western capitalist countries, these had little to do with a 'logic of industrialism'. Any common features which they shared were to do either with the 'underdeveloped' nature of state socialism or with the emergence of state capitalism in Eastern Europe (Cliff, 1974). Accordingly, it would only be with the longer-term development of distinctively non-capitalist forms of production in Eastern Europe that such features as the 'forced' or detailed division of labour and hierarchical systems of management and supervisory control would be abolished. Thus, in the view of many writers, notions of convergent tendencies between these and Western capitalist countries were untenable (Sweezy and Betterheim, 1971; Mandel, 1974).

1

Many such claims were rejected by 'non-Marxists' writing, as they were, in the economic conditions of the 1960s and the early 1970s when economic growth in Western capitalist countries was producing higher living standards and improved levels of social welfare. For them, the very notion of *capitalism* was seen to be of questionable utility because of the ways in which state-financed welfare systems and the intervention of national states in market-based economies were creating 'mixed' social systems which were allegedly very different from their predecessors of before the Second World War (Bell, 1974). If, however, such structural changes were often attributed to the strength of labour movements, the popularity of social democratic ideals and the increasing influence of political regimes in market economies, the driving forces of socioeconomic change were usually seen to be the effects of the so-called scientific–technological revolution. As such, technological change was viewed as the primary motor of social development and the chief determinant of the major structural features of society, irrespective of whether they were state socialist or capitalist (Galbraith, 1968). For some writers there was often the assumption that processes of industrialization were leading to a 'convergent' *industrial society* whose characteristics transcended those which, in one way or another, could be attributed to allegedly different modes of production (Kerr *et al.*, 1973). As such, any differences between Western capitalist and East European state socialist countries were considered to be of relatively minor importance compared with those associated with levels of industrial and economic development. Accordingly, the designation of societies as 'non-industrial', 'industrial' and, often, 'post-industrial' was seen as more helpful for understanding and describing different social structures (Bell, 1974).[2]

Indeed, for those writing in the early 1970s, it was the emergence of an alleged 'post-industrialism' in the more advanced Western societies which was the major focus of attention (Kumar, 1987). It was argued that technological and scientific changes were abolishing the need for industrial and manufacturing occupations and that with the growth of 'science-' or 'knowledge-based' work processes, high-wage 'service' economies were emerging with a growing preponderance of expert, technical and professional jobs (Touraine, 1971; Bell, 1974). From this, it was suggested that these societies were becoming more meritocratic and achievement-oriented and, as such, 'qualifications' rather than gender, ethnic or class-related attributes were more important determinants of personal life chances. Thus, for many writers, social divisions and

2

class-derived ideologies and antagonisms – associated as these were with the inherent forces of capitalism – were being superseded by more 'individualistic' ideologies (Kerr *et al.*, 1973). Accordingly, within 'post-industrial' society any apparent social divisions were associated with occupational and professional differences rather than with class-related conflicts stemming from the social relations of production (Bell, 1974). It was, then, hardly surprising that writers argued the case for cross-societal convergence. As in Western societies, technological change in East European countries would similarly bring about forms of 'post-industrialism' based upon industrial–scientific 'techno-structures' and predominant value systems which emphasized 'individualism' and rational efficiency (Galbraith, 1968).[3]

These, then, were some of the major concerns of those who, writing in the 1960s and early 1970s, were interested in the direction of social change. As such, they were *historical* in their approaches – in order to identify patterns and trends – and *comparative* – in order to illustrate cross-national similarities and differences. It was for these reasons they were interested in the industrialization process, in terms of its impact *upon* and development *within* East European state socialist and Western capitalist societies. Indeed, the debates continue as witnessed in contemporary disputes about the *nature* of East European countries. Do they constitute a distinctive mode of production or are they little more than differing forms of *either* capitalist *or* industrial society (Davis and Scase, 1985)?

But much has changed since the mid-1970s when *Industrial Society* was published. Although many of the issues in comparative sociology remain as pertinent today as then, discussions of the nature of industrialism and theories of convergence are less pronounced. In the study of Western and East European countries, *less* attention is now given to them as expressions of industrialism and, as a result, they are more likely to be considered by reference to their own particular socio-political processes. Indeed, many of the socioeconomic changes which are occurring within both types of society are, perhaps, highlighting their differences. If, in the 1960s, economic growth and technological change within both systems seemed to be producing similarities in social structure, the tendencies of *crises* that have appeared in the 1980s illustrate their contrasts. Indeed, the very nature of these differs between them.

While in state socialist countries the nature of crises are *political*, in Western capitalist societies they are usually *economic* in their

3

origins.[4] By *crises* is meant tendencies within a mode of production which can challenge the very nature of its inherent dynamic. In Western countries, economic crises have become more pronounced as manifested in over-production, large-scale de-industrialization and processes of economic rationalization through corporate mergers and take-overs (Offe, 1985). Declining profit margins in different economic sectors have reinforced these trends and, as a result, major programmes of structural change have brought about increases in levels of unemployment in almost all of the Western capitalist countries during the 1980s (Merritt, 1982; Clegg *et al.*, 1986). Without profits, the capitalist dynamic ceases to function because it is only through returns on capital that there are incentives for investment in the productive process. As such, the production of goods and services and, hence, economic growth is almost entirely dependent upon this. If this ceases to function – at least to the extent whereby capitalism as a mode of production is able to reproduce itself – the whole system may be viewed as in crisis. Accordingly, there will be ramifications for most other aspects of social structure, including political institutions and national states. Indeed, the strategies which the latter have formulated for the purposes of coping with the causes and consequences of crises are very different to those utilized during the earlier postwar decades (Brittan, 1977; Crozier, 1979; Birch, 1984).

In state socialist countries, by contrast, the production of goods and services according to *need* rather than profits means that, potentially, such crises can be avoided. In contemporary East European countries *need* – in terms of the *planned* production of goods and services for distribution and consumption – is determined by enterprise directors, party officials and technocrats within the contexts of various interrelated bureaucratic systems. As a result, definitions of social and economic need and the formulation of strategies for the purposes of satisfying these, are derived largely from bargaining processes between different 'elite' groups (Konrad and Szelenyi, 1979). Rarely will they be unanimous in their opinions as to what should constitute national priorities for production and consumption, with the effect that planning goals will be pursued on the basis of sectional and vested interests and legitimized by appeals to 'the common good' and to 'socialism'.[5] At the same time, such bargaining is largely secretive and non-accountable to broader populations. Thus, in essence, and in sharp contrast to Western capitalism, the production, distribution and consumption of goods and services are shaped by *political* rather than *economic* or profit-making criteria. Accordingly, crises in East European countries tend to be political in their origins if only because the supply of goods and services for meeting needs are largely shaped by politically determined processes (Hirszowicz, 1980). The fact that this often leads to 'inefficiencies', both in terms of the *over-* as well as the *under* production of many goods and services is the source of social tension, political conflict and, occasionally, broader social protests (Harman, 1983). These tend to range from unrest over food shortages and price rises to demands for the political decision-making process to be made more 'open' and publicly accountable; in other words, that the determination of needs should be removed from the secretive and 'monopoly' control of party and state officials and subjected to wider debate (Ascherson, 1981).[6]

Such crises have affected the relationships of East European societies with Western capitalist countries. As a result of 'inefficiencies' within their planning processes, many of them have incurred large foreign debts, compelling them to purchase essential goods from abroad and, perhaps most importantly, to imitate or adopt various capitalist methods of economic production (Wallerstein, 1979). As a result, attempts to improve economic efficiency have often led to the introduction of forms of 'market-socialism'. Criteria of efficiency, measured according to whether or not politically determined plans can be achieved, have been supplemented with capitalist notions of 'cost-effectiveness', 'competitiveness' and 'returns on capital employed'. Accordingly, unemployment is now a feature in some East European countries as labour needs become determined according to economic rather than social or political criteria. At the same time, the adoption of capitalist systems of management have reinforced the development of productive processes characterized by close supervision, measured performance, and piece-rate systems. As such, labour is regarded as a cost of production which must be calculated according to traditional capitalist criteria (see Chapter 7). Small-scale, privately owned enterprises are also being encouraged such that local entrepreneurship, as in many Western countries, is seen as having important functions in meeting economic demands (Davis, 1987). In agriculture, producers are being allowed to retain a larger proportion of their goods for their own personal consumption and for sale in local markets. If East European countries have always possessed strata of independent producers and retained forms of petty, private property ownership, what is distinctive about recent developments is that instead of these being viewed as legacies of 'inferior', pre-socialist forms of production, they are now officially sanctioned and encouraged (see Chapter 7).

In view of such developments, stemming as they do from planning crises within the political structures of the different East European countries, there has, then, been the adoption of many of the practices which determine the production and sale of goods and services in capitalist countries. But this is not to imply a process of convergence; as we stated earlier, theories of convergence are derived from notions that the industrialization process possesses an inherent logic. By contrast, the adoption of many capitalist methods of economic management is the outcome of decisions taken by élites in order to resolve a variety of economic, social and political problems. As such, the tendencies found within many of the East European countries are leading to the implementation of policies which are bringing about changes in many of the assumptions and principles according to which state socialism is presently organized.[7] In this sense, there is during the closing decades of the twentieth century, a crisis of state socialism which is equal to that of Western capitalism; in both, the processes which shape the nature of their respective productive systems are bringing about fundamental changes. It is the outcome and the expression of these which now attracts the attention of sociologists.

If, in Western capitalism, the effects of economic growth and 'affluence' were previously the major issues for discussion and research, the focus of interest now tends to be upon the outcomes of crisis, recession and economic restructuring for life chances and life-styles among different groups in society (Roberts et al., 1985; Rose, 1988). As in the past, aspects of class remain central to sociological analysis but what is noticeable about many contemporary debates is the increasing attention that is now devoted to issues of social polarization and division. Since the 1970s, economic restructuring and the rationalization of productive processes have tended to reinforce social divisions. If, previously, economic growth *appeared* to be creating a large 'middle mass', consisting of those engaged in lower-grade administrative, routine non-manual, and more highly paid manual occupations, subsequent economic changes have reinforced divisions within the occupational orders of capitalist countries.[8] At the same time, the increasing automation of work processes – both within the office and on the shop-floor – together with the increasing implementation of computer-based technologies, has reduced requirements for the skills of many occupational groups. In many work settings there is now less need for routine white-collar workers and skilled craft employees. Instead, small numbers of managerial, professional and technically qualified workers, through the use of 'new technology' and the adoption of sophisticated management information systems, can now exercise tight supervisory control over lesser skilled operatives (Buchanan and Boddy, 1983; Child, 1985). While the former receive high financial rewards and enjoy various fringe benefits, the latter perform jobs that offer few intrinsic rewards, low pay, and provide little in the form of employment security and promotion prospects. There have, then, been shifts towards greater income and economic inequality during the past decade which have exaggerated class divisions in most Western societies (Top Pay Unit, 1988). If the relative affluence of the earlier postwar decades tended to render less visible, class differences, the altered economic conditions of today have reaffirmed their significance. It is for such reasons that discussions of 'core' or 'primary' sector employees on the one hand and 'periphery' or 'secondary' sector workers on the other have been particularly pronounced in sociological discussions (Gordon *et al.*, 1982; Garnsey *et al.*, 1985). While the former enjoy relatively secure, highly paid jobs, often with good promotion prospects the latter, because of their more dispensable skills, are more likely to experience poor working conditions and to be prone to redundancy and unemployment. Indeed, the latter are likely to be workers whose employment prospects are contingent upon the fluctuating demands of large-scale corporations and their *dependent* subcontractor, small businesses (Scase and Goffee, 1987). However, despite such trends, the level of class awareness and, indeed, conflict remains low. In fact, class-related ideologies seem to have diminished since the early 1970s and 'class' as an element of personal identity is probably less pronounced. It reaffirms the extent to which the institutional and ideological structures of Western society are able to inhibit class conscious-ness under material conditions when, it could be argued, they should be more acute (Newby *et al.*, 1985).

Clearly, a number of factors are pertinent, ranging from the effects of high unemployment and the concomitant weakening of working-class trade-union and political movements, to the growth of the 'New Right' as an ideological and political force (King, 1987). All of these have had their effects but it is important to recognize that the emergence of broader forms of class consciousness have been inhibited by processes of economic restructuring. If, historically, workers have been divided on the basis of skill, craft, occupation and industry – as well as in some capitalist countries according to linguistic and religious factors – economic change has made some of these less relevant. Thus, 'craft' is becoming less salient in some industries because of the de-skilling of many work processes (Braverman, 1974). At the same time, however, *age, gender* and *ethnic* divisions are becoming more pronounced (James, 1975; Allen, 1988). If young people, women and members of ethnic minority groups have traditionally made up substantial groupings of the 'reserve army' of Western capitalism, the restructuring of labour markets has altered this traditional function. They now constitute a relatively permanent supply of cheap, de-skilled labour and are part-and-parcel of the secondary sector of labour markets. Thus, they are attractive to capitalist corporations because they are available for work at lower rates of pay than many other groups of employees.

Of course, workers in competition with each other undermine the basis for collective action and for class-based forms of solidarity (Korpi, 1983). Thus, the polarization of labour markets and the fragmentation of the secondary sector according to age, gender and ethnic groupings have given an added impetus to a variety of sexist and racist ideologies, which by dividing the working class, can do little but serve the longer-term interests of capital. Youth and ethnic minority groupings nurture various subcultures which, although functioning as forces of both conflict and social control, have usually served to defuse potential sources of unrest (Brake, 1985). At the same time, women continue to be perceived as having little more than tangential claims on jobs because of a range of ideological and institutional factors which emphasize their primary role within the family rather than in the 'public' sphere of work and employment (Oakley, 1981). Thus, although age, gender and ethnicity have always been important sources of division in society, what is significant about recent trends is how these have now acquired *added* meanings. If, in the late 1960s in some countries, capitalism seemed to be challenged by well-organized protest movements, this is no longer the case. Economic recession and the associated processes of restructuring have altered the 'needs' of capital and, as an outcome of this, a more fragmented and divided working class has emerged.

It is, then, hardly surprising that labour movements seem much weakened compared with their position little more than a decade ago. Within both the political and industrial spheres, their support among traditional rank-and-file members has declined (M. Davis,

1986; Department of Employment, 1987b). Indeed, trade unions and labour parties in many Western countries no longer possess the legitimacy which they seemed to have enjoyed in the more immediate postwar years (Bassett, 1986). A number of factors would seem to account for this, in addition to those associated with the restructuring of labour markets. The increasing international-ization of capital, the growing dominance of multinational corporations within national economies, and the concomitant overproduction of many manufactured goods in world markets, have led to the decline of traditional industrial sectors in many Western countries. It is within these that trade unionism flourished and, were it not for the increasing unionization of women in some service occupations, the decline in trade-union membership would have been even greater (Hunt, 1982). The general rise in the level of unemployment has reduced the bargaining capacity of trade unionism and weakened its ability to obtain concessions from both public- and private-sector employers. Although there may be differences in unemployment rates within different economic sectors, so that some workers have been able to retain their negotiating strength, high levels of unemployment *in general* sustain an ideological framework which affects workers' perceptions of their bargaining capacity. Further, the weakened position of trade unions in many countries seems to be derived from their incapacity to reflect the interests and aspirations of those who are confronting some of the most acute forms of deprivation, subordination and economic marginalization. The difficulties that unions encounter in organizing part-time employees and those who sell their labour as 'self-employed' workers are well known. Equally, trade unionism has always faced problems in increasing its membership among workers in 'service' or 'personal' sector occupations such as retailing, hotel, catering, and transport and distribution, where there is a predominance of small businesses. Even so, trade unionism continues to appeal primarily to male white workers, such that those who are young, female, or black feel estranged from the dominant ideals of trade unionism and perceive themselves to be marginalized within Western labour movements as a whole.

If, then, the restructuring of capital has had these implications, it has also had similar effects for working-class political parties. With the possible exception of Sweden, their level of support has generally declined (Curran, 1984). Again, this is partly due to the structural changes that have destroyed traditional working-class communities and industrial work settings. If, in the past, these fostered ideals and patterns of solidarity which were eroded during the growth decades of the immediate postwar years (Goldthorpe *et al.*, 1969), economic recession and higher levels of unemployment have reinforced this process. The destruction of working-class support systems, often based upon kin, neighbour-hood and community relationships, have compelled many of those economically marginalized to develop more *individualistic* and familial strategies for coping with deprivation (Pahl, 1984; Harrison, 1985). Often they have become disillusioned with collective forms of protest and have little or no commitment to a more broadly defined working-class movement. Indeed, it is doubtful whether those who are most deprived, either as unemployed or through undertaking various secondary-sector jobs, have ever been little more than highly sceptical about what labour movements can 'deliver'. In view of the structural changes that are occurring, the impotence of labour parties is self-evident. They are generally viewed as ineffective in the face of multi-national capital's ability to switch production from one country to another, to impose labour-saving technological processes and, generally, to pursue various strategies of cost reduction. Instead of a commitment to collective action, therefore, more 'individualistic' ideologies are emerging within the working class to which, as yet, labour parties have been unable to respond in politically effective ways. At best, they recognize the dilemmas and realize they are being forced to develop strategies within very different structural and ideological conditions. As such, they are having to reassess their political objectives in ways which, as far as possible, are compatible with their traditional ideals of social democracy and, indeed, of socialism. How, then, is this to be achieved?

For many of the political parties in Western Europe, it entails the formulation of policies which emphasize the desirability of decentralized, employee-owned, small-scale forms of economic organization (Gorz, 1982). It is now often conceded that the creation of large-scale, state-owned monopoly corporations has achieved little in enhancing the level of employee influence over the production, distribution and consumption of economic resources. Hence, the postwar programmes of nationalization pursued by the different labour parties of Western Europe are seen to have failed to have changed the social relations of capitalism (Clegg *et al.*, 1986). Compared with their privately owned counterparts, they possess very few differences except for the fact that they are *formally* more publicly accountable through various statutory regulations, and that they often have greater access to state funding for modernization schemes. However, in terms of their management systems and patterns of decison making, they imitate the methods and procedures of any large-scale capitalist corporation. Consequently, labour movements in many Western countries are formulating alternative economic strategies which recognize that co-owned ventures, organized and managed on a local or regional basis, can produce more 'socialist' forms of production in ways that are more compatible with worker needs for self-management (Gorz, 1982). Indeed, some developments in new technology are enabling many goods and services to be produced using a division of labour organized upon a territorial rather than a factory basis (Murray, 1983). In Italy, 'industrial districts' provide examples of how forms of subcontracting can be organized according to patterns of trading among small-scale, independent and co-operatively owned producers (Bamford, 1987). Similarly, many of the social democratic ideals underlying the setting up of wage-earner funds in Sweden are related to encouraging worker participation in ownership so that employing organizations are more accountable to their employees on a decentralized basis rather than through forms of state ownership whereby 'public control' is 'removed' from the direct influence of employees (Korpi, 1983; Clegg et al., 1986).[9]

In these ways, the labour and social democratic parties of Western Europe are being forced to develop industrial and political programmes which, in many ways, are more compatible to the changing aspirations of their potential working-class supporters. The creation of state-owned corporations of the sort established during the immediate postwar years are no longer regarded as relevant to the emerging needs of employees during the closing decades of the twentieth century. But, even so, the formulation of these policies is taking place among political parties whose general legitimacy and support is low. Many of their traditional and potential supporters perceive them to have little or no influence, if only because of their inability to safeguard basic workers' rights, as well as their being unable to prevent the erosion of many of the concessions which they obtained from capital in the 1950s and 1960s. In Britain, changes in legislation in such areas as dismissal procedures, health and safety, security of employment, collective bargaining agreements, and industrial relations have severely changed the conditions of work and employment for large sectors of the labour force (Wedderburn, 1985). These have allowed capital to reduce its operating costs by cutting 'overheads' through employing labour on a cheap, often part-time, basis, and by using workers who are generally unprotected by *rights* as these have been achieved by postwar working-class movements (Fevre, 1986).

It is as a result of such tendencies that the role of the state is changing in many Western countries. In the 1970s, the national state was of considerable interest to sociologists if only because of what appeared to be its apparent contradictions (O'Connor, 1973). On the one hand the growth of its functions was seen to be compatible with the 'needs' and interests of the working class, while on the other it was seen to provide a variety of necessary conditions for capitalist production. Certainly, it was viewed as inadequate to regard national states *solely* as instruments of *bourgeois* class rule since this was generally unable to account for the growth of state-financed services in such areas as health, welfare, education and old age (Gough, 1979).[10] Indeed, it became increasingly apparent that the expansion of state activities of this kind had created fiscal crises; as public-sector borrowing requirements grew so too did the state's demands upon financial markets (O'Connor, 1973). Thus, those of the 'New Right' and various so-called 'monetarists' began in the 1970s to argue strongly for reductions in the levels of state funding and for the return to 'basic market principles' (Hayek, 1976a and b; Crozier, 1979). In many countries, as a consequence, corporatist structures have been abandoned as levels of state intervention within economies have been severely curtailed.

During the 1980s, therefore, new themes have become popularized for solving the crisis of capitalism; profits and investment will only thrive, so it is argued, when the ideals and practices of classical entrepreneurship and capitalism are more strongly pronounced (Friedman, 1962). Accordingly, the state and organized labour are seen to have only very limited functions and, as such, corporatism or 'tripartism' – as favoured during earlier decades – is now regarded as redundant for solving the needs of present-day economies. If the state does retain any functions these, according to the 'New Right', are seen primarily in terms of providing *minimum* levels of 'back-up' to profit-making organizations and to supporting basic standards of education, health and welfare. In the 1980s there would appear to be, as a result, less apparent contradictions in the nature of the state. The elected conservative and liberal governments of Western Europe, in the light of weakened labour movements, have adapted state institutions so that they more adequately and directly serve the needs of capital. The abolition of corporatist structures, then, adds further to the dilemmas of organized labour and severely limits the extent to which the interests of workers can be protected, if not represented, within legally enforceable state structures. Without these, laws in such areas as equal opportunities, race relations and employment are little more than non-enforceable statutes. At the same time, the abandonment of national and local consultative bodies for developing economic strategies on the basis of consultation between capital, labour and the state, severely weakens the general influence and legitimacy of trade unionism. Sweden, as in so many other aspects of its institutional order, seems fairly unique among Western capitalist countries in the extent to which its corporatist structures have been largely maintained with a high level of trade-union involvement in national and local economic management and planning (Clegg *et al.*, 1986). The Social Democratic Party, unlike its counterparts in most other countries, has remained in government during most of the 1980s while rates of unemployment and inflation have remained low. In Sweden, by contrast with other European countries, the appeal of right-wing ideologies has been limited and, as such, the legitimacy of collectivism, corporatism and trade unionism remains relatively intact. As yet, appeals to entre-preneurship and for a return to 'classical' capitalist principles have been given little credibility as strategies for future economic development.[11] Indeed, they are usually considered irrelevant to the needs of structural rationalization and industrial moderniza-tion. As such, state institutions in Sweden continue to be fraught with contradictions because of the attempts to accommodate the irreconcilable needs of capital and labour.[12] In most other Western countries, on the other hand, these have been resolved to a greater extent by the state siding more explicitly with the interests of capital.

Perhaps the key processes of change during the 1980s are reflected in the growing problems of 'inner cities' (Harrison, 1985). In a sense, they represent the outcomes of broader socioeconomic and political forces as these are occurring within different Western societies. They reflect the growing problems of inequality, of increasing class divisions and the extended economic marginality of different groups within the working class. In these urban areas, the withdrawal of state provision and the underfunding of public services are reflected in poor education, housing and welfare facilities. The rationalization of capitalist production systems has brought about a restructuring of working-class work patterns and life-styles such that local economies have been destroyed and traditional kin- and neighbourhood-based support systems abolished. Individuals are left to pursue their own personal strategies for coping within economic, social and built environments which are both impoverished and alienating (Elliott, 1984). Indeed, it is a token of the effectiveness of various control agencies that social order is only sporadically challenged through petty crime and occasional social protest. The inner cities, in reflecting the increasing polarization of society in terms of the distribution and consumption of goods and resources, ferment 'cultures' of poverty. Hence, attitudes of social disengagement reinforce the predominant ideological and material orders of society which continue to reward the more advantaged while sustaining indifference to, and unawareness of, the problems of more deprived and subordinated groups. Indeed, the ideologies of the 'New Right' which have become incorporated within the programmes of many of the conservative and liberal democratic governments of the West, sustain political cultures which reflect and incorporate such indifference (King, 1987). Accordingly, these political parties are able to argue that the state can do little to improve the conditions of the inner cities; their impoverished conditions can only be ameliorated through the further development of capitalist, market relationships, and the creation of entrepreneurial, profit-making ventures.

Much, then, has changed since the mid-1970s. If, in 1977, sociologists would have predicted such trends, their ideas would have been considered as misguided. The developments which have occurred over the past decade are apt reminders of the extent to which prevailing political ideals and assumptions can rapidly alter, and with fundamental outcomes for social structures. Thus, a perceived crisis of capitalism – as reflected in both academic and political debates during the late 1970s – has brought about political responses which have drastically altered the character of national states, organized labour, stratification systems and class relationships. Indeed, much the same could be said of contemporary developments within Eastern Europe and in China. In both capitalist and state socialist countries, then, these are posing fundamental sociological issues. They raise questions about processes of social integration, cohesion and control. Indeed, they pose issues about the nature of political legitimacy and the extent to which dominant groups are able to sustain their economic and social privileges within different types of social structure and in contrasting national economies. But despite the practical and

14

academic relevance of these questions, the credibility and perceived relevance of sociological analysis and discussion is now less than in the 1970s. It has become a 'marginalized' discipline and, as such, the quality of political debate and the level of general understanding about the organization and direction of modern societies is that much more impoverished.

Notes

1 During the 1970s, sociological debates were often 'polarized' in these terms, despite contrasting perspectives and viewpoints within each of these so-called 'positions'. As such, sociology lost credibility as a 'detached' empirically based discipline.
2 Such typologies of society were fashionable in the 1970s but generally all of them lacked both logical and empirical rigour.
3 Indeed, it was sometimes argued that the abolition of class privileges in Eastern Europe and the creation of non-capitalist institutional orders provided more appropriate preconditions for 'post-industrialism' than those pertaining within many Western countries.
4 It must be appreciated that such a distinction is somewhat arbitrary. Even so it remains helpful to conceptualize the differing nature of 'crises' in East European and Western capitalist countries in these terms.
5 This, of course, raises questions about the nature and degree of 'elite differentiation' within such societies.
6 It is here that *glasnost* and Gorbachev's reforms are most explicitly directed.
7 Similar processes are occurring, often with even more far-reaching effects, in China.
8 The emergence of a 'new' middle class within a classless (!) society was much heralded within political debate at the time, but it generally lacked empirical substance (Westergaard, 1965).
9 So far, wage-earner funds in Sweden have been more effective in funding small-scale enterprises than in changing the nature of control relationships in large corporations.
10 Although, in the last instance, the state must serve the needs of capital (Parkin, 1979).
11 Business start-up in Sweden is generally viewed as a 'deviant act'.
12 Hence the current 'crisis' of Swedish state funding and the alleged need to reduce the public sector's borrowing requirement.

1

The limits and divisions of industrial capitalism

KRISHAN KUMAR

> Revolutionaries sometimes try to prove that there is
> absolutely no way out of a crisis [for the ruling class]. This is
> a mistake. There is no such thing as an absolutely hopeless
> situation.
>
> Lenin, *Report to the Second Congress of the Communist
> International*, 19 July 1920

The decline of Western capitalism?

The 'decline of the West' has been pronounced at regular intervals
since Oswald Spengler's gloomy prognostications of 1918. It was
a favourite theme of Marxist and other literary intellectuals such
as Christopher Caudwell and Ortega y Gasset in the 1930s. Later,
in the 1970s it reappeared in the wake of the oil crisis and a rude
awakening to the problem of the world's future supplies of energy.
Ecological critiques were now joined to more traditional Marxist
analysis to proclaim the bankruptcy of Western capitalism.
Capitalism, as the dominant form of industrialism, seemed
incapable of escaping the logic of its growth process. As an
ecological, economic and social system, it was reaching its limits.
Once more the choice seemed to be that posed by Rosa Luxemburg
at the beginning of the century: socialism – of *some* kind – or
barbarism.

As the millennial year 2000 beckons, such eschatological
speculations are bound to grow. Every civilization known to us –
and *a fortiori* every one we don't know – has after all declined.
Often, like the Hittites or the Mayas, they have disappeared

16

altogether, leaving only a few material remains. Or they go into a state of frozen or suspended animation, like the Polynesians. Of the twenty-six civilizations identified by Arnold Toynbee, sixteen are dead and five 'arrested'. Of the five remaining, one of these, Western civilization, is rapidly swallowing up the rest. Is there any reason to think that Western civilization will prove an exception to the law of decay and breakdown? And as it turns itself into the only remaining civilization, a world system or world civilization, does not its own downfall now threaten the downfall of the whole species?

Most theories of civilizational decline emphasize internal factors, or 'internal contradictions'. Suicide, not murder, is the general verdict. In Toynbee's case, this takes the form of a process whereby a civilization's ruling 'Creative Minority' becomes a coercive 'Dominant Minority', losing its ability to bind the 'Internal Proletariat' to its culture and so unleashing class war. The 'External Proletariat' of barbarians beyond its borders, previously kept in check with little difficulty, can now successfully invade a system fatally weakened by internal strains (Toynbee, 1962). Max Weber too, in his account of the decline of the Roman Empire, picks out the internal contradictions of the slave-based economy of the ancient world as the principal cause. The barbarians overran an imperial system that was already pointing their way, away from a centralized empire based on slave labour towards a manorial system based on family serfdom. 'The Empire had ceased to be what it once was, and the barbarian invasions simply concluded a development which had begun long before . . . When, after one and a half centuries of decline, the Western Empire finally disappeared, barbarism had already conquered the Empire from within' (Weber, 1976, p. 389).

But such theories of decline, with their concentration on internal social mechanisms of contradiction and conflict, have always had to contend with others that emphasize extraneous or natural factors. Social Darwinism looks to military fitness, in an environment of predatory and competitive states, as the key to survival or servility. International war is the testing agency that elevates some societies and enslaves others. Malthusians, from an even more cosmic perspective, have pitilessly observed the levelling of human societies as they come up against the blank wall of starvation. Population increase continually outstripping food supply, successful and growing societies are punished by their own progress, as if for hubris. Nature, in the form of plagues and famines, jerks them sharply back to their primitive starting points.

The sorry cycle then starts all over again. What latter-day doomster has been able to match the Old Testament thunder of the Reverend Malthus himself?

> The power of population is so superior to the power in the earth to produce subsistence for man, that premature death must in some shape or other visit the human race. The vices of mankind are active and able ministers of depopulation. They are the precursors in the great army of destruction; and often finish the dreadful work themselves. But should they fail in this war of extermination, sickly seasons, epidemics, pestilence, and plague, advance in terrific array, and sweep off their thousands and ten thousands. Should success be still incomplete, gigantic inevitable famine stalks in the rear, and with one mighty blow levels the population with the food of the world.
>
> (Malthus, 1985, pp. 118–19)

Decline and downfall, all theorists agree, can however inevitable take a very long time. Weber, as we have seen, speaks of the decline of the Roman Empire stretching over a period of at least a century and a half. Toynbee for his part considers the whole Roman Empire as but the penultimate stage in the decline of a larger entity, Hellenic Society, as it vainly attempts to rally within the framework of a 'universal state'. Hellenic Society had in fact been in decline since the convulsions of the Peloponnesian War of the fifth century BC. 'The Roman Empire itself was a monumental symptom of the far-advanced decline of a Hellenic Society of which this empire was the universal state . . . this empire was already doomed before it was established' (Toynbee, 1962, p. 61).

This is *la longue durée* indeed, taking in over a thousand years; and one wonders how far such a long-breathed perspective is useful to anyone but the most philosophically minded historian. Certainly from the point of view of a comparative historical sociology, centuries rather than millennia might seem a more appropriate time dimension – for instance, the four or five centuries, from the fourteenth to the eighteenth century, that Braudel takes as the period of the 'economic civilization' of commercial capitalism in Western Europe (Braudel, 1970, p. 153). What such a time horizon would sufficiently suggest is that societies can live with their 'contradictions', if not comfortably at least tolerably, for long periods. The signs of decay may be observable only retrospectively, as to an eighteenth-century European like Gibbon musing on Roman history amidst the ruins of the Capitol. Or the persistence of old forms and old values may be so powerful and pervasive as to hide for a long time the seeds of decay. Joseph Schumpeter was convinced that 'there is inherent in the capitalist system a tendency toward self-destruction', and that for those with the eyes to see the signs were becoming evident. But he could also see all around him the evidence of a still confident and prosperous bourgeoisie. 'The middle class is still a political power. Bourgeois standards and bourgeois motivations though being increasingly impaired are still alive. . . The bourgeois family has not yet died', etc. These may, he conceded, be thought of as surface, short-run factors. But 'from the standpoint of immediate practice as well as for the purposes of short-run forecasting – *and in these things, a century is a "short-run"* – all this surface may be more important than the tendency toward another civilization that slowly works deep down below' (Schumpeter, 1976, pp. 162–3, my emphasis).

If a century can be considered a 'short-run', then it would clearly be no contradiction to expect, say, the eventual demise of industrialism through the exhaustion of fossil fuels and mineral resources, while at the same time remaining relatively optimistic about its foreseeable future over the next century or so. The same can be said about the Marxist notion of 'the falling rate of profit' as an inherent long-term tendency of capitalism, and one that will compass its doom. So long as there are fresh fields for capitalism to conquer – and this could, without being too fanciful, now include other worlds than our own – it may be only of theoretical interest to deduce from its working some distant point in time when the accumulation crisis will reach revolutionary proportions.

Still, it is one thing to stave off the ultimate, the terminal crisis. There may be other problems in the meantime scarcely less pressing. While to the out-and-out Darwinian survival may be the only thing that matters, human societies have generally also been concerned with the terms of that survival. Those inmates who survived the Nazi concentration camps endured in conditions that few would describe as human. To have remained alive was certainly a triumph of individual ingenuity and resilience. But many would question whether, if whole societies came to resemble concentration camps, survival on these terms and in those conditions could ever be worth fighting for. Similar things have been said of some of the slave societies of the past. Social survival is the necessary premiss of all human values and purposes. But it is not synonymous with them.

This is perhaps to put the matter too alarmingly. Few societies are so intolerable that some space for humanly valued activities cannot be found. The point is simply that there can be questions about the 'limits' to social development short of the stage where limits become absolute. Societies can throw up a range of problems that suggest, not catastrophe, but systematic failures and lesions of various kinds. Life can be made so unpleasant and uncomfortable, so threatening and debilitating, that people withdraw from society, or seek to escape it. Society may have gone beyond some point – never easy to fix with precision – at which its institutions still function relatively harmoniously, and that can still deliver a relatively fulfilling life to the bulk of the population. The system survives, but shows increasing signs of wear and tear. It is just as important – in the short run, more important – to consider these relative limits and incapacities as to speculate on the long-term capacity for survival of the system as a whole.

In the following sections I consider views of this kind as well as those concerned with long-term survival. I make no attempt, of course, to be comprehensive. I have merely selected some examples which are useful for opening up questions about the future development of industrial societies, and for suggesting some of the newer sources of strain within them.

Capitalism and the world system

Despite, or perhaps because of, its origins in nineteenth-century evolutionary social philosophies, sociology has shown little interest in the transformations of whole social orders, and the mechanisms that bring this about. Following Weber, there has been some concern with origins – at least, the origins of capitalism – although even there the field has largely been left to sociologically minded historians such as R. H. Tawney and Christopher Hill. But to scan the literature on revolution, the concept most directly relevant to breakdown and renewal, is to be struck by the paucity of serious sociological contributions (and one Skocpol, 1979, does not make a summer). To repeat the old but still accurate charge: sociology has been good at explaining order; it has been far less successful in dealing with change.

The exception of course is Marxism. Marxism is the most powerful modern theory of revolution and social transformation. But its limitations as such have also been widely exposed, both in its treatment of past transformations – for example, from feudalism to capitalism – and its anticipation of future ones. Most pertinent to the present concern, it remains true to say that while Marx provided a compelling anatomy of capitalist society, his account of its transformation and supersession in a socialist revolution is, as all admit, incomplete and unsatisfactory.

Marx gives an unrivalled account of the rise of modern society. His writings on the origins and development of capitalism are the best part of his work, and better than anything else yet offered on the subject by anyone. In the *Grundrisse* and *Capital*, in the occasional writings on European politics and society, Marx provides a comprehensive sociology of bourgeois capitalist society that is still unsurpassed, and off which modern sociology still lives (see Bottomore, 1975; Davis and Scase, 1985).

On the future development of capitalism, the case is less clear. Marx's contempt for futurology – 'I don't make recipes for the cookshops of the future' – is to his credit. To have seen something of the barrenness of contemporary futurology must make us grateful that Marx did not indulge in detailed prediction and prophecy (although the attack specifically on utopianism, a different enterprise, was unfortunate and misplaced).

Nor is it true to say that Marx's account does not contain much valuable material on the future of capitalist society. Any developmental or evolutionary theory, as in essence Marxism is, must embody some notion of emergent properties or processes. Of this there is a good deal in Marx, on both general and particular matters. The analysis of technological innovation, de-skilling, and the general proletarianization of labour needs very little to add to it to bring it up to date, as Harry Braverman (1974) so vividly demonstrated. So too with the account of the concentration and centralization of capital, and the projected rise of managerial and monopoly capitalism (Sweezy, 1972; Heilbroner, 1985). Marx had from the first seized on the world character of capitalism; hence the massive growth in the internationalization of capital and the international division of labour would have come as no surprise to him.[1] In a celebrated passage in the *Grundrisse*, even the fully automated society is anticipated, at a time when mechanization had barely got under way (Marx, 1973, p. 705). In the late-twentieth-century world of multinational corporations, the North–South divide, automation, technological unemployment, and a growing underclass of casual, unskilled workers, Marx would have found little reason to think that his analysis of more than a century ago was fundamentally mistaken. What might surprise him, and what surely ought to astonish us, is how little he would have to change or add to his original prognosis.

Would he also have felt the same way about his ultimate prognosis, that capitalism must eventually collapse and give way to socialism? Again, the evidence of the past century would have given him some grounds for reaffirming his belief. The instability of capitalism as a system shows little sign of abating. The 'great thunderstorms' in which the economic contradictions of capitalism express themselves (Marx, 1973, p. 411) have blown up often enough. Crises and depressions, the upswings and down-swings of the business cycle, the 'long waves' of growth and recession, have continued with remarkable regularity since the time of Marx's *Capital* (Maddison, 1982, pp. 64–95). Mass unemployment has been once already, in the 1930s, and returned half a century later to show that Keynesian recipes may not be enough. Technological unemployment, a spectre raised by Keynes himself, threatens a not too distant future of 20–25 per cent unemployed among the adult populations of the industrial countries (Merritt, 1982). The growth and internationalization of capital have brought with them new sources of vulnerability. As the oil-producing countries showed with striking effect in the 1970s, a small group of countries in control of a strategic industrial resource can now exert something like blackmail on even the most powerful capitalist nations. With new countries – Israel, India, Pakistan – now joining the nuclear club, the possibility of other kinds of pressure on the guardians of the world capitalist order increases further.

And yet the oil crisis itself is a good example of how capitalism can weather even the roughest storm. The OPEC countries increased the price of oil fourfold in 1973–4, and doubled it again in 1979, amounting to more than a tenfold rise in the price of oil in the 1970s. This was at a time when Western countries had become increasingly dependent on oil: in 1973, oil imports were more than seventeen times their 1950 level, and oil represented half of total energy consumption, compared with a quarter in 1950. The oil shock produced simultaneously recession and inflation. Capitalist world production fell by 10 per cent in less than a year, and the average annual price increase in Western countries in the mid-1970s was 12–13 per cent. Unemployment rates too began to climb, rising from an average of 2.5 per cent in 1973 in the Western countries, to 5.5 per cent in 1980. Following the dizzying growth rates – an annual average of 5.5 per cent – and virtually negligible unemployment of the 'Golden Age' of 1950–73, the post-1973 period saw the capitalist countries in the worst recession since the 1930s (Maddison, 1982, pp. 142–57). In a series of trenchant essays

22

written in the 1970s, the contemporary historian Geoffrey Barraclough proclaimed 'the end of an era'. 'We stand at a watershed in world history . . . The days of neo-capitalism are numbered . . . Neocapitalism, with its pretensions to have found the answer to Marx, was the expression of a temporary situation, borne along not by its own dynamic but by the upward wave of the economic cycle' (Barraclough, 1974, p. 20; 1975, p. 24; 1976, p. 31).

In the upshot the prophecies of collapse seemed wide of the mark. The West rallied under the leadership of the United States and brought about a remarkable re-stabilization – or at least 'normalization' – of the international economic order. The first step was to separate the non-oil-producing Third World nations from the OPEC cartel, thus heading off a potentially threatening anti-Western coalition and a strategy of 'collective self-reliance'. This was done through a typical mixture of threat, bluster and bribery. The non-OPEC LDCs (least developed countries) were warned that they, not the West, would suffer most from 'trade union' tactics against the capitalist bloc. They were, it was pointedly remarked, critically dependent on the West, especially the United States, for food and technology. Their best hope for economic development lay in a relationship of 'interdependence' with the West, not one of confrontation. The speedier the West's recovery, the likelier the improvement in the LDCs' own prospects.

The pill was sweetened somewhat by the decision to increase lending quotas to the LDCs through the International Monetary Fund, and by the establishment of a 'Common Fund', under-written by the developed countries, to stabilize the prices of raw materials – which made up more than 80 per cent of the LDCs' export earnings – if they fell too far on world markets. But the balance – or rather imbalance – of power was clear. The LDCs' demand for 'indexation' – the tying of the price of raw materials to the price of manufactures – was decisively rejected by the West. So too was a request for an easing of the debt to Western banks. As Barraclough observed, in a somewhat more chastened vein, it was shown 'that if recession is notoriously a bad time for trade unions to fight for wage increases, it is also a bad time for the less developed countries to fight for NIEO' (the New International Economic Order) (Barraclough, 1978a, p. 47).

For their part, the OPEC countries were co-opted into the capitalist bloc through the recycling and absorption of petrodollars into the capitalist economies. Direct and portfolio investment gave the OPEC cartel an increased stake in the United States and other capitalist countries. If Western capitalism was hostage to OPEC, OPEC soon became hostage to capitalism. Vast amounts of technology, machinery, arms and spare parts were purchased by OPEC from the West. OPEC increasingly found its future, both as supplier and customer, annexed to the capitalist bloc. Under pressure from Saudi Arabia and Brazil, the Third World retreated from the radical strategy of 'collective self-reliance' and reverted to the traditional pattern of 'trade and aid'.

Even more effectively the United States asserted its leadership over the capitalist bloc and tightened the integration of the capitalist world. The United States, of all the major capitalist countries the least dependent on oil imports, emerged with greater power than ever before. It had been largely instrumental in separating the OPEC cartel from the non-oil-producing LDCs, and had master-minded the policy of setting the enormous power of the organized capitalist nations against the threats of trade-union action by the LDCs. It had made it clear that the New International Economic Order demanded by the Third World would be only marginally different from the old. The NIEO would remain, as Michael Harrington said at the time, 'impeccably capitalist' (cited Barraclough, 1978a, p. 49; and, for the general account, see Rousseas, 1979, pp. 76–93).

There can be nothing very comforting about this recovery, either in its manner or in its prospects for future stability. It tightens the screws even more on the LDCs. At the same time it does not secure the capitalist bloc from future attempts at pressure by other nations sitting on key industrial resources. The secret is now out, and the rich capitalist countries will be faced with demands from Danegeld at fairly regular intervals from now. The capitalist world system may become more integrated, but by the same token it becomes more vulnerable to pressure at its weakest points. Moreover, as the world recession continues, it intensifies rivalries and the rich capitalist countries will be faced with demands for Danegeld at fairly regular intervals from now. The capitalist world unity of the rich countries vis-à-vis the Third World. The United States, Western Europe and Japan, not to mention the East European states, may see their future, in the short run at least, not as part of an integrated bloc of developed nations – the 'North' – but as separate superpowers pursuing separate strategies of survival and self-interest. Barraclough, tracing at intervals the process of re-stabilization during the 1970s, indeed finally came to see this as the likeliest outcome of the experience of these years.

The liberal world economy, as it had existed for a quarter of a century after 1945, was on its way out.

> What we have to expect in its place . . . is something approximating to a world of regional blocs or superblocs – that is to say, of exclusive trading areas, hedged in by protective tariffs, in which groups of developed and underdeveloped countries are linked together by mutual interests and stand opposed to other groups of developed and developing countries similarly linked.
> (Barraclough, 1978b, p. 56)

The point is that, as Barraclough himself admits, such a system of closed trading blocs worked 'relatively well' in the 1930s (the world war was not a product of this system), and there is no reason why it should not work as well today. That it has certain disorderly and inefficient features is not in question. But then the capitalist system has never been stable, if by this we mean orderly and harmonious. Its history is punctuated by alternating phases of progress and regression, growth and depression. What rather is at issue is its resilience, its capacity for survival as a system in the face of such vicissitudes. On present evidence there is little to indicate that it has reached the end of its viable existence.

There is certainly not the remotest sign of a successor (and in this respect at least, Wallerstein's characterization of the East European states as 'collective capitalist firms' (1979, p. 68), participating willy-nilly in the capitalist world economy, seems quite right). What is to come, that is, so far does not look like socialism, though to many it increasingly looks like barbarism (see, for example, Heilbroner, 1977; Bottomore, 1984, p. 160). The lesson that Stephen Rousseas, for instance, draws from the response to the oil crisis is that capitalism is quite capable of surviving in the new environment, but at the cost of some prosperity and many liberal freedoms. 'Unplanned advanced capitalism' will give way to 'a planned postcapitalist state' under the control of 'cartelized big business' fused with a strong government. Low growth rates, high unemployment, and high inflation will be the norm for a considerable time to come. In the scramble for scarce raw materials and declining energy sources, a new mercantilist world order will emerge (perhaps on the lines of the regionalized world envisaged by Barraclough).

Capitalism has shown over the course of its entire history a remarkable ability to adapt to changing circumstances, and is

25

already beginning to show a similar, though somewhat strained, flexibility in adapting to its biggest challenge of all – effective domestic planning in a finite mercantilist world of increasingly limited resources . . . Planned capitalist society's legitimation would be achieved via media control, surveillance, and a co-optation of the masses through a growth based on the predatory exploitation of weaker nations held firmly under political and military control – the 1973–7 scenario replayed with a vengeance.

The descent into barbarism that Luxemburg so feared could become a reality in a world in which capital accumulation will be severely limited. But the 'barbarism' Luxemburg foresaw as a possibility not to be automatically ruled out by a mechanical dialectic will most probably not entail the 'catastrophic' collapse of capitalism but rather its dialectical transformation into an advanced, planned technocratic capitalism operating within newly defined boundary conditions.

(Rousseas, 1979, pp. 93, 96–7)

Marxism and the collapse of capitalism

It is worth remembering that Marx himself opposed the idea that capitalism would collapse as the result of a mechanical working out of its 'objective' logic. In a famous footnote in *Theories of Surplus Value*, he associated himself with Ricardo, as against Adam Smith, in the view that a fall in the rate of profit due to 'an over-abundance of capital' posed a temporary and transitory, not a permanent, check to capital accumulation. 'Permanent crises do not exist' (Marx, 1968, p. 497n). Crises of overproduction indeed seem to function for Marx much as they later appeared to Schumpeter: as 'gales of creative destruction', providing the opportunity for the clearing out of obsolete and unwanted capital stock and a re-stocking with newer and more productive technology. Marx, that is to say, was not a 'breakdown theorist'. Bottomore fairly expresses what now seems to be the general consensus on this:

None of Marx's partial analyses embody a conception of crises as leading to an ineluctable 'economic breakdown' of capitalism . . . On the contrary, Marx's general view seems to have been that crises, in purely economic terms, are a means of countering dis-equilibrium and re-establishing the conditions for further capitalist development. (Bottomore, 1985, p. 13)[2]

26

Rudolf Hilferding put the Marxist position correctly when he stated that 'the idea of a purely economic collapse makes no sense', and that the collapse of capitalism 'will be political and social, not economic' (Hilferding, 1981, p. 366). It was the growing indignation, power and confidence of the proletariat, stimulated by the life conditions of capitalism, that would ultimately bring down capitalism, not some technical economic malfunctioning of the system. This was the view even of those Marxists, such as Rosa Luxemburg, who modified Marx to the extent of postulating an ultimate and irresolvable crisis of capitalism caused by over-accumulation. Marx, Luxemburg pointed out, had assumed for analytical purposes a fully formed, fully developed world system of capitalism. She quotes the relevant footnote from *Capital*: 'In order to examine the object of our investigation in its integrity, free from all disturbing subsidiary circumstances, we must treat the whole world as one nation, and assume that capitalist production is everywhere established and has possessed itself of every branch of industry' (Luxemburg, 1972, p. 58).

This 'theoretical premiss' can be misleading. It relates only to an abstract, formal, model of capitalism. In reality, says Luxemburg, capital accumulation depends on the existence of non-capitalist strata and non-capitalist countries, both as consumers and as suppliers of certain kinds of commodities and of fresh groups of proletarianized labour. Only when capitalism has completely eliminated all internal and external non-capitalist pockets – and this crucially includes the epoch of imperialism – does stagnation set in and push the system to its limits in a crisis of profitability. This is however only a *theoretical* limit to the system. It is indeed a 'theoretical fiction, because capital accumulation is not just an economic but also a political process'. Well before the outer theoretical limit is reached, Luxemburg expects capitalism to be overthrown. Its bloody progress through the world increasingly provokes 'an endless chain of political and social catastrophes and convulsions'. These, together with periodic economic crises, 'make continued accumulation impossible and the rebellion of the international working class against the rule of capital necessary, even before it has economically reached the limits it set for itself' (Luxemburg, 1972, p. 146).

So Luxemburg too pins her expectations on the development of a revolutionary working class as capitalism enters its 'final phase', the age of imperialism. Final? We have seen enough of capitalism's energy and expansiveness in the past half century to be wary of such eschatologies. Even the bouts of destructiveness, as in the two world wars, have not spelled the end but, confirming Schumpeter's wartime speculations (1976, p. 163 n7), have actually been the springboard of renewed growth. In an unevenly developed world, with vast areas still available for capitalist penetration and exploitation, it was on the face of it hardly probable that capitalism would be in its final phase in the early part of this century. That being so, it has retained a considerable capacity for staving off a revolutionary crisis by the co-optation of its own proletariat and the exploitation of the 'external proletariat' of the Third World.

What else indeed should one have expected from a system endowed with such unique dynamism by Marx? In the *Communist Manifesto*, the *Grundrisse*, and *Capital*, Marx in some well-known pages depicts a force for growth and change whose only limits appear to be the stars. Capitalism, he says, is a stage of society 'in comparison to which all earlier ones appear as mere *local developments* of humanity and as *nature-idolatry*'. Its 'great civilizing influence' comes from its 'universal appropriation of nature as well as the social bond itself'. It penetrates to the heart of nature and society, exploring both in theory and exploiting both in practice to the fullest possible extent.

> For the first time, nature becomes purely an object for humankind, purely a matter of utility; it ceases to be recognized as a power for itself; and the theoretical discovery of its autonomous laws appears merely as a ruse so as to subjugate it under human needs, whether as an object of consumption or as means of production. In accord with this tendency, capital drives beyond national barriers and prejudices as much as beyond nature worship, as well as all traditional, confined, complacent, encrusted satisfactions of present needs, and reproductions of old ways of life. It is destructive towards all of this, and constantly revolutionizes it, tearing down all the barriers which hem in the development of the forces of production, the expansion of needs, the all-sided development of production, and the exploitation and exchange of natural and mental forces.
>
> (Marx, 1973, pp. 409–10, original emphasis)

What could stop such a juggernaut? Evidently no non-capitalist force but only its own 'internal contradictions'. Yet their working out demands a world scale and world dimension to history, both of which seem far from exhausted. In its progress capitalism

28

consumes both history (time) and nature (space). It deals with temporal barriers to its growth by smashing down all pre-capitalist residues – peasants, craftsmen, small traders, local markets, and so on. It deals with spatial barriers by its worldwide expansion and reconstitution of the earth's people and resources. In this aspect its development takes the form of geographical differentiations, which are not 'mere historical residuals' but 'actively reconstituted features within the capitalist mode of production' (Harvey, 1982, p. 416).

Capitalism tends to integrate the world into a single system characterized by an international territorial division of labour. The accumulation process 'spreads its net in ever-widening circles across the world, ultimately enmeshing everyone and everything within the circulation process of capital' (Harvey, 1982, p. 418). This brings in its train new forms of inter-regional competition and conflict. Some regions boom, others decline. But this very source of new strains in the system contains, as David Harvey explains, compensating mechanisms of stabilization:

> The different regional rhythms of accumulation may be but loosely co-ordinated because the co-ordinations rest on the variegated and often conflicting mobilities of different forms of capital and labour. The timing of upturns and downturns in the accumulation cycle can then vary from one region to another with interesting interaction effects. The unit to the accumulation process presupposed in earlier versions of the crisis theory fragments into different regional rhythms that can just as easily compensate each other as build into some vast global crash. The very real possibility exists that the global pace of accumulation can be sustained through compensating oscillations within the parts. The geography of uneven development helps convert the crisis tendencies of capitalism into compensating regional configurations of rapid accumulation and devaluation.
>
> (Harvey, 1982, pp. 427–8)

It may be true that, as Harvey says, the process of uneven geographical development and expansion will not ultimately solve anything, that 'there is . . . no "spatial fix" that can contain the contradictions of capitalism in the long run' (Harvey, 1982, p. 442). But the difficulties faced by Marxists in envisaging and explaining the end of capitalism are greater than they are apt to realize. It is not simply that the 'contradictions' must take much longer to express themselves than they usually allow, not simply that – perhaps as a result of this – the international proletariat has so far shown scant willingness to play its allotted part as capitalism's executioner.[3] There is the more serious difficulty of the uniqueness of capitalism's origins, and the corollary of this, the problem that arises in contemplating its outcome. Both Marx and Weber showed that though there was material progress in many societies above the hunting-and-gathering level, in only one place – Western Europe – was there a 'breakthrough' to the higher level of capitalist industrialism. From there the new system went on to conquer the rest of the world. Elsewhere inertia, social structural, or superstructural forces prevented or counteracted tendencies towards autonomous material growth.

What this means is that the materialist conception of history is reduced to explaining a special case, the once-and-only rise of Western capitalism. This poses a question, as Hobsbawm notes, not just about the origins of capitalism but about its expected course of development and final destination. It casts doubt in particular on the inevitability of the clash between the forces and relations of capitalist production. For 'if it can be shown that in other societies there has been no trend for the material forces to grow, or that their growth has been controlled, sidetracked or otherwise prevented by the force of social organization and superstructure from causing revolution in the sense of the 1859 *Preface*, then why should not the same occur in bourgeois society' (Hobsbawm, 1984, p. 45)? This makes the end of capitalism not only 'conjunctural' but, to a large extent, conjectural. Capitalism's end must remain as open, as undetermined, as its beginning. This certainly gives it no permanent or everlasting lease of life. All civilizations, as we have already noted, like all natural species, are marked out for extinction from the moment of their birth. But, as with species, the when and the how of it remain matters more for soothsayers than for sociologists.

'Disorganized capitalism'

There can be other kinds of 'system failures' than those that end in self-destruction. Societies may build up such an array of problems as to make their effective functioning increasingly difficult and costly. There may be no new system on offer, no victory for any party, but simply an enervating and wearisome stalemate. Temporary patching-up and specious palliatives become the order of the day. Alienation seizes considerable

30

sections of the population, leading to attitudes of cynicism and contempt. There is no recorded instance of a civilization dying of boredom, but plenty of instances – for example, from late Hellenistic civilization – of populations quietly withdrawing their moral support from systems in clear need of renewal.

Capitalism, in the eyes of many contemporary critics and analysts, has become increasingly 'disorganized' (Block and Hirschhorn, 1979; Williams, 1983; Offe, 1985). It does not function as it is supposed to, according to its own self-understanding and self-proclaimed principles. Formal parliamentary democracy has been undermined by the rise of the powerful party–state and the policy-making bureaucratic agency. The principle of majority rule, once an instrument of progress, has become regressive by virtue of its 'equal treatment of the unequal', in an environment increasingly characterized by 'minority' areas and interests related to such divisions as sex, age, ethnicity, region, and family status. Trade unions, far from being associations of the great mass of oppressed workers, have become the bastions of a privileged core of securely employed male workers, indifferent to the claims and interests not just of the unemployed but of more 'marginal' workers such as women, the young and members of minority ethnic groups.[4] Work itself, the uniquely privileged source of ethic and identity in industrial societies, has for much of the population lost its ability to convey meaning and give shape to an individual's life. It has come to occupy a shorter period of our lives, due to longer schooling and earlier retirement. It tends to become intermittent, interrupted by bouts of unemployment. As an experience it has become unfulfilling, shaped by the dictates of the large bureaucratic organization or the capital-intensive factory.

Even at its most successful, capitalism as an economic system runs the risk of undermining its own cultural and political props. Its emphasis on pecuniary goals and 'possessive individualism' steadily drives out all the pre-capitalist residues of moral restraint that are an essential part of its effective functioning (Hirsch, 1977; Kumar, 1983). Its reduction of all relationships nakedly to the 'cash nexus' releases in particular the full energy of the organized working class – but in a capitalist rather than a socialist direction. The working class, schooled by the capitalist ethic and capitalist practice, comes to feel increasingly uninhibited in the use of its industrial power in the market-place. It demands its due; the strike weapon is its bargaining counter. The result is endemic industrial conflict and, with leap-frogging wage settlements, endemic inflation (Fox, 1974; Goldthorpe, 1978; Gilbert, 1981; O'Connor, 1984).

In the context of an expanding economy, growth can be a surrogate for redistribution. That, as Charles Maier puts it, has been 'the great conservative idea of the last generation', no less so for being espoused by many social democrats (Maier, 1978, p. 70). When growth cannot keep up with expectations, as has been the case recently, inflation can for a time disguise the lag. But ultimately its effect is to intensify distributional struggles. Low growth in fact converts all social and political choices and decisions – over environmental pollution, energy use, levels of unemployment – into 'zero-sum' conflicts: ones in which every gain by one group must be suffered as a loss by others, and so all decisions are stale-mated. Society achieves stasis (Thurow, 1981). The state, originally drawn into the market-place to stabilize capitalism and to secure its orderly growth, now finds itself having to adjudicate between competing claims without the economic wherewithal to leave the losers on any issue reasonably satisfied. Capitalist economic growth is in itself destabilizing, but at least while steady it provides the wealth to pay off claimants and still the demands for equality. Periods of stagnation not only do nothing to lessen the destabilizing tendencies of capitalism but actually reinforce them by bringing to the surface tensions and divisions temporarily submerged by capitalism's success.

The most serious problem had already been foreseen long ago by Marx. The French Second Republic of 1848 introduced, for the first time in modern history, universal male suffrage. But in conceding political democracy, Marx argued in *The Class Struggles in France* (1850), the bourgeoisie had entrenched a fundamental contradiction between the political and the socio-economic realms of capitalist society.

> The comprehensive contradiction of this constitution . . . consists in the following: The classes whose social slavery the constitution is to perpetuate, proletariat, peasantry, petty bourgeoisie, it puts in possession of political power through universal suffrage. And from the class whose old social power it sanctions, the bourgeoisie, it withdraws the political guarantees of this power. It forces the political rule of the bourgeoisie into democratic conditions, which at every moment help the hostile classes to victory and jeopardise the very foundations of bourgeois society. From the ones it demands that they should not go forward from political to social emancipation; from the others that they should not go back from social to political restoration.
>
> (Marx and Engels, 1962, I, p. 172; cf. Lenin, 1960, p. 358)

For most of the nineteenth and early twentieth centuries, capitalism was legitimated by the persistence of a 'protective cover' of religious and other pre-capitalist moral conceptions: *noblesse oblige*, economic success as the reward for the moral virtues of industry and frugality, and so on (Polanyi, 1957, pp. 130–50; Bell, 1976, p. 224; Kristol, 1979, p. 245). The contradiction between the political and the economic realms was masked, not just by the slow and uneven growth of democracy itself (Therborn, 1977; Mayer, 1981), but by the operation of customary restraints that inhibited the full impact of the democratic principle on the capitalist economy. Increasingly, two things have happened. The restraints have dropped away, leading to a politicization of the economy – or, what comes to the same thing, the commercialization of politics. The political victors in the electoral struggle have come to regard the economy as fair game: a fit object of manipulation and a source of spoils for their supporters (Brittan, 1975). More positively, the democratic principle of the state is used to counterbalance the unequal and coercive sphere of the private capitalist economy. In either case, the separation of state and 'civil society', critical to the liberal capitalist order, increasingly breaks down.

This has the effect of inducing 'crises' of various sorts, whose precise definition depends largely on political perspective. For liberal individualists, such as Samuel Brittan and Daniel Bell, the politicization of the economy, and of society generally, generates excessive and 'unfulfillable expectations' on the part of all social groups (Brittan, 1975, p. 156). There is government 'overload', and an unholy scramble among organized groups for political influence as the state becomes 'the arena for the fulfilment of private and group wants' (Bell, 1976, p. 232). For left-wing thinkers, the crisis is primarily one of legitimation, caused by the now evident contradiction between the private character of the capitalist economy and the public character of liberal democracy (O'Connor, 1973; Habermas, 1976; Wolfe, 1977). The capitalist economy takes its stand on property rights. It promotes an ethos of individual acquisitiveness at the expense, if need be, of society. Its structural principle is inequality: the vast divide between property-owners and the propertyless. Liberal democracy enshrines the universal rights of persons. Its key concept is citizenship, and its structural principle is equality: the equal rights of all citizens, and their effective embodiment in democratic practice. Kept separate, as they were for over a century, the two spheres can function more or less autonomously, with only occasional

clashes. Brought together, as they have been with the politicization of society, their irreconcilable principles create 'a contradictory totality' which sends shock waves throughout the system
(Bowles and Gintis, 1982; 1986).

The basic problem, from the point of view of capitalism, is what
Claus Offe calls 'the largely irreversible framework of the welfare
state and competitive democracy' (1985, p. 145; see also Therborn,
1984, p. 25). The liberal 'nightwatchman' state of the nineteenth
century has become the democratic welfare state of the twentieth.
The interwar slump and the national mobilization of the Second
World War supplied the main impetus. So far as possible there was
to be no repeat of the 1930s. Keynes and Beveridge showed the
how and the why. Since the Second World War the state has
stepped in as guarantor of an adequate level of demand in the
economy. It has accepted the principle of full employment; and
the practice of 1950–70, when full employment was substantially
achieved, has built this into the expectation of the mass of the
population. The state has also committed itself to minimum levels
of welfare. Moreover, in conceding welfare as a right of citizenship
and not simply an entitlement in return for contributions paid, it
has established the principle of a 'social' or 'citizen' wage which
has brought about 'the partial de-proletarianization of wage labor'
(Bowles and Gintis, 1982, p. 83), and which signifies 'a partial de-
commodification of social relations' (Therborn, 1984, p. 29; see also
Offe, 1985, p. 97). Welfare capitalism is still capitalism; but it is
capitalism modified by a welfare ethic and a democratic practice
which confront it awkwardly with principles drawn from other,
non-capitalist, traditions.

By its own expenditure and employment, the state has seen to
it that these welfare goals have been achieved for much of the
postwar period. State expenditure accounts for between 40 and 60
per cent of Gross Domestic Product in Western European
countries, and state employment for between 25 and 30 per cent
of total employment. Since the 1970s, moreover, welfare
expenditure and employment have come to predominate in the
state sectors of all advanced industrial societies, amounting to
about a half of all public expenditure and a half of all public
employment. Thatcherism and Reaganism have had, despite
official rhetoric, remarkably little effect on this general pattern.
Public expenditure in Reaganite America rose from 35.4 per cent
of GDP in 1980 to 38 per cent in 1982: 'Reaganomics' unrolled a
vast carpet of public borrowing and spending that left the federal
government with the biggest budget deficit in America's history

and made the United States, for the first time since 1914, a net debtor to foreign nations. In Thatcherite Britain public expenditure went up from 42.6 per cent of GDP in 1978 to 46.5 per cent in 1982, dropping only to 43.2 per cent in 1986. And while there has been some shift in the composition of public expenditure – towards 'law and order' spending – it remained the case that 60 per cent of Conservative state spending in Britain in 1986 was on social security, health and personal social services, and education and science.[5]

Welfare state capitalism is 'the integrating principle of the modern economic era' . . . 'The era of the welfare state is synonymous with the era of advanced capitalism' (O'Connor, 1973, p. 72; Gough, 1979, p. 74). This suggests, as indeed is clearly the case, that whatever ideological difficulties this may pose are more than offset by the real degree of stabilization and regulariza-tion that the welfare state confers on capitalist development. Private capital clearly benefits from state unemployment and sickness insurance, public housing, a national health service, and a national education system – as well as, more obviously, from state subsidies to industry and state infrastructural projects such as motorways. It fares even better if in addition it can 'socialize' the expenses of clearing up the industrial waste and pollution for which it is largely responsible. All this contributes to capitalism's well-being by providing valuable social capital investment as well as the 'social consumption' that is necessary to secure the satisfactory reproduction of the labour force. It also aids capitalism's legitimation by substantially softening the blows of *laissez-faire* capitalism of the older kind (O'Connor, 1973).

But the integration of welfare and capitalism is, equally clearly, not an effortless process. There is a genuine conflict of principles at stake. The welfare state is the product not just of capitalist needs but also, perhaps more so, of the political struggles of working-class parties and movements (Gough, 1979, pp. 55–74; Bowles and Gintis, 1982, pp. 64–84). Hence the possibility and prospect of a 'fiscal crisis', a growing gap between state expenditure and state revenue, caused by the escalation of working-class demands on the capitalist state. State expenditure may be necessary to capital accumulation in the twentieth-century world, but by the same token, it may inhibit capital accumulation by reducing the quantity of surplus value available for reinvestment. While this is not necessarily an insuperable problem – much state expenditure is fed back into the capitalist sector (Gough, 1979, pp. 108–17) – the full generalization of the welfare ethic in the context of political democracy has appeared to some thinkers on the left to pose a major potential challenge to capitalism. It would mean the starkest opposition of 'person rights' to 'property rights'. 'Demands posed as universal rights and movements constituted by the universal discourse of liberal democracy are prone to become class demands and class movements' (Bowles and Gintis, 1982, p. 92). In such a development a key role is marked out for public-sector employees. They have grown with the welfare state, and have a vested interest in its expansion. They are powerfully unionized, and have been among the most combative and politically conscious of all organized workers in recent years. Of all social groups, they are the ones most imbued with the 'service ethic' and most hostile to the calculative rationality of capitalist accumulation (O'Connor, 1973, pp. 236–43; Gough, 1979, pp. 141–4; Therborn, 1984, pp. 33–5; Offe, 1985, pp. 139–40).

Lenin thought that 'a democratic republic is the best possible political shell for capitalism' and that, 'once capital has gained control of this very best shell', its rule becomes unshakeable (1960, p. 312). What Bowles, Gintis and others seem to be saying is that the democratic shell, far from being a protective cover, has the potentiality to crack the capitalist kernel – or, to change the figure, that democracy is a dagger pointed at the heart of capitalism. Democracy can indeed be uncomfortable for capitalism. Hitler and Franco, not to mention Napoleon III and, in a somewhat different way, Stalin, all show that capitalist development can proceed at a brisk pace when unhampered by democratic constraints. Capitalism can certainly consort with democracy; but at various times and places it has shown that it may find dictatorship a more congenial 'political shell'.

But discomfort is not the same thing as danger. Capitalism may be able to do without democracy, but this does not mean that democracy can through its regular operations displace capitalism. The limits of democratic intervention are tragically illustrated in the case of Allende's Chile. Without the accompaniment of an organized revolutionary movement – of which, to repeat, there is no sign in the contemporary capitalist world – democratic pressure on capitalism may be no more than an inconvenience, easily containable. This has been strongly put by James O'Connor, who was the first to raise in an influential way the possibility of a 'fiscal crisis of the state' in the era of the democratic welfare state. 'Budgetary needs may remain unsatisfied and human wants may go unfulfilled, but if those who are dependent on the state do not engage in political struggle to protect or advance their well-being, the fiscal crisis will remain relatively dormant' (1973, p. 226).

Nothing in O'Connor's analysis in fact suggests an inevitable or insupportable crisis. On the contrary, what emerges as the dominant tendency is the reconstruction of capitalism around what O'Connor calls the 'social–industrial complex'. The most advanced sectors of monopoly capital have already envisaged a 'revision of the social contract' in response to the demands of welfare and other reformers, such as the environmentalists. Since the business community best understands the capitalist system's problems, David Rockefeller urged in the *Wall Street Journal*, it must 'share in designing the solutions. So it is up to businessmen to make common cause with other reformers . . . to prevent the unwise adoption of extreme and emotional remedies' (quoted in O'Connor, 1973, p. 227). Monopoly capital can accommodate itself quite comfortably to the new social environment. Basing itself on the customer–contract model, capitalism can carry out, to its own profit, many of the requirements of the welfare state: for health services, housing, recreation, education, scientific and technical research, and armaments (for the welfare state is also the 'warfare state'). It can even become a partner in law enforcement and social control, in the provision of private police forces and private prisons. In the social–industrial complex, private capital does; the state sanctions and pays.

There will, no doubt, be budgetary pressures and crises all the time. But this will not give rise to a horizontally linked, self-conscious class, rather to vertically integrated groupings of service suppliers and their respective clients and customers. The tendency, in other words, will be to segment and subdivide a potential mass opposition. Only a 'mass socialist movement', O'Connor concludes, can overcome this divisive effect of the emerging social–industrial complex (1973, pp. 249–55; cf. Gough, 1979, pp. 138–41).

'Structural helplessness'

O'Connor wrote over a decade ago. Today the tendencies might seem to be going the other way. In 1980s Britain, under Conservative rule, widespread 'privatization' of state enterprises and state services is taking place. Private home ownership, at the expense of both the public and private rented sectors, has been achieved by two-thirds of all households. One-fifth of the population owns some equity shares, largely through the sale of public enterprises. There is much talk of a 'welfare backlash' and a decisive breakdown of the Keynesian welfare state that was the linchpin of the political consensus of the postwar period (see, for example, Miller, 1986).

But do not many of the elements also point to the very 'social–industrial complex' that O'Connor projected? Are not many of them examples of the state's farming out activities to monopolistic sections of private capital? 'Privatization' takes place generally without any corresponding increase in competition. The degree of monopolistic control remains as high after 'privatization' as before (for example, British Telecom, British Gas, British Airports Authority). The market remains as rigged and regulated by state policies – on such matters, for instance, as consumer credit and currency rates – as it has been since the war. State hand-outs to industry remain a ready recourse, as in the large public subsidies to British Shipbuilders, British Steel, British Leyland.

There are other, more direct, indications of the continuing strength of the state–business nexus. Private industry is invited to fund special schools for achieving 'scientific and technical excellence', with a remit from the state to oversee critical aspects of the curriculum and staff recruitment. Universities and poly-technics are directed to establish customer–contract relationships with private industry as well as government departments. Welfare services are not abandoned – and it is clearly recognized that it would be electorally damaging to do so, given the strong support for the welfare state among the population at large.[6] The state even boosts, and boasts about, its spending on some of the most popular parts, such as the National Health Service. But with noisy self-advertisement it farms out to private enterprise certain ancillary activities, such as hospital catering and cleaning. In all this Conservative spokesmen make great play with the language of the market and 'the spirit of free enterprise'. What they do not point out is how dominant the state remains by virtue of its continuing high level of expenditure and employment. Nor do they remind us – although some Opposition parties have done so – that what the state gives away it can also take back.

It is easy, in the midst of events, to overestimate their importance. This is the journalistic fallacy. The move to the 'radical right' in several democracies marks important changes in the moral and ideological climate of those societies (and no-one should underrate these 'non-material' factors). Part of the appeal of the New Right is the nostalgic evocation of the past: past glory – 'putting the "Great" back in Great Britain', making America 'stand tall' again; and past values – reviving authority, regenerating the family, marriage and religion. But, however important the past as a storehouse of cultural symbols, there can be no real going back to the political economy of the past – no 'rolling back of the frontiers of the state', no 'dismantling of the welfare apparatus'. The marriage of large-scale monopoly capital with the state has gone too far, and is far too important to both, to be annulled by party rhetoric and short-term party manoeuvring. This has been implicitly acknowledged by New Right leaders, as the level and direction of state spending – noted above – make clear.

Thatcherism and Reaganism are both populist, and draw on anti-state sentiment; but they are also both authoritarian (Phillips, 1982; Hall, 1983; Moe, 1985). This leaves the state with a wide discretion, and undiminished power, to intervene according to the perceived needs of the time. At one moment it may be largely the area of ideology and social control – the educational system, the media, local government, police and prisons, and all the paraphernalia of the warfare state (arms spending, internal and external surveillance, and so on). At another moment it could take a turn towards corporatism – always, despite current ill-favour, a temptation for all power groups in the zero-sum conditions of advanced industrial societies. The strength of 'apple-pie authoritarianism' (Phillips, 1982, p. 32) indeed lies in its expansive capacity to blend old and new: anti-state rhetoric with massive centralization, *lassez-faire* individualism with organic Toryism, nostalgic patriotism with a hard-headed wooing of foreign multinationals.

As many have pointed out, the political economy of authoritarian populism is distinctly unhelpful and profoundly frustrating to certain sectors of capital – notably, in the American as much as the British case, manufacturing (Jessop *et al.*, 1984; Leys, 1985; Krieger, 1986, pp. 159–65). This suggests that when the necessary 'restructuring' has taken place, longer-term tendencies will reassert themselves and the continuities with the 1960s and 1970s will be more evident. A Japanese-style corporatism, rather than either the divisive Social Darwinism of the right or the more politicized European corporatism, may well then appear to monopoly capital the most attractive political form. The Reagan–Thatcher phenomenon has the appearance of a temporary holding operation, a hiatus between one phase of capitalism and another, 'post-industrial', phase. In the interregnum, as Gramsci noted, 'a great variety of morbid symptoms appears'.

The strains imposed upon society by the New Right experiment will not necessarily be repaid by a new, streamlined, effective capitalism. The costs in terms of unemployment and social divisiveness may be too high. The new international division of labour may make it more difficult for any but the most powerful capitalist nations to prosper, pushing many erstwhile leaders, such as Britain, further and further down the economic slope. But it need hardly be said these days that such stresses will not necessarily benefit the left either, whether we consider the prospects for old-style socialism or the newer, greener, vision of a 'sane, humane, ecological' future (Robertson, 1985). Where the red and green critiques remain important, however, is in providing an insistent counterpoint to the erratic, crisis-strewn progress of capitalism. They raise questions about the kinds of 'contradictions' that may not necessarily lead to breakdown but rather reflect a certain 'structural helplessness' (Offe, 1985, p. 63) in the face of accumulating problems and frustrations within the capitalist world order.

How, for instance, will the capitalist (or any other) world deal with the now-visible 'energy gap' that by common expert consent will confront industrial civilization early in the next century? How far can nuclear power, with its attendant risks and danger, supply the want and at what costs to political freedoms? What of the continuing environmental destruction and depletion of natural resources? How practicable though are alternative sources of energy or alternative, 'low-energy' life-styles? The current answers are not reassuring (Hodgson, 1983; Edmonds and Reilly, 1985; United Nations, 1987).

What also of the continuing moral, social and psychological costs of capitalism? A growing literature points to the insufficiency of capitalism to satisfy consumption wants and human needs at anything but the crudest material levels. The 'dizzy pirouette of wants and commodities' created by advanced capitalism has led to the fragmentation and homogenization of needs, and 'the dissolution of the commodity into an unstable network of characteristics and messages' (Leiss, 1978, p. 103). Not only are needs and wants thus no longer satisfied by commodities, but needs themselves are distended and distorted by capitalist requirements to the point where some of them inflict physical and psychological damage on individuals while others – such as the needs for community, care, and respect – receive no recognition whatsoever (Williams, 1983; Ignatieff, 1984).

Disraeli thought that modern society had mistaken comfort for civilization; to this Tibor Scitovsky (1977) adds the equally penetrating criticism that affluent Western society has mistaken comfort for pleasure – or rather, allowed active pleasure to be displaced by mere comfort. In a similar vein Hirsch (1977) points to the disappointments of consumers who fail to get the quality (or 'positional') goods and services that they had legitimately expected as they progress economically; while Hirschman (1982) adds the melancholy twist that inevitable disappointment and disillusion are in store if and when those consumers get the very goods they have set their hearts on.

Market mechanisms and mentalities invade every sphere of life – not simply work and politics, but recreation, friendship, family and marriage. All are subjected to the capitalist rationality of 'least cost' and 'utility maximization'. But the market is a poor mechanism for handling the non-material and the social spheres of human life. It cannot easily deliver 'positional' and public goods, and it is inefficient in its own self-professed goal of maximizing personal well-being and happiness. Discontent and divisions among many are the other side of material abundance for some (Sen, 1983).

The end of societies is as slow as their beginning, frequently more so. Revolutionary cataclysms may hasten it, though they may also, as Tocqueville noted, give existing social orders a new lease of life. If, as many historians from Marx onwards have suggested, capitalism took three or more centuries to emerge from feudalism, why expect its decline and demise to take so much less? Industrial capitalism was established, on a reasonably general scale, only by the end of the nineteenth century. In the course of this century it has extended its reach and intensified its hold. The very novelty of its full operation, and the dynamism intrinsic to its mode, have misled some into seeing the emergence of a 'post-industrial' society – barely half a century after industrial society itself had in any real sense come of age. This would be rapid change indeed and, one might add, unprecedented. Social orders change somewhat more slowly than intellectual fashions. Post-industrial theorists have sought to foreshorten capitalism's past and fore-close its future every bit as roughly and arbitrarily as revolutionary socialists (Kumar, 1978; Badham, 1986).

Some thinkers indeed have been pointing to signs of the renewal rather than the replacement of capitalism. Those convinced of cyclical phenomena such as Kondratieff 'long waves' have suggested that far from facing long-term decline we may be on the threshold of a new upswing in the economy. 'Information technology' and its associated cultural infrastructure will provide the spur to a new swarm of technological innovations which will revitalize the world economy, just as cars and electrical goods pulled the economy out of the global recession of the 1930s (Freeman *et al.*, 1982; Bell, 1985; Gershuny, 1987).[7] Other thinkers, also depending to some extent on a hopeful view of the new technology, have discerned a 'second industrial divide' marking the long-term evolution of capitalist society. Computer-controlled 'flexible' production in small 'high-tech cottage industries', as in the new industrial districts of central and north-eastern Italy, is bringing about a regeneration of the work environment and may allow capitalism to go beyond the alienating 'Fordism' of classic large-scale mass production (Piore and Sabel, 1984).

Marx wrote, with a significance still often unappreciated, that 'the bourgeois period of history has to create the material basis of the new world' (Marx and Engels, 1962, I, p. 358). Driving the point home in his account of the continuing worldwide expansion of capitalism, David Harvey remarks that 'the "historical mission" of the bourgeoisie is not accomplished overnight, nor are the "material conditions of a new world" created in a day' (1982, p. 436). We can expect, as ever before, massive disruptions and bloody turmoil as capitalism continues to transform the world. It remains the case that, half a century after Keynes warned us of it, 'avarice and usury and precaution must be our gods for a little longer still' (Keynes, 1972, p. 331). The discontents and disappointments of industrial life can be expected to increase *pari passu* with world industrialization. But whether, when, and from where the new society will emerge as the fruits of this travail are questions clothed in obscurity.

Notes

1 'The modern history of capital dates from the creation in the sixteenth century of a world-embracing commerce and a world-embracing market' (Marx, 1954, p. 146).

2 Cf. Cohen: 'Marx was not a breakdown theorist . . . There is no economically legislated final breakdown' 1978, pp. 203–4. See also Maddison, 1982, p. 18; Rousseas, 1979, pp. 11–14; and the discussion in Hobsbawm, 1984, pp. 44–8; Wood, 1984, pp. 102–7; Heilbroner, 1985, pp. 178–9, 194–208; Shaikh, 1985, pp. 138–43; and O'Connor, 1987, pp. 49–107. Compare also Marx's caution that the 'law' of the falling rate of profit 'acts only as a tendency', and that 'it is only under certain circumstances and only after long periods that its effects become strikingly pronounced' (Marx, 1959, p. 233). For a more 'determinist' view of the economic contradictions of capitalism, see however Marx, 1973, pp. 411ff., 748–50.

3 For a helpful critical discussion, with copious citation, of the immense literature on proletarian class consciousness, see especially Przeworski, 1977; Lipset,

1981; and Marshall, 1983. On the British working class specifically, and the sectional divisions, fragmentation and privatization that many have discerned in its recent development, see Hobsbawm, 1981; Williams, 1983; Marshall *et al.*, 1985; Newby *et al.*, 1985; and Pahl and Wallace, 1987.

4   The proportion of the workforce that is unionized averages about 30 per cent for the major countries of Western Europe (the main exceptions are Belgium and the Nordic countries, which are higher, and France, which is lower) (Therborn, 1984, p. 11; Offe, 1985, p. 336 n13). In the USA, with a historically low rate, the proportion in 1984 was under 20 per cent (Davis, 1986, p. 147); in the UK, with a historically high rate, the proportion is now close to the European average – 31 per cent in 1985 (Department of Employment, 1987b, pp. 84–6).

5   For the figures in this paragraph, and commentary on them, see Rose, 1980; Therborn, 1984, pp. 27–9, 34–5; *Times*, 24 January 1985, and 8 November 1986; Davis, 1986, pp. 235–6; Krieger, 1986, pp. 91–101, 159–76; Parry, 1986, pp. 208–9; Kavanagh, 1987, pp. 212–30; Central Statistical Office, 1987, p. 114.

In view of common misconceptions, a number of things need to be said about 'the Thatcher effect' in Britain in the 1980s. First, the annual average growth in public spending since the Conservatives came to office in 1979 has exceeded that of the Labour government of 1974–9: 1.3 per cent a year under the Conservatives compared with 1 per cent under Labour (*Times*, 8 November 1986). Second, any changes in the size and composition of public expenditure – which, due largely to increased unemployment, are not great – and such discontinuities in social policy as there are, began under Labour, before the Conservatives took office (Gough, 1979, pp. 131–41; 1983, pp. 148–9; Hall, 1983; Krieger, 1986, p. 84). Third, much of the more publicized Thatcherite legislation, such as the 'anti-union' laws, have had little impact on actual practice (on industrial relations, see Milward and Stevens, 1987; Goldring, 1987). Mrs Thatcher has been very successful in altering the moral climate of British society; she has been less successful in altering its structural continuities. For a balanced assessment, see Kavanagh, 1987.

For Reagan's parallel difficulties in holding back public expenditure in the USA – due partly to successful congressional pressure in maintaining domestic social programmes – see Mills, 1984; Bawden and Palmer, 1984; Krieger, 1986, pp. 154–86; Hogan, 1987. These show that federal social programme spending as a proportion of GNP has barely shifted under Reagan from its postwar high of 11 per cent in 1976.

6   This is shown not just for Britain (Krieger, 1986, pp. 88–90; Kavanagh, 1987, p. 217; Taylor-Gooby, 1987), but also in continuing public support for the social programmes of the New Deal and the Great Society in the United States (Navarro, 1985). Neither in the United States nor Britain is endorsement whole-hearted and clear-cut. As both Taylor-Gooby and Navarro show, public support for welfare is selective and pragmatic, not ideological or 'universalist'. The Thatcher government's practice has echoed this closely: 'government provision of social services within an anti-welfarist ideology, benefit but no beliefs, welfare but no welfare state' (Krieger, 1986, p. 89; see also Parry, 1986, p. 209).

7   But, compare Hirschman's comment on the Kondratieff cycle, 'whose duration is so long (50–60 years) that, given the limited historical experience with capitalism so far, we cannot be quite sure whether it really exists' (1982, p. 4). For a discussion of 'long wave' theory, see Kitwood, 1984; and see also, on the 'information society', Lyon, 1986.

2

Corporatism and the New Right

DAVID McCRONE, BRIAN ELLIOTT and
FRANK BECHHOFER

Introduction

A basic and pervasive tension between the interests of capital and
labour is an inevitable feature of Western capitalist societies.
Historically, governments have sought to manage this conflict in
different ways, but gradually, in most Western countries in the
twentieth century, various forms of what has been called
'corporatism' have appeared alongside efforts to stabilize relations
between capital and labour. Corporatism is a term given to
these efforts through which governments seek to bring together
in an institutionalized way state agencies, bodies representing employers and others representing the interests
of workers (McLennan, 1984; Schmitter, 1985; Williamson,
1985).

In this chapter, we shall look briefly at how corporatism has
developed in Britain since the 1920s and then at some of its
criticisms which began to surface during the late 1960s and early
1970s. Thus, the complex of boards, commissions and other
institutions through which governments have brought together
representatives of capital and labour, and endeavoured to plan the
United Kingdom economy have been attacked from both the 'left'
and the 'right'. The left has often expressed considerable
scepticism, if only because of fears that, by belonging to various
governmental consultative and planning bodies, the working
class would be 'incorporated' into capitalist society, acquiesce in
schemes designed chiefly to benefit capital, lose its vision of an

alternative socialist order and, thereby, its capacity for radical action. But the most sustained and vigorous attack has been launched since the mid-1970s by a new and self-consciously radical New Right. To the politicians grouped around Margaret Thatcher and Keith Joseph, corporatism has been regarded as a manifestation of a strategy, a philosophy and a set of practices which has failed. While corporatism certainly did not give rise to the New Right, it exemplified a view of politics which had been tried by both Labour and Conservative governments and which, in the eyes of the New Right, had failed. Attempts by postwar governments to *plan* the economy, to bring employers' associations and trade unions together in various diverse bodies to negotiate forms of economic rationalization and to construct the welfare state were depicted as misguided and, ultimately, counter-productive. Corporatist structures and strategies were seen as part and parcel of efforts to construct new forms of social and economic consensus to override market forces. Thus, with the agreement of both capital and labour, the state had intervened extensively in economic life, created different national-ized enterprises, set up a large number of regulatory bodies, and manipulated a high level of aggregate demand through public expenditure. To the 'new conservatives', these post-war strategies had been unsuccessful and, through the writings of Hayek (1976a and b), Friedman (1962) and others, they redis-covered a faith in the 'free market'. Consequently, they argued that only market forces could restore the efficiency and com-petitiveness of the British economy and, from the 1970s, those who thought of themselves as part of the New Right argued for a radical reconstructing of the economy and society on 'market principles' and, therefore, for the dismantling of corporatism.

In this chapter, we shall attempt to explain these powerful and determined attacks of the Right and to understand theories, values and ideas which shaped their criticisms. How did they mobilize themselves and various other forces and how were they able to articulate a critique of practices, relations and assumptions which had endured for such a long period of time? However, we will also argue that corporatist tendencies may eventually be reasserted due to the modernizing ambitions of politicians, business and labour leaders, and because the social gains achieved under postwar corporatism are valued and will be defended, not only by the traditional labour movement but also by many other social groups in society.

The British road to corporatism

The regimes which developed in the most thoroughgoing way the systems of central control, of state co-ordination of functional groups – the regimes from which corporatism has acquired its most pejorative associations – were those of Hitler and Mussolini. Their authoritarian governments used corporatism as a means for modernizing their societies between the wars. The fascist leaders were men of the 'machine age', intent on harnessing technology in order to improve living standards and, in the case of Germany, to rebuild the industrial, technological and military might of a nation conquered in the Great War. This strategy required the mobilizing of economic resources by the state in the pursuit of economic and political progress. This association of corporatism with autocratic and militaristic regimes meant that, after 1945, few of the liberal democracies regarded this system of political and industrial management as appropriate to their needs. The concept of 'corporatism' was tainted by its association with fascism and deteriorated, as Winckler has put it, into 'a term of promiscuous abuse' (Winckler, 1977). But, in fact, in many Western societies, the conditions of war had led to a considerable degree of central control, and the creation of many state structures with corporatist tendencies. The need to co-ordinate production efforts and to resolve differences of interest between employers and employees in particular laid many of the foundations for corporatist structures. In postwar attempts to rebuild shattered economies, a good many governmental boards and public co-ordinating bodies were kept and others created.

While it is usual to point to the post-1945 period as the one in which Britain became a 'corporatist' society, there is evidence that the corporatist tendency had its roots much earlier in the century. Keith Middlemas (1979, p. 20; and 1986), for example, argues that 'corporate bias' entered the British political system in the industrial and political crisis of 1911. Then, the state was faced with a wave of strikes, a great clamour for social legislation (the National Insurance Act was passed in 1911) and mounting civil unrest in Ireland. The Great War gave added impetus to a more centrally directed economy by means of the War Cabinet Manpower Committee, the Industrial Unrest Commissions of 1917, and the National Industrial Conference. Thus, in order to avoid industrial and social breakdown, the state had to find ways of reinforcing its authority through a series of compromises with different groups in society. So it was that, by the 1920s, the Trades Union Congress

(TUC) and employers' associations – the National Council of Employers' Organisations (NCEO), the National Association of Manufacturers, the British Employers' Confederation (BEC), and the Federation of British Industry (FBI) – became 'estates of the realm'. Indeed, the challenges from labour, which occurred between 1915 and 1922, and the 1926 General Strike made the search for a strategy of crisis avoidance all the more urgent. Middlemas (1979, p. 20) argues that trade union and employers' associations were elevated from 'interest groups' to 'governing institutions': 'Equilibrium was maintained because the governing institutions came to share some of the political power and attributes of the state, itself avid to admit bodies to its orbit rather than face a free-for-all with a host of individual claimants'.

The state, through its civil servants, mobilized groups on the basis of 'the national interest'. Middlemas (1986, p. 10) points out: 'those who aspire to and are able to compete at the "altruistic" level of the national interest enter the environs of the state'. Those who remained outside the invisible boundary were defined as self-interested lobbies or pressure groups. Into these charmed environs in the second decade of the twentieth century were admitted the representative organizations of business and labour.

It was, however, the Second World War which gave a massive boost to 'corporate bias' in Britain, for the wartime government actively sought to bring labour, industry and the City round the governing table (see the Appendix for a chronology of corporatism since 1939). These new 'governing institutions' were co-ordinated by senior civil servants acting as brokers in the new government departments of Supply, Munitions, Transport and Aircraft Production. The committee structures assembled in wartime survived the end of the war and were carried over into peacetime production in which, remembering the depression of the 1930s, full employment was the lodestone. In 1947, the Economic Planning Board was formed, and the FBI, the BEC and the TUC all joined, despite the rivalry of the two employers' associations (a second merger attempt between the FBI, representing larger businesses, and the BEC, representing smaller ones, failed in the same year). The TUC used the 'war memory' to remind the government of its importance in the production process, an easy task given the Labour government's commitment to tripartism. The higher reaches of the civil service were none too averse to this arrangement because they were equally hostile to socialism (as opposed to labourism) and to advocacy of the free market.

On the Right, the Conservative Party had been won over by the

1945 defeat to the approach outlined in Harold Macmillan's *Middle Way* (1938), written while its author was in the political wilderness and deeply affected by his observation of mass unemployment in his Stockton constituency. After 1945, Churchill's Tories were quite at home with the concept of 'the mixed economy' and Labour politicians, who had inherited the wartime structures they had helped to create, saw no difficulty in this version of 'socialism'. When Labour lost office in 1951, the bargain held for the rest of the decade until shop-floor demands for higher wages placed the TUC in a difficult position. While unwilling to cede its role as a governing institution responsible for wage moderation, it could not ignore grass-roots pressure. Among business, too, the smaller and more militant BEC threatened to break the consensus, while the larger FBI was more accommodating. Small business eventually complained that the price for the corporatist bias was too high, although arrangements like Resale Price Maintenance were to the liking of small traders. Its abolition in 1956 did much to cut adrift this sector and drive them into a more critical view of the corporatist arrangement.

From the 1950s, critics pointed out that Britain was falling behind its competitors, and blamed the cosy system of corporatism for inducing stagnation rather than innovation. Above all, they said, the inflationary pressures of wage demands and the increasing push for state welfare made many demands on government. The mainstream reaction was to try to formalize the system by arranging deals or 'social contracts' between governments, employers and unions. Critics argued that corporatism had become a device which allowed two sets of con-servatisms to coexist: that of business, wanting security and established markets; and that of labour, wanting comfortable continuities in employment and working conditions. At the heart of the system, the civil servants with their chronic dislike of socialism and free market economics were also judged to be a force resistant to change. The public service, as J. P. Nettl (quoted in Wiener, 1981) noted in the mid-1960s, had become a role model for business leaders, and the cultural dominance of Whitehall had encouraged business corporations to mimic its consensual outlook and behaviour. As this process became more established in the 1960s, so its critics on the Left and Right were better able to identify what they were against. So the stage was set for assaults from both directions on the temple of corporatist consensus.

The political critiques of corporatism

On the Left, the 1950s and 1960s saw serious attempts at reconstructing the project of socialism, both politically and ideologically. At a political level, the failure of Labour to win office from 1951 until 1964 generated both revisionist and radical formulations of socialist ambitions. Among the trade unions, a new phase of shop-floor militancy developed in the context of fifteen years' full employment and, as a result, the TUC found itself pressed between the demands from above to hold the line on wage increases, and those from union members below seeking higher wages. A new breed of union leaders emerged, particularly in the big general unions like the Transport and General Workers Union, with leaders like Frank Cousins and Jack Jones. Such leaders were more willing to allow shop-floor workers to express their demands, and were very suspicious of the corporatist consensus. Among leftist intellectuals, as well, the suspicion was growing that corporatism was 'a political structure designed to integrate the organized working class into the capitalist state' (Panitch, 1980). Corporatism, they argued, was essentially a *class* concept, a means of waging class warfare by a capitalist state when market conditions (such as unemployment) could not be relied upon to subordinate labour. These critics argued that corporatism had come about in the years since 1918 because the state had to come to terms with the power of organized labour. A system of industrial conflict-management was evolved by the state in conjunction with employers' organizations; one which remained relatively low-key as long as trade-union demands were moderate. The 1960s and 1970s, however, saw an explosion of rank-and-file militancy, and governments struggled to impose wage controls as a means of containing inflationary pressures. In this leftist analysis, Labour governments were particularly reprehensible because they manipulated the political sympathies of organized labour and played upon the weakness of pusillanimous union leaders. The 'social contract' of 1974–5 represented the peak of this 'bargained corporatism' (Crouch, 1979). The Labour government sought to introduce wage controls and the unions acquiesced in these for the benefits of new labour legislation, notably the Trade Union and Labour Relations Act and the Employment Protection Act of 1975. The Left judged the collapse of this settlement in 1978–9 ('the winter of discontent') as the inevitable outcome of capitalist contradictions.

If corporatism is simply a capitalist strategy for controlling labour, as some on the Left have argued, it is hard to explain why the Right has taken such exception to it. What disturbed the Right was the fact that, as they saw it, labour had become 'an estate of the realm', a governing institution and part of the ruling apparatus of modern Britain. Above all, the Right argued, the state, at the behest of labour, had placed such controls on the operations of capital (especially with regard to Planning Agreements in the mid-1970s) that private property and the market system were in danger of being swept away. The state, then, had become directive rather than simply supportive. As a result, the 1970s witnessed a series of sustained critiques from the Right, many couched in apocalyptic tones. Writing in 1977, for example, Robert Moss presented what he called a 'dystopia' – a prophecy of what Britain would be like if present trends continued. In this grey, totalitarian Britain, he imagines, farms have been collectivized, personal wealth, including jewellery, has been expropriated; and a gin and tonic costs £250. Moss was not alone in painting this bleak scenario. Brian Crozier (1979), who headed the Institute for Strategic Studies, had his own global version in which democracy gives way to authoritarian or totalitarian rule. Such lurid scaremongering reflected the mood of the Right in the 1970s. The first half of the decade was marked by economic and social developments, by economic conditions and crises that caused profound unease among a good many Conservative politicians. Heath's government of 1970 set out to pursue sustained economic growth through market mechanisms rather than state-led investment. This, the so-called 'Selsdon Man' phase, perhaps the most radical strategy of any government since 1945, was in trouble by 1972. The reform of industrial relations generated intense opposition from trade unions. Pay settlements were high, unemployment and inflation rising, and, judging that its free-market policies had failed, the government changed direction, introduced a full-blown statutory prices and incomes policy, and went for state-led development through projects like the Channel Tunnel and a third London airport. This strategy was to no avail when the quadrupling of oil prices by OPEC coincided with the miners' strike of 1973–4. The defeat of Heath in general elections held in February and October 1974, marked the discrediting of his 'right-progressive' strategy, and opened the way for a new brand of Conservatism, character-ized by its commitment to neo-liberal economic ideas, and its antipathy to many of the social and moral changes of the previous decade. Although Sir Keith Joseph was the intellectual leader of this 'new' Conservatism (though much of what he argued had earlier been outlined by Enoch Powell), it was Margaret Thatcher who became leader of the party and the politician who popularized and, in many ways, personified the philosophy of this New Right.

The Labour government which was elected in 1974 adopted an interventionist, corporatist style of administration. It was through this that the 'social contract' with the trade unions was born. The Labour government, in return, introduced a number of labour laws: the Redundancy Payments Act, the Employment Protection Act, Contract of Employment Act, Trade Union and Labour Relations Act, the Equal Pay Act, the Social Security Act and the Race Relations Act. The policies which these laws reflected were anathema, not only to a small set of Tory politicians, but also to a wider group of business leaders, journalists, academics and opinion makers. From 1974 to 1979, a network of individuals and organizations identifying themselves as a New Right emerged, voicing fierce criticism of the Wilson and Callaghan governments. In the closing months of 1978, with high inflation, high interest rates and extensive labour unrest, the prophecies of economic and social doom were given some credibility. Thus, the political success of the New Right in 1979 owed much to the process of mobilization which took place throughout the second half of the 1970s. Business, both large and small, felt it had much of which to complain. Both corporate leaders and self-employed entrepreneurs considered themselves unfairly hit by the new legislation and high rates of inflation. They complained of over-regulation and over-taxation. As the old entrepreneurial middle class felt its influence wane, so it perceived that of the new bureaucratized, professional middle classes grow, largely fostered by the expansion of state services. And, of course, the traditional 'class enemy' – the organized working class – had been strengthened by the new wave of legislation promulgated by Labour governments.

Small and independent business felt the burden of Labour's laws more than most; for example, measures such as the 8 per cent levy on National Insurance for the self-employed, and the introduction of licences for subcontractors, known as the 714 certificates. In a remarkably short period of time – from 1974 to 1975 – new organizations sprang up to represent small businesses (King and Nugent, 1979; Elliott et al., 1982): NFSE (National Federation for the Self-Employed), ASP (Association of Self-Employed People), NASE (National Association of the Self-Employed), IBPA (Independent Business Person's Association) and the Forum for Independent Business. Even older established organizations were re-invigorated; the Association of Independent Businesses (AIB) representing medium-size manufacturing companies, while a new break-away organization, the Union of Independent Companies (UIC) fought for the middle ground. Many of these threatened to outflank the CBI, which was seen to be too identified with big business, and even included within its ranks state industries. The AIB, itself, was the descendant of the older Association of Independent Manufacturers which had refused to join other business groups to form the Confederation of British Industry (CBI) in 1965.

The prognosis for business in general was poor. Inflation in the middle years of the 1970s was high: 16 per cent in 1974, 24.2 per cent in 1975, 16.5 per cent in 1976 and 15.9 per cent in 1977; and, as a result, creditors found the value of their capital dramatically eroded. Inflation was corroding the morality of enterprise, for it sharply reduced the value of savings and undermined the need for planning. Government restrictions on incomes had eroded wage differentials and corporate managers, in particular, had found their relative rates of pay falling. Company profits, too, began to collapse; from about 8 per cent per annum (pre-tax and corrected for inflation) in the early 1970s to less than 3 per cent by the end of the decade (Useem, 1983). Leagues and lobbies emerged, too, to speak for the middle classes in general (Elliott *et al.*, 1987). The Middle Class Association had been formed by two MPs in the early 1970s and, although it did not survive for long, it was succeeded by the National Association for Freedom (NAFF, latterly the Freedom Association), which became a major force in right-wing politics, using the law courts in an expensive and public way, notably in the Grunwick dispute of 1976. On the extreme fringes, more militant and militaristic bodies emerged, mobilizing 'apprehensive patriots'. So GB75 was formed by Colonel Stirling, Civil Assistance by Lady Birdwood, and old organizations received a new lease of life as the right-wing rhetoric about a supposedly imminent revolution began to be taken seriously by some sections of the middle class. All saw themselves as defending what were defined as 'freedoms' and regaining those which had been lost.

Providing intellectual force for much of this middle-class discontent was a collection of diverse intellectual ideas. Simply put, the emerging New Right drew upon three ideological strands (Elliott and McCrone, 1987): the *libertarian*, which argued for personal as well as economic freedom; the *neo-liberal*, which focused on 'setting the market free'; and the *conservative*, which sought to impose tighter social and moral discipline on society. Of these, it was the neo-liberal which emerged as the dominant strand during the mid-to-late 1970s. Libertarianism appears not to have made any serious impact on the Conservative Party. But what was of great importance was the cadre of right-wing intellectuals, particularly those associated with the revival of interest in neo-liberal economics and the 'Austrian school', centred around the ideas of Friedrich von Hayek (1976). This revival of liberal political economy owed much to the Institute for Economic Affairs (IEA), AIMS (a business pressure group), the Adam Smith Institute and Sir Keith Joseph's Centre for Policy Studies. The oldest of these groups, notably the IEA and AIMS, had been calling for the 'freeing' of business from the state since the 1940s. Their critique started from the premiss that state intervention in business affairs and social welfare generated inefficiencies and waste. Only the market provided a mechanism for allocating goods in an efficient and rational way. The more the state intervened, the less well the economy and society could work, since 'controls' and 'subsidies' distorted the 'proper' working of the market, and generated unrealistic expectations among producers and consumers. The views of Brittan (1977, p. 119) and other neo-liberals were fairly unusual among Conservative thinkers if only because they wanted to pursue the implications of the primacy of the market-place to personal behaviour. Brittan recognized that advocates of competitive private enterprise, as he called them, and libertarian radicals had common interests: 'If only these two groups could overcome their mutual prejudices – in one case about non-bourgeois lifestyle and, in the other, about the profit motive – the remainder of the twentieth century could see an unexpected turning of the tide, towards individual freedom and limited government' (1977, p. 127).

In other words, personal liberty or 'permissiveness' was at one with competitive capitalism. 'Doing your own thing' was both the ethos of the market economy and the basis of personal life. Neither 'mainstream' conservatives nor socialists were prepared to accept this tenet, since they both started from collectivist assumptions. What Brittan and the economic liberals wanted was not simply a market *economy* but a market *order*; a complex network of exchanges between individuals organized in different markets. Because this order is fragile, it has to be protected by the state – its only useful function. Thus, in the neo-liberal view, the state has frequently exceeded its legitimate role because it has bought off the growing social expectations of the electorate. Accordingly, universal franchise has put particular pressure on the institutions of liberal democracy, and the state has somehow to manage these electoral expectations (Hailsham, 1978). The market can be threatened by democracy, for democracy, neo-liberals argue (Brittan, 1977, p. 281), harbours the politics of 'excessive expectations'. It responds to popular pressures which raise expectations and, in postwar Britain, as in other liberal democratic societies, people's aspirations have been heightened by a decline in social deference. Groups pursue their self-interest in the political market-place, and excessive burdens are then placed upon the distributive role of government. Politicians are forced to react to short-run popular demands, because electorates have short-term expectations. Thus, at each turn of the ratchet, governments pursue the politics of appeasement and seek to buy off pressure by allowing sectional interests to share in policy making. Ultimately, the state loses its capacity to manage effectively and the corporatist society is born. Such, at least, are the arguments of many of the ideologists of the New Right.

This critique is reinforced by the thesis of 'overload' or 'ungovernability', which was fashionable among political scientists in the 1970s. Anthony King, for example, in a tract called 'The problem of overload', reached similar conclusions to the neo-liberals. Writing in 1976, he stated: 'Britain has become harder to govern. The reason it has become harder to govern is that, at one and the same time, the range of problems that government is expected to deal with has vastly increased, and its capacity to deal with problems, even many of the ones it had before, has decreased. It is not the increase in the number of problems alone that matters, or the reduction in capacity. It is the two coming together' (p. 25). The solution to this dilemma, according to King, is for government to act upon the demand side of politics by reducing the expectations of the electorate: 'Governments have tried to play God. They have failed. But they go on trying. How can they be made to stop? Perhaps over the next few years, they should be more concerned with how the number of tasks that government has come to be expected to perform can be reduced' (1976, p. 29). Little did he know at the time of writing that Mrs Thatcher would take his prescription seriously.

The concept of 'state overload' had become part of the recognized currency of many of the neo-conservative critics of liberal democracies in the latter part of the 1970s. In the United States, for instance, Bell, Kristol and Moynihan built it into their critique of liberal society (for a critical overview, see Birch, 1984). But other writers, such as Habermas (1975) and Offe and Keane (1984), drawing upon a Marxist tradition, also regarded the process as yet another contradiction of capitalism and as a manifestation of its crisis of legitimation. Certainly, the 'overload' thesis chimed in nicely with the prevailing political and ideological conditions of the 1970s. Both Conservative and Labour govern-ments effected U-turns in their policies. 'Hyperinflation' seemed to be the price of political and economic weakness. 'Individual freedom' and 'getting the state off people's backs' became increasingly popular as political slogans. Economic liberalism was back on the agenda and the state seemed set for decline.

By the late 1970s, then, there had emerged a 'New Right' armed with the necessary ideological weapons for attacking corporatism. Petty capital had felt the burden of state fiscal policies and begun to organize. Some simply wanted a seat at the decision-making table – the so-called 'Third Force', sitting alongside big business and organized labour – while others of a more libertarian persuasion were more intent on sweeping away the whole corporatist structure. Think-tanks and policy institutes emerged, offering more robust criticisms of government intervention. The attrition of company profits, hyperinflation and the imposition of various government controls had brought big business on the side of those demanding 'freedom' of the market. Following the lead of the more right-wing Institute of Directors, the CBI was arguing by the late 1970s that social welfare, in particular, and public expenditure, in general, were inhibiting wealth creation and it, therefore, threw in its lot with the policies of the Thatcherite Conservative Party.

These policies were heavily influenced by 'monetarism', an economic doctrine whose modern formulation owed most to Milton Friedman and the Chicago School, and which claimed that tight governmental control of the money supply could defeat inflation. Monetarism, as Gamble puts it, was 'the battering ram that made the breach' (1986, p. 32) in the walls of Keynesianism and postwar social democracy. What began as a narrow technical debate between economists took on the character of a full-blown political strategy in which cutting public expenditure and, particularly, the Public Sector Borrowing Requirement, would restore 'sound money'. Corporatism had built into it an assumption of full employment and when, by the late 1960s, both unemploy-ment and inflation began to rise, the simple trade-off between them seemed no longer to be possible. If it was the Labour government of the late 1970s, under pressure from the International Monetary Fund, which adopted monetarism as an expedient financial strategem, it was their Conservative successors who embraced it with enthusiasm and adopted it as their economic policy for the first two or three years of Margaret Thatcher's first administration. It promised not only to restore the profits of business but also, so its advocates believed, to serve to undermine the whole postwar political consensus.

While Friedman and his colleagues were fairly sanguine about the consequences of governments simply adopting the monetarist models and prescriptions, Hayek and his followers wanted a frontal assault on the corporatist institutions which actively prevented the freeing of the market. And pride of place went to trade unions and the interventionist state. Monetarism caught many union leaders off-guard because they were beguiled by the notion that incomes policies were part of the disease and not the cure. Free collective bargaining was a necessity in the new economic order and, after the so-called 'winter of discontent' in 1978–9, it seemed a way out of the impasse. Hayek's aim, on the other hand, was to curb what he perceived to be excessive trade-union power by removing legal immunities, closed-shop and picketing arrangements and, above all, by banishing them from the negotiating table of central government. Just as businesses would have to accept the threat of bankruptcy to control their activities, so labour would have to adhere to the rules of the market-place. Neither of them, therefore, could be allowed to remain 'governing institutions'.

The related strategy of the elected Conservative government of 1979 was to attack public spending – something which was made easier by the Labour government's earlier actions – and to cut taxation: a view derived from their commitment to supply-side economics. For this government, the role of the state was to ensure that the market had 'freedom to work' and to enforce laws of contract. But it did not necessarily mean that the state would disappear, for as Stuart Hall (1986, p. 15) has pointed out: 'It is possible to *use* the state strategically to *divest* the state. The idea that "neo-liberalism" meant the abolition rather than the *recomposition* of the state was always an illusion.'

The election of Mrs Thatcher in 1979 resulted from the disenchantment of the electorate with the 'winter of discontent' and with the Labour government. Her first administration witnessed a marked shift in the level of consultation with representatives of capital and labour. While previous governments had placed considerable emphasis on discussions with both parties in the forum of the National Economic Development Council (NEDC), the new government largely ignored it. Other tripartite agencies survive but only to become the means of implementing government policies in the labour market. Agencies such as the Manpower Services Commission and the Scottish Development Agency continued to function but with more market-oriented policies. The second Conservative government, elected in 1983, pursued a strategy of deregulation and the privatization of state monopolies – from council housing to British Telecom and British Gas. The accruing profits enabled there to be substantial cuts in income tax in 1987 and an appeal to 'popular capitalism'. The election of a third Thatcher government in 1987 would seem to spell the demise of corporatism; the market rules, and the state is simply its handmaiden.

Thatcherism: towards the regeneration of corporatism?

Despite such trends, neo-liberals continue to doubt whether Mrs Thatcher's governments have been sufficiently liberal and anti-statist (Brittan, 1985, p. 52). While it is true there has been an extensive programme of 'privatization', this has not extended competition to any great extent, if only because privatized monopolies have rarely been broken up. Nevertheless, as Stuart Hall (1986, p. 14) points out: 'Thatcherism's "anti-statism" is no mere ideological figleaf. In relation to the economy, the state sector, economic regulation, the "swollen" welfare state (swollen by so-called "unrealistic" popular aspirations), it signified something real and profound – the project to reverse the post-war Keynesian welfare-corporatist consensus.'

There can be little doubt that the Conservative regimes of the 1980s have been committed to withdrawing the state from central areas of economic life and to exposing the economy to international market forces. The destruction of 'quangos' – 'the outriders of the corporate state' as the Freedom Association called them (The Free Nation, 1978) – the deregulation of financial markets, the privatization of state assets and services, and the attack on public employment in both local and central government, are all evidence of the dismantling of corporatist structures. But herein lies a very real contradiction if only because the power of the state has, in many respects, been *extended* rather than diminished. Though the state has withdrawn from some spheres of activity – from some forms of public ownership and from much economic planning – it has intervened much more directly and vigorously in attempting to undermine the power of organized labour. This has been undertaken through industrial relations legislation and through 'set-piece battles' with employees in the automobile, steel and coal-mining industries. The state has extended its powers over local government through 'rate-capping', the system whereby restrictions are placed upon the revenue-raising and, therefore, the spending powers of local authorities. Some local government services have been privatized and a number of local authorities have even been abolished. The aim has not been simply financial control; the attack has been upon local government as an arena for the pursuit of socialist policies, and in which organized labour has been able to pursue policies often radically different from those of the new conservatism. The government's own expenditure patterns (HMSO, 1987) demonstrate how the state has spent *more* not *less* since 1979. Thus, general government expenditure rose by 13.6 per cent in real terms between 1979 and 1987, an increase discounting for inflation of £19.2 billion. By 1990, the government plans an increase of 17.4 per cent over 1979; for an avowedly anti-statist government, this is surprisingly high. Table 2.1 describes expenditure patterns for government departments since 1979.

Table 2.1 Expenditure patterns for government departments, 1979 to 1987

Government departments	Main gainers (%)	Main losers (%)	
Employment	90	Energy	−78
Home Office	50	Trade and Industry	−65
Social Security	39.5	Housing	−60
Arts	30	EEC	−24
Defence	30		
Agriculture	23		
Health	25		

Source: HMSO, 1987.

Of course, the sharp rise in the level of unemployment accounts for increases in spending on employment and social security benefits, while Conservative governments' commitment to law and order and to defence accounts for increases in those areas. At the same time, the withdrawal of the state from the oil industry and the dismantling of regional grants and aid explains why the Energy and Trade and Industry departments have suffered so heavily. But Thatcher governments have also found it necessary to use authoritarian and repressive measures to impose 'freedom' on the economy, and to maintain deregulation of the market. These governments have claimed that only an 'enterprise culture' will generate long-lasting changes in attitudes and behaviour and, as a result of this 'moral crusade' in the interest of economic freedom, the control instruments of the state have been increased. The size of police forces has been expanded, new powers of arrest and detention have been legislated, and most evidently in the miners' strike of 1984/5, police have been deployed in new ways. The concentration of political power in Westminster has been a marked feature, making Thatcher administrations, in many ways, the most 'centrist' governments Britain has witnessed in peace-time. An array of mediating institutions have had their sphere of influence reduced or taken away and central government policies for education, health and welfare have asserted the principles of direct state control. The effect has been that civil society has found its defences greatly weakened with a kind of 'authoritarian centralism' put in place.

Does this mean that a new kind of corporatism has crept back in by stealth? Does it signify that Mrs Thatcher is a corporatist? There are those who at least see this as a possibility. As Goldthorpe (1985, p. 342) observes, some British Marxists advance the argument that: 'sooner or later a "monetarist corporatism" must emerge'. This, however, is implausible, for the reasons Goldthorpe states: 'Thatcher and her ideological mentors saw far more clearly than Marxists were apparently able to do the radical potential of new corporatist tendencies based on union involvement in political bargaining, and have unremittingly opposed them' (p. 343). The critique of corporatism is an important component of the New Right's ideology and it would be ingenuous to suggest that it has been subverted by recent Conservative governments intentionally, or that it has crept back unnoticed. Corporatism provides opportunities for organized labour to obtain concessions from both capital and the state and Thatcher regimes are certainly opposed to this. But by concentrating power within an increasingly centralist state and by weakening civil society, Thatcherism could be laying the foundations for a more thoroughgoing and highly developed corporatism, should a government with different political goals come to power. Moreover, there seems to be ample evidence from other liberal democracies that the exaggerated faith of the New Right in the free market may not really prove very effective in promoting the desired conditions for economic growth and prosperity. Most national economies, with such varied political systems as those of Japan, Sweden and West Germany, rely on strong state infrastructures for economic development. The market left to itself does not necessarily stimulate economic growth in the appropriate areas. Middlemas (1987) has argued that even the present British government has begun to recognize the need for maintaining a forum for the discussion of national economic objectives with various producer groups. Admittedly, it has reduced the importance of the National Economic Development Office (NEDC) by curtailing its meetings to four times a year, and by abolishing 22 of its 36 industry committees ('little Neddies') (*Guardian*, 1987), but it has stopped short of abolishing this quintessential corporatistic body altogether. Indeed, says Middlemas, there is, at least implicitly, a new common agenda for potential corporatist bargaining, reinforced by the mutual inter-dependence of large firms, the banks, financial institutions and major trade unions. Setting this agenda are the Bank of England, the Department of Trade and Industry, and the Manpower Services Commission with its 'broadside interventionism' in the fields of employment, trade and education.

The centralizing tendencies of the present Conservative government could make the re-emergence of state co-ordination of the economy potentially easier. Corporatistic strategies and institutions retain a lingering charm and appeal. The desire to address the plight of the inner cities may well require considerable state co-ordination of private and public agencies, a door through which we may glimpse the shadow of corporatism once more. At the same time, there seems to be little support among the electorates of the different Western capitalist countries for the wholesale withdrawal of state-financed welfare programmes. Mrs Thatcher's government has been careful, so far, not to privatize, in any significant ways, the health, welfare and education services. Public opinion seems to be firmly behind the retention of strong state provision in 'key' welfare services. If there was a tide of sympathy for cutting taxes at the expense of services in the late 1970s and early 1980s, this now seems to have turned. By 1985, only 6 per cent of the population favoured tax reductions at the expense of cuts in social spending (Bosanquet, 1986). The Conservative government has – to date – had to maintain much of the welfare state, itself a reflection of the broader social consensus alongside which many of the corporatistic structures were established.

What has led many observers to regard Thatcherism as a 'revolution' is that it departs so significantly from previous economic strategies of both Conservative and Labour governments. Mrs Thatcher has sought to mobilize 'bourgeois values' – for example, those of 'thrift', 'independence' and 'self-reliance' – alleging that they represent traditional ideals when, it seems, they have enjoyed only brief currency in British economic, political and cultural life. Outside observers, such as the American historian, Martin Wiener (1981, p. 166), realize the scale of the task facing Mrs Thatcher. He argues that large sectors of the English middle class and of the aristocracy have always found industrial activity uncongenial. He speaks of the 'gentrification' of the middle classes in the nineteenth century, a process whereby the 'new' bourgeoisie sought to imitate the life-style and social values of the old. Thus, the historic antipathy to wealth creation through manufacture coincided in the 1960s and 1970s with an explicit organized opposition to the results of technical and material advance, an anti-growth and anti-technology movement which fed upon the older anti-industry tradition. Wiener concludes:

> At the end of the day, it may be that Margaret Thatcher will find her most fundamental challenge not in holding down the money supply or inhibiting government spending, or even in fighting the shop stewards, but in changing this frame of mind. English history in the eighties may turn less on traditional political struggles than on a cultural contest between the two faces of the middle class.
>
> (1981, p. 166)

Consequently, Mrs Thatcher embraces 'liberal' values of the sort which seem to have only a precarious position in English cultural life. It is true that modernization and the pursuit of economic growth has been whole-heartedly adhered to by governments since 1945, but the form of institutional innovation has been decidedly corporatist. It seems that the recent Conservative administrations have accepted the goal of modernization in more thoroughgoing ways than any of their predecessors, but they do so with only limited middle-class support. This is possibly because these governments have rejected the conventional means – through corporatist consensus – and, therefore, they have to resort to appeals to 'traditional' bourgeois values, reinforced by strong statist sanctions in order to induce an 'enterprise culture'. But the difficulties of pursuing such a 'fundamentalist' liberal revolution are clear. Modern states are themselves major players in the world economic system; there is a strong popular commitment to the welfare state and to the virtues of public expenditure; and English culture seems particularly resistant to *'laissez-faire'* forms of modernization. Further, liberal economics does not have deep roots within the Conservative Party. Mrs Thatcher's own victory over Mr Heath for the leadership in 1975 was not achieved as a result of a wholesale ideological conversion of the party but, rather, almost by accident. Thus, there remains within the Conservative Party a strong commitment to more state interventionism as a basis for developing a more coherent industrial strategy. The Labour Party is committed to 'building a national consensus for industrial recovery', to strengthening the Department of Trade and Industry, and to ensuring that government works in partnership with private industry in order to provide investment. Indeed, virtually all the political alternatives, both within and outside the Conservative Party, point to the re-establishment of corporatist styles of government. In many ways, of course, Mrs Thatcher has done the groundwork for this, if only because 'top-down' or 'state' corporatism is now easier to implement. At the same time, demands for 'bottom-up' or 'societal' corporatism have not been eradicated while the British electorate continues to be committed to public spending and the welfare state. Consequently, it does not seem impossible that some form of corporatism will re-emerge on the political agenda before the end of the century as governments in the late twentieth century are compelled to find institutional and political substitutes for, and complements to, market mechanisms. It would be ironic if Mrs Thatcher is later seen to be its midwife.

Appendix: A Chronology of Corporatism

1939–45: Coalition government

Wartime economy: close relationships between government and producer groups (business and labour). Ministry of Labour under Ernest Bevin dominant. New government departments of Supply, Food, Transport, and Aircraft Production.

1941: National Production Advisory Council (NPAC); National Joint Advisory Council (NJAC); Ministry of Labour and National Service (MLNS).

1942: Ministry of Government formed to co-ordinate role and function of all ministers.

1944: TUC's 'Report on Reconstruction': proposals to formalize links between government, business and labour (not accepted by government until 1962, as NEDC).

1945–51: Labour government

Production Authority Planning (government, unions and industry).
1947: Economic Planning Board (FBI, BEC and TUC); Central Economic Planning Staff (an early 'think-tank').
NJAC, EPB and NPAC acted as instruments of tripartite consultation.

1951–64: Conservative government

Some reintroduction of *laissez-faire* (e.g. denationalization of steel), but largely the retention of tripartite arrangements especially with producer groups.
Butler's 'Industrial Charter': Industrial Policy Committee and retention of NJAC and NPAC.
'Indicative Planning' on the French model: regional policy and the redirection of industry, the demise of Joint Production Committees in the early 1950s notwithstanding.
Political ideology of 'Butskellism' (the similarity of ideas between the Conservative, Butler, and the leader of the Labour Party, Gaitskell): the 'pragmatic and undogmatic statism' of Harold Macmillan (Middlemas).
National Economic Development Council (NEDC) formed in 1962.

1964–70: Labour government

1965: George Brown's National Economic Plan.
The Confederation of British Industry (CBI) created.
1966: Statutory Prices and Incomes Policy.

1970–74: Conservative government

Phase One (1970–2): 'Selsdon Man': free market economics.
Phase Two (1972–4): 'U-turn': Industry Act and tripartite agreement with CBI and TUC.

1974–79: Labour government

'Social Contract' with unions.
Industrial strategy and new incomes policy.
Planning Agreements with business.

1979: Thatcherite Conservative government elected

The dismantling of corporatist structures begins.

3

Employment relationships in economic recession

GRAEME SALAMAN

It is frequently argued that the 1980s have witnessed a radical shift in relationships between management and labour: that organized labour has been weakened and management strengthened so as to alter the balance of power and advantage between these two parties. It is further argued that this has been exploited by management to improve profit and efficiency. This argument is assessed in the present chapter. It will be suggested that, empirically, these developments have been exaggerated; that, conceptually, they are simplistic; and that, theoretically, they are contradictory and flawed. Although there have been changes in the nature of worker–management relations, these need to be more precisely identified and carefully assessed.

The structure of the chapter is as follows. In the first section, those factors which are seen as constituting or supporting a class attack on labour by strengthening employers and weakening labour are identified and briefly discussed. Such developments are essentially significant for their potential role in determining or, at least, enabling changes in worker–management relations of the kind which are described in later sections. The section that follows addresses the key role of management strategy. This, it is claimed, is significant since it translates pressures on, or opportunities for, management, into management practice and intention. It, therefore, requires our critical attention. In the next sections, four key areas of alleged changes are assessed. In each of these, the precise forms of change are identified and the alleged developments evaluated in an attempt to clarify what, if any, changes are actually taking place. The final section of the chapter then puts forward an appraisal of the conceptual and theoretical weaknesses of the overall thesis.

Background

Three developments have been widely regarded as making possible a class attack on workers, by successfully undermining the basis of worker solidarity and strengthening capital: (1) unemployment, (2) government economic and financial policy and anti-union legislation, and (3) the development and application of information technology. These are seen as occurring against a background of economic recession.

Western Europe has been in economic recession for over ten years. In the United Kingdom, one in five jobs in manufacturing has been lost since 1979. In the private sector, increasing competition, declining profitability, reduced demand for firms' output and the increasingly uncompetitive nature of much of British industry, have put severe pressure on management to rationalize and achieve 'economies'. Between 1979 and 1981, average profits fell by one-half, capital investment in manufacturing by one-third (McInnes, 1987, p. 65). In the public sector, 'cash limits', the control of public-sector borrowing requirements, the imposition of 'efficiency' standards, and the application of performance-related accountancy standards have exerted great pressure on management in nationalized industries.

Early in 1985, unemployment figures, according to the Department of Employment, stood at 13.9 per cent or nearly 3½ million people. The TUC would put the real figure much higher – at well over 4 million. This high level – which is higher than the OECD average – reflects the values and policies of the Thatcherite Conservative government in the 1980s which uses unemployment as a tactic in its attack on organized labour. Indeed, it is often argued that such tactics not only reflect class values, but also achieve class purposes by reducing labour costs, changing trade-union attitudes, and permitting the 'rationalization' of work practices.

The world of work and employment is, of course, highly politicized. 'The profitability crisis of British industry in the late 1960s . . . came to be defined as a political problem. Successive governments saw the control of incomes as crucial in resolving this issue' (Terry, 1983, p. 83). Recently, political interest has focused less on incomes policies *per se*, and more on reducing the role of the state, allowing market forces to operate more effectively, and reducing the capacity of trade unions and shop stewards to resist incomes policies and oppose management's 'right to manage'.

Conservative policies on trade unions regard them as interfering with the 'free operation' of the labour market. Developments in industrial relations legislation since 1980, therefore, have reversed previous approaches to industrial relations and tend to be concerned with four major objectives: '(i) restriction of employment protection; (ii) restriction of the immunities; (iii) debilitation of the unions; and (iv) repeal of the auxiliary legislation' (Wedderburn, 1985, p. 39). The first has weakened the legal rights of workers and their representatives concerning various aspects of employment, redundancy and unfair dismissal. The second has removed unions' traditional immunity from liabilities of breach of contract in trade disputes. These removals rendered unions liable to legal action over forms of picketing, and over 'secondary action'; changed the definition of 'trade dispute' to cover only disputes between workers and *their* employer; made illegal any action on employers to force them to negotiate with unions; and extended the powers of employers to dismiss those taking part in industrial action (Wedderburn, 1985, pp. 41–2). The debilitation of unions has been encouraged by abolishing the 'closed shop', through supporting individuals' 'right to jobs' even when they have refused to join trade unions, and by legal control over the frequency and manner of elections of trade-union officials. Finally, Conservative anti-union legislation has dismantled the body of legislation which supported the processes of collective bargaining and the resolution of employer–employee differences. These changes have been supported by reductions in income maintenance programmes: the 'earnings related supplement' has been eliminated, and unemployment benefit is now taxed. The result has been that unemployed incomes as a proportion of net average earnings fell from 70 per cent in 1971 to 32 per cent in 1982 (Grunberg, 1986, p. 507).

The development of information technology is also often seen as an attack on workers – through its effects in reducing jobs, de-skilling work, and buttressing management control. Jenkins and Sherman (1979) suggest a job loss of 5 million over 25 years in the United Kingdom as a result of various applications of information technology. It is predicted that information technology will also have devastating consequences for the quality of jobs as manual, specialist and, finally, management functions are replaced by computer systems. Thus, the almost totally computerized factory is a distinct possibility.

Consequences for management–worker relations: the role of management strategy

The developments outlined above occur within a context of economic recession which supplies management with the urgent need to achieve improved profitability by various means: rationalization, improved unit costs, improved quality and output. Management's capacity to exploit these developments is increased through the simultaneous strengthening of its bargaining capacity and the weakening of the ability of trade unions to protect the interests of their members. Under such circumstances, it is argued, a 'new realism' is born whereby workers are prepared to accept changes which they would have resisted previously. At the same time, there is the emergence of 'macho management' that actively seeks to achieve purposes previously considered unattainable. However, such an argument rests upon notions of management *strategy*. Because of its centrality for the argument being considered here, this requires some discussion.

There are two views of management strategy. The 'hard' view sees management as vindictively taking advantage of present circumstances to take vengeance for previous defeats and compromises. Support for this is drawn from evidence of attempts to restrict the influence of key individual shop stewards, as in the motor industry. The 'soft' view, on the other hand, sees management as simply and necessarily reflecting and seeking to achieve system requirements.

It is not simply a matter of 'macho' managements taking advantage of large-scale unemployment and a government which is hostile to trade unions to settle old scores, though there may well be some managers who think and act in this way. Rather, it is the situation in the product market which is forcing change on management. Markets have declined; there has been an intensification of competition both at home and overseas; and there is great uncertainty . . . The case for tough policies seems increasingly unanswerable as short-term benefits in productivity improvements and union acquiescence become widely reported.

(Purcell and Sisson, 1983, p. 117)

Both of these perspectives accept that the balance of power between management and workers has shifted, and that this makes it easier for the former to achieve its goals. Both regard management as 'reflecting' system imperatives by means of various 'strategies'. These refer to various *attempts* by management or elements of management to clarify its purposes, and the means for their achievement, in a coherent form (although such efforts may clearly be of varying success, be short-term rather than long-term, and be highly bounded, sectional and 'irrational'). At the same time, strategy involves the notion of choice. Within capitalism, corporate managerial strategies will reflect an appreciation of various conditions which are recognized as those of corporate survival. These include an acceptable level of profitability, and are usually expressed in terms of 'profitable growth' or improved return on assets (Child, 1985, p. 110). However, these 'general objectives' do not supply guidelines for their achievement. The process of identifying, assessing and achieving these goals is mediated by management skill, knowledge, assumption and, indeed competence.

For management, the workforce, the design of work, and the cost and productivity of labour, and so on, are merely some of a number of salient considerations requiring strategic handling. They are only *some* of the variables which affect the determination of profit. Indeed, financial success depends on factors other than labour. Thus, management must develop strategies for product development, marketing, new projects, stock control, and product or market diversification. In particular, it must try to establish market niches and achieve some degree of price protection. Even so, a specific strategy towards labour is also crucial. Thus, it is appropriate to consider those areas where, it is claimed, management strategy, in response to enabling circumstances, has successfully achieved significant change. There are four such areas: (1) the design of work; (2) the nature and conduct of industrial relations; (3) the restructuring of the employment relationship; and (4) the installation of information technology. All are seen as areas of major change where management priorities have been successfully achieved. In the four sections that follow, these areas of change will be identified and assessed.

Economic recession and the redesign of work

It is often argued that the recession makes it both necessary and possible for management to redesign work. 'As economic crisis deepens and the social structure of accumulation begins to become unfavourable, capitalists are in ever greater need of collective strategies capable of restoring the rate of profit' (Gordon *et al.*, 1982, pp. 30–2). These strategies are seen directly to address the design of work, and frequently include: the introduction of cost-reducing technologies, the reconstruction of the division of labour, the intensification of control mechanisms, and the flexibility of the production process (Coombs, 1985, p. 168). The last of these *may* be achieved through the elimination of 'restrictive practices' and the achievement of flexible working. The recession certainly offers the incentive to redesign jobs and, because of relatively weaker trade unions, the opportunity to do so. An index of management concern with work restructuring is the upsurge in productivity bargaining – agreements that embody changes in work practices. Frequently, these involve flexible agreements, where sets of previously discrete work roles are combined into new individual or group jobs (Kelly, 1985). The use of team working – involving greater flexibility of team members and collective responsibility for quality control and problem solving – is particularly advanced within the car industry, but it is also apparent elsewhere. In the United States, Ford, General Motors and Chrysler all have 'worker participation' schemes (Katz and Sabel, 1985). Nichols notes that during the 1980s many British companies have made formal agreements for increased craft flexibility (Nichols, 1986, p. 203). British Leyland's declining share of the United Kingdom car market (from 38 per cent in 1970 to 18 per cent in 1980) together with dramatic differences in its efficiency compared with other European manufacturers and the company's consistent pattern of annual losses after 1978, forced it to take urgent action. During the 1970s, costs were reduced by reduction in pay levels. These fell from being 18 per cent above the average for all manual workers to only 5 per cent in 1984. The closure of plants also contributed to improved efficiency. But it was also necessary to reorganize management and to change working practices and industrial relations (Marsden *et al.*, 1985, p. 90).

Other industries in Britain, for example, British Rail, British Coal and British Steel show a broadly similar pattern with plant closures, job losses, attacks on traditional job demarcations and skill boundaries, changes in job content and enforced flexibility of working practices, and changes in wage structures. A survey by Edwards (1985a) found that in 84 per cent of plants studied, changes in working practice had been introduced over the previous two years. The most frequent were those associated with the introduction of new technologies, increased efficiencies with existing equipment, and more flexible working practices. These were only possible because of the declining power of trade unions. Indeed, it has been argued that such changes are directly associated with an explicit attack on organized labour and its institutions, and the re-establishment of management's 'right to manage' in the workplace.

The 'new' industrial relations

'Reforms of labour practices that should have taken place decades ago have been achieved in a matter of months. . . Many firms have found new scope for co-operation between management and employees.' So, argues Mrs Thatcher (quoted in Nichols, 1986, p. 175), radical and necessary alterations in relations between management and workforce are being achieved under circumstances of recession, unemployment, Conservative policy and information technology. There are two separate aspects of the argument. First, it is claimed that there has been a change of style in industrial relations, with management more prepared to 'regain the initiative' and unions and workforce more prepared to concede: hence, the emergence of 'macho' management and the 'new realism'. Secondly, that the content of agreements with unions is now clearly in management's favour with the power of shop stewards and unions reduced as a result of management's offensives. But have these claimed changes actually taken place?

Some management language suggests a new level of aggressiveness towards unions and workforces. Current circumstances allow management to adopt an approach to industrial relations rarely considered under earlier economic conditions – a direct attack on unions and on shop-floor solidarity. Some managements, particularly BL (British Leyland), have developed the strategy of 'reducing the numbers of full-time shop stewards and restricting the mobility of others, by attempts to "by-pass" them by obtaining workforce opinions directly through ballots and referenda, and by the unilateral imposition of sets of working agreements designed to reduce or eliminate "restrictive practices" ' (Terry, 1983, p. 90). But most employers have not adopted such tactics. There is evidence that the number of stewards actually increased between 1980 and 1984 (Millward and Stevens, 1986, p. 86).

Certainly there is a pressure on management to reorganize

working relations in a more authoritarian manner, and to replace labour with capital (information technology). The majority of British managers display a general hostility to the power of trade unions, antipathy to forms of participation that limit managerial decision-making, and limited enthusiasm for collective representation (Poole et al., 1982, p. 304). Yet, in practice, senior managers give considerable weight to industrial relations matters, feel that they have a clear policy in this area, and think that industrial relations are central to their long-term plans (Edwards, 1985b). The number of large, multi-plant enterprises is growing, and multi-plant companies pay more attention to industrial relations than single-plant companies. This probably encourages a more professional, long-term strategy on industrial relations (Brown, 1981).

The very possibility of corporate strategic policy, itself, may predispose towards strategies aimed at reducing the power of trade unions (Poole, 1986, p. 53). This is encouraged by the tendency for management to move the level of strategic decision-taking away from the plant to the company level, which, in turn, stretches the solidarity of labour. The development of single-employer bargaining whereby each employing company establishes its specific terms and conditions rather than applying an industry-wide multi-employer agreement is also significant. By 1981, multi-employer agreements covered only a quarter of the manual and a tenth of the non-manual workforce in manu-facturing establishments (Brown, 1981, p. 118). Such national multi-plant agreements, being less responsive than workplace agreements, tend to set a floor for wage levels and, thus, stop downward wages drift (Turner et al., 1977). Their decline permits greater 'flexibility' in wages.

The extension of payment systems such as measured day work, group and plant bonus schemes based on job evaluation and work study is also important since such schemes bring pay structures under management control. Yet, although some aspects of the 'macho' thesis are supported empirically, it is unwise to assume that actual management behaviour is as assertive as public pronouncements might suggest. In fact, union involvement in organizational decision-making tends to be slight. Wilson and colleagues report that, of 150 examples of what managers regarded as cases of strategic decisions, unions were involved in only 29. Furthermore, the form of their involvement was slight and reactive rather than proactive (Wilson et al., 1982). Brown and Sisson argue that the vast majority of employers have an approach to unions which can be described as 'pragmatist' or 'opportunist'; that is, an essentially 'ad hoc' or 'fire-fighting' approach. Changes in practice, they argue, should not be 'interpreted in terms of a new breed of "macho" managers breaking new ground. They are more to be seen as a desperate reaction to an appalling product market situation. Their industrial relations specialists, if they have not themselves been made redundant, must shudder to think what is going to happen if ever there is an upturn' (Brown and Sisson, 1984, p. 22). Similarly, Rose and Jones argue that, while management power has increased at the expense of labour, this is not *necessarily* the result of strategy or purposive offensive. Management behaviour between and, indeed, even within firms with respect to work reorganization, industrial relations and employment practices is highly variable (Rose and Jones, 1985).

The 'machoism' of current management is probably exaggerated, though it exists, certainly on the level of rhetoric. What is more important than mere 'vengeance' or settling of scores is a new determination – and a new capacity – to achieve changes in work practices. This is often associated with the installation of information technology which critical commercial pressures are seen to require, and other circumstances make possible. Assuming some level of rationality and strategy on both sides, it is probably true that 'capital and labour act toward each other on the basis of a careful assessment of their relative power . . . the frequency and form of workplace collective action . . . being determined by the organisational strength of each side and by the tactical calculations made by each side of the costs and benefits of taking action' (Grunberg, 1986, p. 504). Such calculations, which are quite possibly haphazard, incomplete, inconsistent and even contradictory, are altered by economic and other circumstances . . . The evidence is overwhelming that Thatcherism has not changed the institutions and procedures of British workplace relations' (McInnes, 1987, p. 106).

It is also argued that under current circumstances, unions are more prepared to concede to management's demands: the 'new realism' which fits the managerial 'machoism'. There is evidence that changes in working practice, and in the use of information technology, for example, are regarded by management as having met no significant resistance. Edwards (1985a, p. 7) notes that, in his sample, all but four of the managers who reported introducing such changes remarked that their introduction had been successful and that the workforces have been prepared to accept change. Similarly, Marsden and colleagues report the importance, in management's effort to restore 'the right to manage' at BL, of the fear of unemployment, and the severity of the competitive situation facing the company (Marsden *et al.*, 1985). Hyman and Elger (1981, p. 120) describe how, in British Rail, British Steel and BL, 'the unions have largely acquiesced in rationalisation programmes, at the cost of massive job loss and with few obvious compensations for their members'. In the motor industry, employment declined by nearly 40 per cent between 1978 and 1983. The majority of these job losses were voluntary; indeed, sometimes volunteers outnumbered the targeted job losses (Marsden *et al.*, 1985, p. 64).

This pattern of accommodation is particularly common in the public sector. It is, of course, necessary to separate the public and private sectors with respect to industrial relations developments under Thatcherism. Since, for example, the public sector is more directly exposed to incomes policies (if not in name) of various sorts. The nationalized industries, dependent upon government subsidies and exposed to market forces, are, in effect, exposed to government income restraint. On the other hand, within the private sector, for those still in work, real earnings have risen appreciably. As Martin (1986) notes: 'Wage increases have probably been more important than either the threat of unemployment or government policy in reducing strikes in private manufacturing industry'.

Yet these developments are not evidence of management attempts to 'smash' the unions (although there are clearly cases – Wapping, or the Miners' Strike – where this was an objective). Chadwick (1983), for example, found, in a survey of plants in a Midlands town, that efforts to regain control over work were successful, but had been achieved while supporting the credibility and retaining the existence of the local trade-union organization. Those who, like Bassett (1986), argue that there has occurred a major and structural transformation of industrial relations with the re-establishment of management authority, relate this directly to the destruction of shop-steward power, and to the reduction of union strength. There is certainly some evidence for this and, again, it applies particularly at BL. It is possible to identify structural developments which weaken shop-steward power: the move away from manufacturing towards less unionized sectors, and the shift of industry from traditional union areas to green-field sites or locations in the south-east of England. However, one review of the evidence finds a less clear picture. On the *organizational* aspect, it argues: 'in plants where stewards exist, there have been no changes of any significance' (Terry, 1986, p. 173; see also Batstone, 1984). But, as Terry notes, this conclusion, in itself, is insufficient as an indicator of reduced shop-steward and union strength, and leads to a further issue: how effective are shop stewards in influencing decisions? Relevant here are statistics on union membership, strike rates, and so on, which, presumably, offer some measure of shop-floor power. It is true that over the years 1980–1, for example, union membership fell by a million, and while this decline has implications for union power and finance, it is more a reflection of job losses (with consequent abandonment of union membership) than of declining membership among the employed (Brown and Sisson, 1984, p. 30). Trade-union density has declined in manufacturing but increased in service industries. There have also been changes in strike rates which reflect the decline of strike-prone industries and of manufacturing. But they must not be exaggerated; the United Kingdom's 'league position' in European strike rates has gone up from seventh to fifth. And the proportion of workplaces experiencing strikes increased by a half from 1980 to 1984 (McInnes, 1987, p. 107).

On the substantive level, it is not easy to assess the importance of workforce and union attitude and strength. Some research (Edwards, 1985b) argues that worker resistance is regarded as relatively insignificant by management. But Batstone argues that '62 per cent of managers feel that working practices could be improved . . . [of those] 73 per cent say that trade unionism is a big or fairly big factor in preventing changes in working practices' (Batstone, 1984, p. 29, quoted in Terry, 1986, pp. 173–4). Probably these differences reflect the fact that most managers could envisage *some* room for improvement, and would appreciate a completely clear hand in the design of work, but also that, in practice, union resistance can, these days, be overcome one way or another more frequently than previously. They may also reflect Nichols's point that Batstone's study was limited to large plants and excludes the public sector (Nichols, 1986, p. 191).

As Martin has noted, it is possible, from research and more general impressions, to obtain two contrasting pictures of current developments in British industrial relations under Thatcher. From a sufficient distance, one notes the increase of management power at the expense of unions, the acceptance of redundancies, of changes in working practices, of strike-free deals, single-union arrangements, the acceptance of information technology, attacks on individual shop stewards, the overt bypassing of formal industrial relations structures, plus the increasing use of the media, the police and the courts to destroy union organization and finances. Yet, a closer view suggests that the institutions, organization and practices of traditional industrial relations in Britain seem remarkably intact, bearing in mind the public–private divide. But, perhaps, the change has been one of attitude, of capacity, of will. The institutions remain, but 'social institutions can remain unchanged on the outside while their actual function and significance changes completely: form may survive, content evaporate, shop stewards might survive, but only on management sufference, tolerated because of their insignificance' (Martin, 1987). But this may overestimate the extent to which workplace relations were in adversity *before* Thatcherism and allows the possibility that, under different circumstances, new life may be breathed back into these somewhat moribund institutions. It also suggests that 'will' and attitude might be affected as much by definitions of the situation as by the situation itself. Grim as this is, it is difficult to resist what is portrayed as 'common-sense', the march of progress, and the facts of life. While for management the benefits of opportunism, of a unitarist conception of work organizations, of strategies of coercion, of 'brutal managerialism' must seem undeniable, in the short term.

The restructuring of the employment relationship

The third claimed change which is seen to result from the factors listed and discussed earlier concerns the definition and organization of the employment relationship. The division of the workforce by availability of jobs, the nature of jobs and their employment conditions is no new dynamic but, under Thatcherism, it is claimed, many organizations are, as a matter of strategy, seeking to redefine the employment relationship for many employees, such as to reduce overheads, the costs of labour and to achieve greater flexibility in the manner in which it is deployed. As Brown (1986) notes, part-time work has increased from 15 per cent of all jobs in 1971 to 25 per cent of employment in 1985. Self-employment has risen from 7.4 per cent to 10.8 per cent in 1985. Homeworking and temporary work have also increased. 'Employment flexibility' often means subcontracting services, previously supplied by regular employees, to outside companies – catering, laundry services, cleaning, even some clerical work. In this case, the employer no longer has any responsibility for the workers involved. Frequently, this transition involves a reduction in security, wages and a deterioration in terms and conditions of work, and to the use of female workers. It is the case, then, that there is a prevalent management strategy to decrease the amount of 'primary' employment conditions and to expand 'secondary' employment, with all its inherent disadvantages. Employers are likely not only to 'privatize' services, thus, allowing other subcontract firms to design secondary employment conditions, but also to design the jobs which remain and the conditions of work and employment in ways which not only achieve greater flexibility, but also target particular ('attractive' or 'congenial') sections of the population (times of work, full-time or part-time, and so on) and which draw on and confirm the established stereotypes of gender, race and age (see Garnsey et al., 1985, p. 69). But the expansion of secondary employment is not solely a consequence of management strategy in manufacturing, but also a consequence of the decline of manufacturing and the expansion of the service sector where employment conditions are more likely to be secondary, where part-time female work is more common, and 88 per cent of part-time workers are women (nearly 50 per cent of working women work part-time). Part-time work is concentrated in small firms of fewer than 25 employees, 80 per cent of part-time work is in the expanding service sector (Beechey, 1986b, pp. 93–4). The use of contracted-out services not only offers cost savings, with the employer no longer taking responsibility for the many supplementary costs associated with formal employment but also offers an opportunity to avoid the implications of collective agreements on work, pay, or conditions by using labour not covered by such agreements. The establishment of 'greenfield' sites and new industries also offers such an opportunity, although, here, labour may be formally employed but under new terms (Nichols, 1986, p. 194). However, McInnes warns against accepting the increasing flexibility thesis unquestioningly. Unemployment clearly discourages those in employment from moving to other work: a net reduction in labour market flexibility, while functional flexibility is limited by skill shortages. If secondary employment has increased, this is not necessarily a result of management strategy, but of sectoral change (McInnes, 1987).

The impact of information technology

The application of information technology is frequently regarded as having widespread and damaging consequences for the quantity and quality of jobs. The benefits of information technology are much publicized and it is assumed that management will rapidly seek to apply information technology in order to achieve these outcomes. The costs for jobs are equally publicized. But are these consequences empirically apparent? Here, three interrelated issues are considered: management strategy with respect to information technology; the consequences for employees of the installation of information technology; and the role of unions in such processes.

Management develops various strategies concerning the use of information technology. But management motivation may not simply reflect the claimed benefits of information technology (see Senker, 1985, p. 5); and management 'rationalities' may differ from the strict accountancy logic of return on investment. Buchanan's research into management objectives in installing information technology suggests it pursues a variety of objectives, that information technology allows these various objectives to be translated into work systems, and that information technology at work potentially *increases* operator skill and control (Buchanan, 1983). The application of information technology at work depends on the assumptions, values and objectives within which management operates (Buchanan, 1986, p. 68). Child offers a classification of management strategies in installing information technology and notes that 'The increasing flexibility of technology renders it far less of a constraint upon, and more of a facilitator of, working practices which emerge from the political processes of management's relations with labour' (Child, 1985, p. 116).

Child identifies four management strategies: the elimination of direct labour, contracting-out of work or services (thus reducing overhead costs), polyvalence or the development of flexible multi-skill workers, and the degradation of jobs. These strategies 'reflect' different objectives and different competitive conditions, while having broadly similar consequences: the segmentation of the labour force and the quantity of labour in the external labour market, both of which weaken labour (Child, 1985, pp. 132–3).

In practice, researchers have noted that managers may have ambivalent, even negative, attitudes towards the installation of information technology. 'Opposition from top management is seen in Britain as a very important difficulty by 5 per cent of the establishments, slightly less than the trade unions, but the figure may under-represent the extent of the problem since a proportion of the respondents would probably regard themselves as top management and would be unlikely to see themselves as a major obstacle' (Northcott *et al.*, 1985a, p. 38).

Assessments of the likely impact of information technology at work vary. One study, on the basis of a review of 'before and after' results in eight companies, reports that 'improvements in virtually every business ratio are achieved by using advanced manufacturing technology and, even during the period of introduction, significant improvements in annual operating profits accrue, helping to make the investment largely self-financing' (Advanced Systems Group Report, 1985, p. 7). The Director of Systems at Ford Europe insists that the use of information technology within Ford is fundamental to three strategic objectives – bringing quality products to the market faster, achieving high quality, low cost products, and getting closer to the customer – that is, responding faster to customer demand. However, at Ford Europe, job losses are calculated by the Personnel Director as about 25 per cent. These lost jobs are mainly the unskilled jobs, the remaining jobs being frequently upgraded in skill content.

Many writers insist that information technology will be used, as all forms of work technology are used, to cheapen and control labour. Empirical studies of the impact of information technology suggest that management is certainly highly conscious of the likely effect of information technology on work organization and on 'management' problems and often installs information technology in order to 'rationalize' production, rather than directly to reduce labour. But the evidence suggests that the managerial benefits of information technology in manufacturing are very much to do with reducing the capacity of the workforce to interrupt or delay management priorities, and to improve efficiency and quality and to reduce costs. Even if management does not deliberately set out to cheapen labour or to maximize control, the ostensibly technical priorities and consequences reported in the research have implications for employees' skill levels, work autonomy and capacity to control uncertainty. The implications of information technology for jobs and job skills are not inevitable or uniform. Such applications can increase or decrease skill, and there is scope for management to choose between these two options. Of course, information technology is not neutral; it has the capacity enormously to increase management control over work. But management can choose how to apply information technology; in itself, it does not contain inexorable logics for job design. Such choices are political in outcome and in origin. Jones, for example, reports on the basis of his study of the introduction of numerically controlled (NC) machine tools into the British engineering sector, that no one cited labour costs as an influence in buying NC even when pressed. More frequently mentioned were time savings (the reductions in between machining or 'floor to floor' time). NC was often thought to have implications for the quality of work which could not even be envisaged with conventional work. Repeatability of items and degree of standardization of components were also frequently mentioned, especially in the context of shortages of skilled labour (Jones, 1982, p. 191). Francis and colleagues report, on the basis of their study of computer assisted design/ manufacture (CAD/CAM) and management information systems (MIS) in engineering plants, that most decisions to take up the new technology were triggered by specific problems, such as when growth in product markets leads to the need for extra production capacity or if technical changes in the product, or new product opportunities, require new methods of manufacture. Changes in factor costs, usually due to an increase in labour costs or a marked decrease in capital costs, often due to technical change, were also important (Francis *et al.*, 1982, p. 185). Among reasons for installing information technology were a general impression that the industry would have to install new technology in the future (as the capital/labour costs increased) and that there was a strong preference for a less labour-intensive technology because this would reduce management/industrial relations problems (Francis *et al.*, 1982, pp. 185–6). While controlling the 'refractory hand of labour' may have been a major motive for innovating production processes in the past, it is now usually of lesser importance (Francis *et al.*, 1982, p. 187). Managers are primarily interested in the final outcomes of the labour process. Their concern with its actual content, where it exists, follows from a practical concern with productivity, quality and predictability (Coombs, 1985, p. 145). But what are the effects of the installation of information technology on employees' jobs and skills?

Despite the predictions of massive job loss associated with the installation of information technology, the evidence to date suggests a less extreme picture, though one with the basic element of some job losses supported. Available studies do not support the thesis that information technology will inevitably result in massive unemployment (Francis, 1986, p. 23). One reason is that in many cases the application of information technology is not part of an overall strategy of reorganization but is, rather, carried out in a somewhat piecemeal manner within the parameters of existing structures and practices. One such constraint is the attitude of unions and the existing – and desired – state of relationship between management and workforce. And even when information technology has direct consequences for labour productivity, the methods of reducing staff that is frequently employed, 'natural wastage', delays the impact of job loss. It also has other effects. One survey (Northcott and Rogers, 1984) found that in the factories which had reduced employment as a result of information technology, for every person actually dismissed there was one job lost through voluntary redundancy and seven jobs lost through natural wastage. This method of job loss poses little threat to those with jobs and so helps to explain the relative lack of resistance to information technology in the workplace and from unions; but job losses through natural wastage protect the interests of those currently employed in the establishment at the expense of throwing the costs on to other groups – those unemployed and looking for a new job, women wanting to return to a job when their children have grown older, and school and university leavers trying to enter the job market for the first time. These groups are not able to block the adoption of new technology nor able to make their disadvantage evident or significant politically (Northcott and Rogers, 1984, p. 84).

So far the evidence does not support the predicted job loss if the general thesis that information technology will result in job loss is supported. Some lost jobs are exported to other non-information-technology firms and some of the employment effects are simply delayed through the manner in which information technology is installed and the manner in which job losses are handled. The tactic of natural wastage does not solve the problem, it simply moves it outside the firm. As far as the impact of information technology on skill levels is concerned, Sorge *et al.* (1983) note that the skill implications of the installation of information technology in British and West German companies are influenced by the existence of traditions of training and of skilled workers. In the West German factories, management is more likely to use information technology to enhance skill because of the craft traditions, whereas in the British factories information technology is used to de-skill. In banking, the de-skilling option can even be short-term and counter-productive (Smith and Wield, 1987).

The installation of information technology need not necessarily result in de-skilling. That consequence is a result of the strategy deployed. Research emphasizes the role of management choice between using the introduction of the new technology as an opportunity to build upon the skill and experience of workers or using the new technology as a means of reducing skills and replacing them with procedures and systems devised by an array of 'experts'. The first of these options does not necessarily imply altruism on the part of management. Rather these policies provide employers with a valuable increase in flexibility of deployment (Gill, 1985, pp. 79–81). There is no unilinear tendency towards de-skilling (Francis, 1986, p. 102). Jones notes that as far as the application of NC to machine tools is concerned, it is difficult to assess the implications for skill because, overall, there are skill losses and skill gains. Jones also notes that the effect of NC on skills varies from plant to plant. Northcott *et al.* (1985b, pp. 84–5), on the basis of a survey of manufacturing plants employing 20 or more staff during 1981–3 and 1983–5, note that use of information technology in work processes resulted in the loss of 3000 skilled jobs and of 18,000 unskilled jobs. But these figures do not cover changes in skill levels of surviving jobs. This survey suggests that when information technology is used in work processes, even where there has been no overall change in total employment, there has tended to be change in the composition of jobs. The disappearing jobs tend to be the unskilled ones and the ones based on traditional manual skills, while the new ones tend to be of kinds needing new skills – particularly knowledge of electronics, programming and the other special skills associated with the new technology.

The responses of trade unions also differs from the expected. Northcott *et al.* (1985), on the basis of their international comparison of micro-electronics in industry in the United Kingdom, France and West Germany, investigated the major disadvantages and problems in the use of microprocessors in work processes. Bottom of the list of thirteen identified factors comes opposition from various groups within the organization. Eight per cent of British users, 14 per cent of West German and 15 per cent of French identified 'opposition from shopfloor or unions' as a source of difficulty. Opposition from other groups within the companies, or from management itself, was regarded as more important than opposition from the unions. It was mentioned by 9 per cent of the sample. A similar picture emerges from a survey of studies of employees' responses to the installation of information technology at work (Northcott *et al.*, 1985b), which notes that the general experience is that the introduction of micro-electronics has been accepted at the place of work, often with enthusiasm (Northcott *et al.*, 1985b, p. 16).

These authors list three factors as contributing to this response: the generally positive form of response of trade unions and the TUC, the relatively muted impact of information technology on job satisfaction and on job losses, the relatively slow speed of installation of information technology in the United Kingdom (Northcott *et al.*, 1985b, p. 16). To this we might add the particular strategies used by many employers (see above), which protect those currently in work at the expense of those outside the company or outside the world of employment, plus the fact that the majority of British unions are in favour of technological innovation, seeing technology as socially neutral (Robins and Webster, 1980). And while the number of new technology agreements covering information technology applications is extremely low, research into actual processes of information technology installation suggests that, on occasions, unions may achieve more, and that managements may be prepared to achieve less. Rose and Jones (1985, p. 98), for example, report on an 'almost random character' of unions' preparedness and capacity to resist, acquiesce in, or bargain about management initiatives. A key factor may be the existing structure of 'bargaining institutions, job control structures, union jurisdiction, and inter-union relations; managements are still prepared, indeed, often deem it necessary to elicit cooperation from union representatives with differing degrees of consultation and participation in the implementation of change' (Rose and Jones, 1985, p. 99).

Discussion

The thesis that Thatcherism is radically transforming work relations has been found to be empirically unsatisfactory. Many of the claimed developments – 'macho' management, the new 'realism', the destruction of unions and shop stewards, the elimination of job controls, the imposition of information technology with devastating consequences for job losses – are, at best, tendencies rather than achievements, occurring within a context of surviving institutions, relations and practices. 'There is no widespread incidence in large manufacturing enterprises of either intensified, degraded, simplified work, or union representation that has been neutralised and divided by management schemes' (Jones and Rose, 1986, p. 55).

Yet the erosion of will and confidence of workforces in the face of management demands owes much to the perceived impossibility and futility of opposition, for the Thatcherite initiative occurs at the levels of ideology and understanding: the rhetoric of BL and macho management swamps the realities of many other workplaces; in the face of the claimed neutrality and inevitability of information technology and workplace rationalization, and their contribution to the endemic sickness of British industry, resistance is seen as hopeless and, even, utopian. Within the Thatcherite thesis, a variety of social and economic contexts are linked directly and unproblematically to forms of successful response, as if these responses could simply be 'read off' directly by management from the identified contextual developments.

This form of argument is unsatisfactory. It assumes that management clearly identifies external threats and opportunities, that management knows how to respond strategically to such developments, that such strategies are bound to be successful. Thus, management is defined as omniscient and super-effective, merely reflecting systemic requirements. This fails to explain how the difficulties management must now resolve ever occurred in the first place. This view is profoundly naive about the imputed form of management rationality. Management thinking – or strategy – is defined as homogeneous, uniform, accurately reflecting external conditions, the necessary courses of actions and the means of achieving them. Senior management is faced with increasingly severe competitive pressures. But do managers always agree on how to respond appropriately to such threats? And do such pressures lead directly and unequivocally to clear courses of action? And are such strategies successful? It is true that, under conditions of economic crisis, firms will *seek* to restructure in ways which are *intended* to eliminate 'slack' through closer co-ordination of subsystems and through more efficient utilization of resources and assets. But there is no guarantee that such strategies will be successful. In particular, it is likely that strategies for the management of labour and formulating workplace relations will remain characterized by contradiction and uncertainty. 'The entrepreneur cannot read off from market forces what must be done nor is it possible to arrive at a fully comprehensive plan which lays down to a workforce precisely what they must do to maximise efficiency' (McInnes, 1987, p. 130).

Management's search for work flexibility is understandable as an attempt to dismantle institutional barriers to management control, yet the 'management of uncertainty remains incomplete, tentative and beset with contradictions and inconsistencies due to profound uncertainties of management on the structure and function of a flexible industrial relations system in a post-crisis accumulation model' (Streek, 1987, p. 286). An important consideration is the *possibility* of management strategy on workplace relations and the design and control of work, which could, in principle, be successful. Hyman argues that strategic choice itself reflects various and contradictory pressures on management. Management strategy can best be conceptualized as 'the programmatic choice among alternatives, none of which can prove satisfactory' (Hyman, 1987, p. 30). A crucial aspect of the contradiction facing management concerns the management of labour.

There are other problems. It is assumed that management itself is an undifferentiated category and that managers of all sorts and specialities will respond in a similar way. This ignores the possibility of management 'irrationality', and assumes that, ultimately, the specialist interests of all branches of management will coincide. For example, all the evidence of management decision-making suggests that management is differentiated into specialisms which supply their members with different conceptions of interest and world views, thus leading to differentiated views of and responses to the same external events. This structural fragmentation is evident in management responses to the crisis, with different and potentially competing views – reflecting discrete and diverse ideologies and interests – being held by finance, production, general management, personnel, and industrial relations experts. Buchanan (1983) argues that managers' responses to information technology are influenced by their position and experience within the organization and by their different perspectives and attitudes. Since the installation of information technology has significant consequences for the distribution of information and influence, its installation is a political issue.

Further, this view implies a naive conception of the origins of management–workforce relations and the design of work. It assumes that only one factor determines the organization of work: the relative power of the participants, so that management will respond in a mechanistic and specific way to system requirements – that they will take advantage of the opportunities offered to correct the compromises of the past. But, even if this view of the past is accurate, it is not clear that the factors which encouraged compromise earlier have changed. This is to assume that the nature of work design, the state of relations between workforce and management, are simply and entirely a result of the power

84

and determination of management 'weakness'. It is to ignore the ambiguity and contradiction of the management of labour and the historical pattern of compromise and mutual adjustment. Paradoxically, this view incorporates, but goes beyond, an extreme reading of Braverman (1974); for it implies that management–workforce relations are not only determined by, but have as their objective, relations of power and control. This misses a number of points, among them that the essence of work is production, not control, and that the relationship between production and the form of control is complex and contradictory. It also misunderstands the complexity and origins of workforce–management relations. Management preparedness to tolerate less authoritarian forms of management, the existence and role of shop stewards, and greater job control on the shop-floor are the result not of workforce strength but of management philosophy and attitude and, indeed, of management's conception of management *per se*.

Yet many writers have analysed the problems of British industry in terms not of *workforce* strength, but *management* strength, and management attitude and approach. For example, the attempts by employees to establish some degree of job protection, and to erect job demarcations represent an attempt to counter the arbitrary authoritarianism of management, just as workforce 'instrumentalism' follows employees' mastery of the rules of the game established by management (Hobsbawm, 1968). The thesis ignores the massive institutional (and taken for granted, and anonymous) power of management while exaggerating the more publicized responses of organized labour and using workforce 'strength' to justify the increase in management domination (Fox, 1985, pp. 45–61)!

Furthermore, the 'problems' of British industry can be ascribed not to worker recalcitrance but to the refusal of British management to take thorough responsibility for the management of work: the consequences of this failure then being attributed to the workforce. Anthony argues that British management has persistently failed to take responsibility for 'the control and direction of labour', and has devised strategies of insulation, all of which involve the development of intermediaries (labour contractors, foremen, specialists). Thus, management continues to avoid addressing, or achieving, the 'foundation' of management – the issue of legitimacy of management authority and expertise. The result is ' "man mismanagement", a condition that has done more to produce lack of interest, low productivity, and industrial conflict than any assemblage of wreckers and dissident agitators could have achieved' (Anthony, 1986, p. 3). Thus, the link between recession and the eliciting of a particular management response ('macho' management) follows only within a particular (if implicit) view of the nature and determinants of management–workforce relations and the design of work. Other reactions are possible, following from alternative approaches.

The responses described and prescribed by the Thatcherite approach may be unsuccessful in practice since they are based upon erroneous analysis. Support for this is offered by Marsden *et al.* (1985) who note that even at BL, where 'macho' management was first launched in the United Kingdom, various investigating committees identified the major sources of poor productivity as essentially centring around the acceptance of allowed non-productive time and of regularly exceeding that time. But the analysts conclude: 'Any assumption that inefficiencies were simply a question of too many stoppages and excessive manning levels is misleading' (Marsden *et al.*, 1985, p. 93). Furthermore, like many other researchers, these authors argue that the effects of strong shop-steward organization for productivity are not obvious. Shop-steward systems can, indeed, contribute to good industrial relations. 'Macho' management at BL may well be a factor in explaining the continuing problem of numerous short strikes at BL (Marsden *et al.*, 1985, p. 92). Similarly, Nichols argues that because the Thatcherite thesis is based on a flawed analysis, it explains poor productivity levels by workers' attitudes, encouraged by protectionist working practices and excessively powerful unions. This is then supposed to have led to an appropriate and counter-productive response, namely 'macho' management. But Thatcherism has failed empirically; it has failed to deliver the goods if only because productivity has not increased dramatically. It is barely back to 1979 levels. Even if there have been some changes in work which support 'macho' management, these have not drastically improved productivity. The main achievement of Thatcherite prescriptions is not productivity but social and economic destruction (Nichols, 1986, pp. 239–40).

This failure is the result of a naive analysis of the nature of relations between management and workforce, for work relations are defined solely in terms of power, of coercion and resistance. The increased strength of management, made possible by external factors, facilitates what has long been necessary: the re-establishment of management dominance and, thus, ultimately, improved efficiency. This domination is necessary because of an inherent conflict of interest between management and workforce. It is not necessary to force people to do what their interests already predispose them towards. Power is needed at work because of class-based recalcitrance. Furthermore, the exercise of class power by management is, within the thesis, all that is necessary to achieve improved output and performance from workers: the new realism consists of a new level of compliance to management domination. Performance arises from obedience to management directives.

This *classist* view of work relations is naive about workplace relations and about the sorts of workplace changes desired by management in the recession. The achievement of acceptable levels of work efficiency depends upon three elements: specification of work, the capacity to perform the work, and the motivation to do it. Management efforts to control the work of employees involve interventions on all three levels. Various control strategies have different implications for employees' skill levels and their involvement in their work, as well as for the ability of management to achieve dominance over employees' activities. Burawoy (1983, p. 590) has noted that early forms of factory control – *despotic regimes* – based on coercion, give way to *hegemonic regimes* where consent prevails and where the application of coercion itself is the subject of agreement. Management is faced with two contradictory imperatives: to reduce employees' discretion and, thus, limit their capacity to interfere in the achievement of management targets, by locating the control of employee effort in management itself; and to encourage and channel the potential intelligence and creativity of employees in the service of efficiency and quality. There are no jobs where there is not some element of skill, however 'tacit' and officially denied (Manwaring and Wood, 1985). Management control and employment and industrial relations strategies have significant implications for the balance that is achieved between these two requirements. As many writers have noted, oppressive 'de-skilling' forms of control destroy consent, develop indifference and carelessness, and relate to levels of worker resistance and quality of work performance (Edwards and Scullion, 1982).

Hyman and Elger (1981, p. 121) suggest that 'overt managerial pressure and dictation can prove counter-productive, provoking uncontrollable resistance'. Possibly more significantly, such forms of control may result in increased machine down-time, reduced efficiency, increased absenteeism. 'Shifting fashions in labour management stem from this inherent contradiction:

solutions to the problem of discipline aggravate the problem of consent and *vice versa*.' He concludes, 'pragmatism may well be the most rational management principle. And it may indeed be questioned how far the elaborate and internally consistent programmes of "management science" have ever guided actual management practice' (Hyman, 1987, pp. 6–7). 'Macho' management, then, is likely not to be universal, and to be counterproductive, and for this reason alone is probably not as popular with management as commentators suggest. It is particularly inappropriate when management is seeking to improve levels of efficiency and of flexibility and quality of work, for these depend on employee willingness. While there is certainly evidence of 'a trajectory from delegation to "regaining control by sharing it", to brutal and assertive managerialism' (Hyman and Elger, 1982, p. 119), it is to be expected that such strategies may succeed in eliminating workers' job controls; but they will not succeed in improving work performance or efficiency. These points are not lost on managers themselves. Managers are aware of the necessary connection between desired changes in production and products (that is, the 'worker participation' programme of the US auto industry) and changes in industrial relations. Katz and Sabel (1985, p. 303) report that General Motors, in 1984, 'began to clarify its view of industrial relations reform. Instead of treating labor predominantly as a cost, the company began to consider reform of labor relations as part of an overall strategy of flexible production, linking new technologies, polyvalent workers, and more specialized products.'

The thesis that Thatcherism works at work is thus deficient because, while *representing* class forces and reflecting the tendency of managers to take advantage of their advantage to seize the initiative and readjust relations between workforce and management and, thus, 'confirm and reinforce the traditional pattern of adversary relations and institutional mistrust between capital and organised labour' (Fox, 1985, p. 429), it fails to comprehend an adequate class *analysis*. It ignores contradiction and thus, by simplifying, distorts. The contradictions are many. While claiming to represent new practices, it is actually significant mainly as ideology. It is certainly true that under circumstances which greatly increase management strength *vis-à-vis* labour, the ambitions and capacity of management grow enormously, while labour's resolution and strength decline. But these changes have not been transformed automatically into 'macho' management; many of the institutions and practices from more accommodating times persist and influence the outcome of current events. It is true that management has taken advantage of circumstantial opportunities to achieve changes in work and technology, but these changes themselves reflect an awareness of the continuing, possibly increasing, dependency of management on workforce attitude, flexibility and skill. It is true that management has sought to exploit opportunities to gain increased efficiencies. But it is not clear that management's conception of the origins of previous inefficiencies, or choice of current strategies of improvement, are markedly superior to earlier inadequate solutions (or that they actually work). Is it simply management capacity which has been responsible for Britain's poor industrial performance? Thatcherism is claimed to represent a radical break with earlier patterns of compromise and concession at work but, in fact, it simply articulates the historic pattern of oscillation from coercion to consent, with all the inherent problems of each form, or combination of forms, of control. It claims to resolve class conflict with the achievement of total management supremacy, yet, even during the period of maximum disadvantage to labour, it is far from obvious that organized labour is vanquished. And when circumstances change, politically and economically, we shall be able to assess how far, if at all, current patterns of accommodation on the shop-floor reflect real changes of attitude or tactical retreat.

4

From 'informal economy' to 'forms of work': cross-national patterns and trends

R. E. PAHL

There has been a remarkable increase in interest in what is loosely termed the 'informal economy' in the current decade. International conferences held in West Germany, Italy, the United States and elsewhere have drawn together scholars from a number of disciplines who feel that they have something in common to discuss.[1] Similarly, governments and intergovernmental organizations have commissioned, and in many cases published, reviews that purport to bring together a cumulative international understanding of a phenomenon that has aroused considerable public interest.[2] Popular reviews of the underground economy, the hidden economy, the shadow economy, or of economies with similar, sometimes colourful, labels are matched by more scholarly attempts to assess the methodological adequacy of attempts to give some order of magnitude to the range, scope and incidence of the phenomenon.[3]

Research on 'the informal economy' ranges from detailed case studies of informal economic activity in Bogotá, Budapest, or Bari to macro-economic analyses, purporting to demonstrate the scale of the phenomenon in the United States, Britain, or the Netherlands (Bromley and Gerry, 1979; Renooy, 1984; Galasi and Sziráczki, 1985; INCHIESTA, 1986). Sometimes these studies are overtly oriented to political or public policy issues and the phenomenon being investigated may be perceived as a managerial problem to be reduced, a solution to be adopted, or an ambiguous feature of a society that is, perhaps, best left alone (OECD, 1986b; Pahl,

1987). Sometimes the phenomenon is treated historically and context is seen to be salient (Ditton, 1977; Pahl, 1984). However, more generally, studies are presented ahistorically and serious cross-national research barely exists. This is understandable, since the phenomenon is a catch-all concept which has inevitably eluded precise and universally acceptable definition. Cross-national research is hazardous enough when dealing with phenomena that can be relatively easily defined; without agreement on what it is that is being compared those engaged in such an exercise would be prudent to be wary. Not only must the scientific object be carefully defined but the nature of the comparative research must also be clarified. Kohn has usefully suggested that there are four types of cross-national research. First there is the type where the nation is the *object* of study; the second type is where the nation is the *context* of study; thirdly the nation may be the *unit of analysis*; and, finally, studies may be *transnational* in character (these distinctions are elaborated in Kohn, in press). Most comparative research is focused on type two – the nation as context of study. However, studies of the informal economy may be directed at specific countries – say Italy or Hungary (Mingione 1988, Sik 1988) – because they are interesting in some way. For example, the interrelations between formal and informal work in these two contrasting contexts may tell us much about the distinctive nature of these two societies. 'What distinguishes research that treats the nation as the unit of analysis is its primary concern with understanding how social institutions and processes are systematically related to variations in national characteristics' (Kohn, in press).

Despite such cautionary caveats, there is now some widespread agreement, certainly in Europe, that the analysis of work and employment in both capitalist and state socialist societies has been too limited in the past. Informal forms and new patterns of work, both within and outside employment, need to be explored in order to reveal elements of social change that traditional approaches have ignored. Traditional and conventional divisions of labour in society are being renegotiated: informal employment and work outside employment are essential ingredients in this process that need to be understood (Gorz, 1982; Gershuny, 1983; Pahl, 1984, ch. 12). The conflation of work with employment in the manner of outmoded texts on 'the sociology of work' is now seen to be a curious archaism. The puzzle is why sociologists held such limited conceptions of work for so long.

It it not possible to provide comprehensive documentation here of the large and growing literature that has developed over the past decade in Europe and the USA – particularly since the path-breaking work by Ferman *et al.* (1978). Rather, I will attempt to provide some analytical signposts in the swirling fogs of conceptual and definitional confusion. I will then conclude by suggesting a means of moving beyond formal taxonomies of informal economic activities to a more sociologically grounded approach.

Approaches to the informal economy

In order to clear the ground, a number of general points need to be made. First, the notion of an informal economy in the more developed societies implies the reciprocal of a formal economy. This is because the rules, regulations and procedures that govern the formal economy create the conditions for evasion or circumvention; since such formal rules are endlessly changing – as the state shifts between modes and styles of regulation and deregulation – so the 'informal economy' waxes or wanes. If states and international organizations are serious about enforcing their systems of regulation, or if they wish some better measure of imputed tax loss, then there will be a concern to pay economists and others to compile comparative statistics showing the general order of magnitude of the economic activity which they think should be in the national accounts but which they cannot easily discern. A report published by the OECD in 1986 concluded that there could be '2–4 per cent of concealed employment in work-hours of the total labour input in work hours, for the more industrialised countries, though this could be as high as 8 per cent' (OECD, 1986b, p. 69). Clearly, comparative statements at this level of abstraction – Kohn's transnational comparative research – are very general and may not have much scholarly or practical value – although a focus on forms of regulation and deregulation could, in fact, provide a useful basis for cross-national research, as I argue below.

Compiling indicators of the informal economy as in some way the reciprocal of the formal economy implies, secondly, that the latter provides some kind of bench-mark. Yet if one takes the economies of, say, Kenya, Afghanistan, Hungary and Denmark, it is evident that differences between state socialist and liberal-democratic societies or between different forms of post-colonial developing societies are more salient than the simple formal–

informal dichotomy. Statistics indicating similar orders of magnitude may conceal more than they reveal. The remarks by Stefan Nowak are pertinent here:

> How do we know we are studying 'the same thing' in different contexts; how do we know that our observations and conclusions do not actually refer to 'quite different things' which we unjustifiably include into the same conceptual categories? Or if they seem to be different, are they really different with respect to the same (qualitatively or quantitatively understood) variable, or is our conclusion about the difference between them scientifically meaningless?
>
> (Nowak, 1976, p. 105)

Regulation and deregulation may respond to global processes but are bound to be context-specific to an important extent. Mel Kohn sums up the issue: 'there is no way to be certain whether the apparent cross-national differences are real or artifactual' (Kohn, in press).

Thirdly, the idea that there are multiple *economies* within any one social formation needs to be scrutinized carefully. Under modern Western capitalism there is a common currency, banking system and conception of market relations: it is hard to see the basis for a separate economy. An innovative attempt to distinguish four sub-economies in the United Kingdom economy was put forward by Davis as long ago as 1972. His description has not been usefully superseded.

> The market sub-economy is governed by laws of commercial trading, employment, labour relations and so on, and includes all transactions in services and commodities. The redistributive economy is governed by laws of taxation and welfare and state expenditure. The domestic economy is governed ultimately by family law, but more immediately by customs and expectations, more or less idiosyncratic, about the relations between members of a family. It includes all productive activities which are not mediated by a market – making and mending, food-processing, and so on – as well as the greater part of consumer activities. The gift economy is governed by rules of reciprocity, and includes all those transactions which we call giving a present, making a gift, and so on.
>
> (Davis, 1972, p. 408)

Davis makes it clear that he does not claim that his list is exhaustive. Others have contrasted the state planning system of socialist societies with the parallel, often informal, market systems in the same society.[4] Paradoxically, therefore, the notion of separate economic spheres, or 'economies', may have more salience in state socialist societies and I discuss this in more detail later.

Fourthly, there is a deceptive neatness in referring to all that work outside formal employment as being *the* informal economy. The use of the term 'informal economy' would be appropriate, first, if the informal activity referred to a truly separate sphere independent of another economy. This might occur in a centrally planned economy where economic activity operating according to market principles existed alongside or parallel to the 'official' formal economy. Here the emphasis is on the different form or type of economy. A second way in which the term might be used would be to refer to all those economic activities that are, as it were, shadows of the formal. Thus, someone who is self-employed may declare only part of his or her activities to the tax authorities, to be recorded as part of the formal economy. If that person does more of the same or a different activity, but does not declare whatever profits or earnings this extra activity generates, then this may be termed shadow work in the informal economy. Thus each type of formal economic activity will have its informal counterpart. The first use of the term 'informal economy' emphasizes the noun, the second use emphasizes the adjective.

Apart from these two distinct usages the phrase can also include various forms of work that are not either part of a parallel economy or a shadow of the formal market economy. They are best understood as distinctive *forms of work* and it would be confusing and conceptually sloppy to lump all these various forms of work together. It would certainly compound the error to refer to such a lump of disparate forms of work as a separate economy. Those who attempt to do this would have to bring together a range of activities from occupational crime, through domestic labour to quasi-hobbies such as gardening. Work with one's own tools in one's own time to produce goods and services for one's own household can be undertaken by affluent workers in the richest cities and by impoverished workers in the poorest cities in the world – it is evidently bizarre to provide a similar label for such disparate activities. Evidently, some forms of work are culturally specific: do-it-yourself activities, for example, may flourish more in Britain and less in Japan. One of the consequences of summing up a range of activities under the general heading of informal work is that quite different forms of work may be cumulated to apparently similar general orders of magnitude as between different societies. In order for such comparisons to be meaningful it is crucial that the umbrella concept be disaggregated into its constituent elements. It is only when specific *forms of work* have been conceptually distinguished that one can then have any firm purchase on comparative analysis and I return to this below (see also Pahl, 1984, ch. 5).

In order to give some flavour of the range of contexts in which the terms 'informal work' and 'informal economy' are used, a number of different issues and debates may be mentioned. Each has its own literature and I refer to these simply for the purpose of illustration and with no claim to comprehensiveness. The same activities may be referred to as part of an informal economy by some authors, an informal sector by others, or simply informal work, *travail au noir*, or *Schwarzarbeit* by yet others.

1   Reference is made to a range of activities that can be termed survival strategies of poor people, whether in the slums of Third World cities or in the Italian South (Mingione, 1983). Debate centres on whether this is an obligatory option or is the result of a choice between alternative ways of getting a livelihood.

2   New or alternative modes of service provision in advanced industrial society encourage the spread of work outside employment (Skolka, 1976; Gershuny, 1979). Self-provisioning, do-it-yourself, using new technology to produce entertainments and services privately that were previously only available publicly, and so on, are all facets of a debate that, by implication, can be applied to all industrial societies. Those with the highest levels of material production may be expected to show the tendency most markedly (Gershuny, 1983; Pahl, 1984). The so-called 'new service economy' is heavily weighted towards self-servicing. Debate centres on the degree to which the informal provision of services may increase with increasing affluence.

3   Work outside employment, also referred to as 'the informal economy', has been heralded as the source of a new liberated life-style in which people are freed from the burdens of oppressive capitalist relations or the constraints of ponderously bureaucratic systems of allocation. Work in the 'realm of necessity' is reduced and work in the 'realm of freedom' is expanded, to take Marx's terminology. The new order can be observed emerging now in existing forms of alternative life-

styles.[5] Debate centres on how far these are significant straws in the wind or insignificant epiphenomena.

4   There is a debate on how far caring, communal work outside the formal welfare state may be an alternative way of producing communal services and support systems. Such work should be distinguished from the support networks of the poor and deprived but is rather a product of material prosperity, greater availability of time and skills, and an ideology of altruistic caring and concern. Self-help groups and various forms of co-operative organization figure strongly in this perspective (Heinze and Olk, 1982). Critics see it as a likely basis for the greater exploitation of women (Ungerson, 1987; Parker, 1988).

5   Another contentious area relates to the degree to which the informal economy (or sector) may be a source of dynamism in both capitalist and socialist societies. Post-Fordism in the West is linked with greater 'flexibility', including subcontracting, home working and the growth of a peripheral, temporary or part-time labour force.[6] Debate centres on whether the so-called 'Emilian model' of subcontracting, of which much has been made, has application in other contexts (Sabel, 1982). What may be liberating and wealth-creating under one set of social relations may be oppressive and impoverishing under another. The line between tax evasion or employing cheap labour – in defiance of labour protection legislation – and being a wealth-creating entrepreneur establishing small enterprises and helping to make capitalism truly dynamic is hard to draw. Similarly, as Stark (1986) has shown for Hungary, the line between a loyal manager in the state's economic system and a swashbuckling pirate, undermining the system through informal internal subcontracting, is also hard to define.

This last example illustrates very well the ambiguity and contradiction inherent in the label. It would not be difficult to set up a number of paradoxical dichotomies. As we have seen, the informal economy can be adduced as a term of approbation – linked to notions of liberation, freedom, self-expression, non-alienated labour, and more *gemeinschaftlich* and expressive activities. But, similarly, the informal economy can carry connotations of illegality, exploitation, oppression and instrumental coercion. It can be a symbol of dynamism and of decline, of progressive and regressive structures and behaviour, an indicator of hope or of despair. Thus modernization may, on the one hand, be seen as a way of reducing 'less efficient' personalized and informal practices and procedures by expanding centralized marketing and banking systems. An alternative trajectory of social change sees the informal economy or sector as being based on an entrepreneurial style that will be important in breaking the mould, of cracking over-rigid organizational or political structures and thus pointing the way to a more efficient future (Piore and Sabel, 1984). A middle position, tacitly adopted by the Irish and Italian governments, would see the creative tension between formal and informal practices as an essential ingredient of a 'good' economic system: the problem is largely to get the balance right. However, simply focusing on degrees of regulation or deregulation may produce comparative statistics of interest to politicians and administrators but may have very little sociological significance.

In an article concerned with Western capitalist societies, the authors claim that 'informality seems to be growing, at least in some sectors' (Portes and Sassen-Koob, 1987, p. 41). (Such an unexceptional observation has, for some years now, been part of the conventional wisdom amongst those working in this field, see O'Higgins, 1980, 1985; Barthelemy, 1982; Heinze and Olk, 1982; Mingione 1983, 1985; Pahl, 1984; Gaertner and Wenig, 1985; OECD, 1986b.) In support of the statement, Portes and Sassen-Koob present data from the US Bureau of Statistics to show that a large proportion of the US workforce is employed in very small establishments (VSEs), that is, those employing less than 10 workers. The authors show that substantial job losses in New York City between 1970 and 1980 have been partially offset by a rapid growth of VSEs, especially in the diversified consumer services sector. Such an account is unexceptional. However, very surprisingly the authors proceed to use the growth of these small businesses as a proxy for the growth of the informal economy.

In doing this they fail to distinguish between different kinds of small enterprises and distinctive forms of social relations. On the one hand, perhaps, firms could be based on new high technology, in which a small group of professional people generate a high value-added component from their product or service – thus ensuring that they all become very rich; on the other hand, they could be small sweat-shops, where the owner may make good profits but his workers receive meagre wages. In both cases the form of work could be more or less formal. At one extreme the first type of VSE could report accurately all its dealings to the appropriate tax authorities and the second could, legally, employ part-time women workers, say, for whom the employer has few formal obligations. At the other extreme the first type of entrepreneur could make substantial profits but only a small proportion of these are officially declared. In the second case the sweat-shop owner could employ people for long hours on low wages, fail to fulfil his employer's obligations in terms of health insurance, safety regulations, holiday entitlement and so forth and under-declare the number of people he employs.

Secondly, the authors assert that 'displaced workers to escape chronic unemployment and to supplement paltry tax relief expand the supply of labor available for informal activities' (Portes and Sassen-Koob, 1987, p. 55). However, there is now a substantial literature that demonstrates unequivocally that unemployed people in many European countries are *least* likely to be engaged in informal work (Foudi *et al.*, 1982; Economist Intelligence Unit, 1982; OECD, 1986b; Pahl, 1987).

Finally, by conflating VSEs with informality and the informal economy, the authors ignore all the other forms of informal work that may be increasing in industrial society (Skolka, 1976; Gershuny, 1983; Pahl, 1984; Redclift and Mingione, 1985; INCHIESTA, 1986).

The authors are certainly right to consider the social implications of regulation and deregulation in given contexts and, hence, the role of government in determining levels of informal employment. They note that 'the mutually reinforcing fit between workers' needs and firms' strategies could not very well occur in a politically hostile environment' (Portes and Sassen-Koob, 1987, p. 56). Unhappily this is the conclusion rather than the starting point of their analysis. The legal deregulation of forms of work previously regulated is associated more with radical conservative govern-ments than with the more liberal neo-Keynesian or corporatist strategies of Sweden or Austria. If exploitative forms of informal work are more likely in New York than in, say, Amsterdam, then that issue needs to be addressed. Yet sophisticated comparative analysis (Pickvance, 1986) is only possible when there is common agreement on what it is that is to be studied.

A true 'informal economy' in a state socialist society?

Though it is reasonable to be highly sceptical of claims to find more than one economy in Western Europe, the issue becomes less obscure in state socialist societies, whose economies are centrally planned and where a real distinction can be made between that sector and the private market sector. The editors of a collection of articles examining this phenomenon conclude 'the second economy forms an economic sphere separate from the state sector and entirely different from it in operational principles as well. In this respect the economy of the present socialist system is a dual one' (Galasi and Sziráczki, 1985, p. 20). They go on to elaborate this distinction, arguing that the first economy is state *directed*, with budgetry dependence on the state. The second economy, by contrast, may be *regulated* by the state but the units use their own means of production and can decide for themselves when and for how long they operate. The two economies have differing rules of operation and there is a kind of competition between them. The state would like to maintain the second economy in a secondary role but, as we shall see, it is not always able to achieve this and *both* economies attempt to evade the regulations that are intended to keep their activities distinct.

A crucial problem posed for the state is that the same amount of work yields more consumable income in the second economy than in the first. It is calculated that about a quarter of the total time given to the first economy is devoted to the second and about a fifth of the GNP is generated in that sphere.

One area in which the second economy flourishes is the building industry. One survey of 600 families in 1978 showed that 40 per cent helped to build other people's homes and of these over a quarter had helped to build two or more houses. In industrial services – the repair and maintenance of vehicles and household and electrical appliances – the gross performance value of the second economy is close to that provided by the state service network. As Stark remarked, 'As bread-winners and as bread buyers, Hungarians live in a dual economy' (Stark, 1988).

Of particular interest, however, is the way the two economies interweave amongst different categories of employees in the first economy. As in the West, key workers are in a privileged position. Again the key concept is flexibility: key workers are those who are able to maintain continuous production through strategies of improvisation – that is, *ad hoc* solutions to shortage of materials or parts and the maintenance of the plant. Firm-specific skills are required, including the ability to get spare parts through their personal contacts in other workshops and having special tools that belong to them personally, that enable the work to be done quickly and more easily. These firm-specific skills enable these key workers to advance up the internal hierarchy and to earn bonuses with the help of their personal tools. Jealous of their privileged position, these elite workers practise strategies of social closure that make it difficult for other workers to break in and share these privileges. Such workers do so well out of the first economy that they have little incentive to work in the second economy.

Below the elite workers are the middle-level workers who are blocked from further advance. Their best strategy is to control their wage–effort ratio so that they get a stable wage level with moderate effort. Since the same amount of work yields a higher income in the second economy, they have a strong incentive to use their job in the first economy as a kind of long stop and to devote considerable effort to developing their position in the private sector. This involves overcoming substantial problems, including the lack of capital, transport, materials and market information. Conditions in the second economy are necessarily highly unstable and returns are bound to fluctuate.

Below the middle-level workers are women, young male workers just starting their careers, and newly arrived immigrants from rural areas who have neither firm-specific skills nor contacts in the second economy. Such categories are doubly penalized and need multiple incomes and other household members in order to survive satisfactorily.

A fourth category of worker is those with specialized skills that firms need, but for whom there are few jobs available. The consequence is that the jobs remain outside the firms' main organizational structure and the opportunities for advancement are limited. Hence, such workers are virtually obliged to move between firms as a way of advancing their careers and improving their salaries. They become like medieval journeymen gradually accumulating knowledge and experience as they move about. Firms intent on keeping these skilled and potentially mobile workers will be more flexible and tolerant towards them. They may allow them more free time, pay them overtime rates, and allow them to use the firm's machines and lorries, so that they can earn extra money doing repair and maintenance work in the private economy.

The strategy of moving between employers as a means of raising wages is also practised by workers without specialized skills but who become 'work-horses' and get increased wages at the expense of their wage–effort ratio. Since there is no organized trade-union activity in Hungary to ensure some kind of parity between firms and workers the free bargaining that is inevitable, given the labour shortage, leads to workers being driven hard, and they respond by moving between firms in an attempt to raise their wages.

A final category – the so-called marginal workers – are employed in seasonal work such as the canning and sugar factories and in construction. Not unreasonably, such people are not committed to state employment and withdraw to the household to work on their private plots. These workers – mainly women – become used to an alternating pattern of working partly in the state labour market and partly in their own private sphere of small-scale commodity production. This pattern, common in England in the eighteenth century (Berg, 1988; Malcolmson, 1988), can also be found in Italy and Spain today but without the sharp distinction between the state sector and the private sector.

From 1982 there was a rapid expansion of partnerships of employees of state enterprises who, in effect, took on sub-contracted tasks for the firms that employed them. The firm would offer a fee for the total job to be completed and this sum would be distributed, after tax, to the workers concerned. These VGMs became an extremely dynamic element in the Hungarian economy. They more than trebled in number in 1983 – from 2775 to 9192 – and by then existed in 56 per cent of industrial enterprises and 67 per cent of building industry enterprises. However, these highly specialized and skilled work groups involved about one out of every ten manual workers by 1986: by December 1986 there were 21,490 partnerships with a total of 267,000 members (Stark, 1988, n. 13). These VGMs illustrate very neatly the interpenetration of the two principles of state planning and market rationality in Hungary. Given the labour shortage already mentioned and the necessary regulation of wages by the state, it is easy to understand why VGMs have spread so rapidly. The fees paid to VGMs count as 'costs', not wages, and thus legitimately circumvent the regulation of earnings. In practice VGM members get paid at least twice as much as they would get for work performed during normal working hours and some get paid four times as much. Some VGM members may even get more from their partnership work than for their formal job.

The scheme appealed to both management and workers. It was initially unnecessary to bring in external labour which was even more expensive than internal partnerships, and the skilled workers who were partners in the VGMs became more committed to their enterprise as their incentive to look elsewhere for earnings was undermined. This latter point appealed to the central state management, since VGMs were seen to be an acceptable alternative to the liberalization and increasing inequality generated by the second economy. They also appealed to the workers, as Stark (1988) explains:

If the washing machine repairman in a state firm could gain clients and spare parts from his regular job for his off hours 'private practice' and if the peasant could intensively cultivate his own hectare of land, how was the furnaceman in a steel mill or a machinist making sophisticated machine tools to use his special skills within the second economy? The VGM provides such an opportunity to gain additional incomes in the off hours. As one young machine designer explained:

> The VGM is a more civilized form than the second economy. I can earn extra money according to my skill and not on a lower level. If you do the work at your same level, you regard the extra money as less humiliating. Let's say, if I need the money, I don't have to wash little Aunt Mary's windows or unload wagons but I can do the work that I like and know well. There aren't too many possibilities to do design work in the black for enterprises. To design and make a tool can't be done in 'schwartz'. But in the VGM I continue my regular work and so it can bring about some professional development too.

Similarly, an older machinist stated:

> I can't grow vegetables in a bathtub. Those who live in the countryside have household plots and can earn some money from these, but we in the city don't have these. In the VGM, though, I can stay in the same place, use my same skills, and work with my same friends.

Or, as a Central Committee member explained to me in an interview, 'The VGMs are the household plots of industry'.

The state planners held the somewhat utopian view that the partnerships would inject a new entrepreneurial spirit into enterprises, which would help to resolve production bottlenecks. They certainly revealed the hidden labour reserves of the large firm. As Stark summarized the situation: 'whereas workers in capitalist economies differ in the extent to which they are protected from the market, workers in the socialist economy differ according to the extent to which they can participate in the market' (Stark, 1988).

By the mid-1980s it seemed as though VGMs were becoming too successful. The partnerships began using their own equipment to produce for the market and began to operate independently of the enterprise that housed them. They seemed to be developing so efficiently and rapidly that it was hard for observers to keep track of developments. Early in 1986 there was some indication that VGMs were operating in more overtly market conditions. When visiting the outside of a major steel plant in northern Hungary I observed an elaborate notice board prominently situated outside the main entrance. The group of Hungarian sociologists who were with me were astonished to see some seventeen advertisements for tasks, including white-collar work. Here was a major state employer in effect advertising for VGMs to come into the plant from outside.

It has been estimated that 40 per cent of the wage labourers in Hungary's first state economy get extra income from the second economy, amounting to 25 per cent of their total wages. Overall three-quarters of all families receive some income from the second economy and it has been suggested that these incomes amount to almost half of the socialist sector's wage-type outlay (Gabor, 1985). The conclusion of one Hungarian social scientist is remarkably similar to the situation in contemporary Britain: 'Groups with high extra income seem to get high extra earnings from every source, while those with low extra income get low extra earnings' (Galasi, 1985, p. 305). Polarization between work-rich, multiple-earning individuals and households and those with low and limited sources of income appears to be growing in Hungary. The new inequalities generated through these internal labour markets are also now much more visible to those who are excluded from the opportunities provided by the VGMs.

Employment flexibility and concealed employment

In Western Europe the growth of part-time work in the service sector and the development of a crucial distinction between core and peripheral workers in 'flexible firms' is creating new divisions within the traditional working class (OECD, 1986a). In Eastern Europe the differential access to income-generating opportunities in the second economy is similarly creating new divisions. The growth of concealed employment and self-provisioning in Western Europe in no way compensates for the growth of unemployment. Rather than one form of work being a compensation for reduced opportunities in access to other forms of work, the situation appears to be one of social polarization, where those on upward benign spirals cumulate more forms of work and sources of income in their households, whereas the reverse is the case for those caught in malign downward spirals (Pahl, 1988b).

In both Western and Eastern Europe the forces for change are more market-driven than consequent on state intervention in the regulation and organization of relations between households and the formal economy. More traditional divisions between capital and labour in the West and between collective and individual goals in the East are now being replaced by divisions based on the work strategies of enterprises and workers. Thus as *The Economist* noted in 1983:

> Expensive, full-time workers are being turned into cheaper, independent subcontractors by a growing number of companies in Europe. Skilled, white collar workers can cost employers up to three times their basic salary in office space, fringe benefits and other overheads. By turfing them out and signing contracts for their services, companies can cut costs and still retain people they can trust.

In Hungary, as we have seen, the state has encouraged a substantial degree of private entrepreneurial activity, ownership and management. However, it is clear that the new 'entre-preneurial socialism' produces wealth that is creating a category of *nouveaux riches*, matched by an impoverishment of another part of the population – that is, low-status public officials and others who do not have access to lucrative unofficial activities. Marginal workers and various minority groups are part of a significant impoverished minority.

These new divisions are not revealed in conventional socio-logical analysis which lays disproportionate weight on the 'official' occupational status of a household's 'chief earner'. Clearly, the actual occupation of a worker may be much less significant than his or her position in the enterprise, the composition of his or her household, and a variety of other factors relating to the capacity to engage in concealed income-generating capacity in the West or in the second economy in the East. Distinctive household work-practices are emerging which require extremely detailed socio-logical reporting and analysis to reveal (Pahl 1984, 1988b). Such strategies involve multiple earners, distinctive occupational milieux that provide good access to concealed employment in the second economy in different contexts and, finally, home owner-ship as a focus for self-provisioning. These household work strategies can intermesh with firms' strategies when a male 'chief earner' becomes a core worker and his wife and young, unmarried children who have left school become low-paid peripheral workers, providing component wages for the household. It may suit wives to work part-time – particularly at certain stages of the life cycle – and young school-leavers may prefer a low-paid job to no job at all. The shift in Western economies from manufacturing to services has strengthened women's position in the labour market (reflected in the reduction in the pay differential between the wages of men and women, see Adams *et al.*, 1988).

If the old image of patterns of inequality was of geological strata with one layer superimposed on another with a 'structural fault' between the working class and the middle class (Parkin, 1972), the new image is perhaps more appropriately a patchwork quilt, where the same colours reappear in different places. Core workers and work-rich households can be in a variety of contexts, depending on the industrial and urban geography of the nation concerned.

In this new context national statistics tend to be positively misleading as they suppress real variations in favour of an unreal uniformity. Detailed studies based on distinctive local labour markets, showing the distribution of all forms of work and indicating the underlying social and economic processes, will help to build up our understanding of the patchwork quilt, based upon the new divisions that are emerging.

Returning now to the problem of comparative cross-national research, rather than carrying out even more individual research projects on apparently the same issue in different contexts, the first step, as I have suggested, is to clarify more precisely what it is that is to be the object of analysis. One suggestion is to focus on 'concealed employment', that is, 'employment (in the sense of the current international guidelines on employment statistics) which, while not illegal in itself, has not been declared to one or more administrative authorities to whom it should be made known. Thereby leading to the evasion of legal regulations, the evasion of taxes, or the evasion of a reduction of social security entitlements' (OECD, 1986b, p. 67). That is evidently a pragmatic and workable definition but it seems more a definition of administrative convenience than of sociological bite. Since the whole notion of an informal economy or sector is almost impossible to define in a way that could sensibly encompass the wide range of empirical diversity, I suggest that it is time that sociologists cease being parasites on economists' concepts. Most of the early impetus to measure the *informal economy*, certainly in the United States, came from economists (for example, Gutmann, 1977; Feige, 1979). However, the detailed exploration of *informal work* has been undertaken by sociologists. Hence, *I now want to argue that comparative analysis may be most fruitfully advanced by sociologists by focusing on work rather than on the economy*. In this way we may hope for some genuine advance in comparative sociology as opposed to managerial statistics.

Defining forms of work by the social relations they are embedded in

It may be objected that attempts to define informal work may be as readily frustrated as those attempts to define the informal economy. I now put forward my proposal for an analytical framework which would be based partly on an actor's definition of the situation and partly on the understanding of the social relations in which a given task or activity is embedded. Only when both of these objective and subjective conditions are known is it possible to determine what kind of work is being done. However, the charm of my approach is that it provides categories which may be compared cross-nationally. The size of these categories will depend on a whole complex of variables but with some measure of orders of magnitude, a framework for comparative analysis can be established. These social relations can be structured by the patterns of domination generated by the capitalist economic system, the principles of both the market and of reciprocity, and by the social hierarchies of age, gender, kinship, neighbourhood and informal group. An individual may apparently be engaged in a work task but simply observing that individual may provide little understanding of what kind of work it is or, indeed, whether it is work at all. Not all purposeful activity is work; but if it is non-work or play we again cannot be sure until we know more of the social relations in which the play activity is embedded. We see people at an embassy drinks party: one person may be there sharing a convivial activity and engaging in a pure form of sociation or play. Another person may work for the British Council or the embassy staff and is heavily and intensely involved in the employment for which she is paid. There *is* a distinction between work and play but it is not based on the intrinsic nature of the task or activity. In order to clarify this and to introduce further complexities a particular example may be explored in some detail.[7]

Consider an image of a woman ironing. She is standing by an ironing board on which there is a garment – a blouse or a shirt. Is she at work or is she at play and, if the former, what kind of work

106

is she engaged in? The answer will depend on the social relations in which her task is embedded. Let us explore some possibilities.

First, the woman could be a full-time wage-worker producing garments as a domestic outworker. If she has been hired on a piece-work basis she could have an incentive to iron as many garments as quickly as possible. Alternatively, she may have been hired on a fixed contract with no incentive to increase the number of garments she irons, although there may be some quality control so that the style or quality of her work is more important than her pace. Her approach to her task is likely to be related to the contractual arrangements that exist between her and her employer. She may be working part-time, she may be working shifts which include a period at home, or she may be doing casual work, covering for regular employees at a holiday time or taking on extra work at a particularly busy period. Whatever the precise details, she is, in all these cases, basically a wage-labourer: she is selling her ironing skills to an employer who provides her with the materials and also, possibly, the tools. If she had an accident and lost her sight or injured her ironing arm her labour power would disappear or be reduced.

There is a further twist. We may learn that she is basically a wage-labourer, determined by the social relations in which her task is embedded, but we cannot be sure that her employer is honest. It is possible that this female outworker is not recorded in the firm's official returns to the appropriate government depart-ment. This may be a strategy to avoid, on the one hand, the obligation to pay certain taxes or insurance contributions, and also to avoid granting certain rights and benefits to the employee, such as the number of days' holiday with pay, rights to sickness benefit and maternity leave and insurance in the event of, say, an accident with the iron. If the worker is being hired informally or illegally that will not affect the basic social relations of wage-labour; it will, however, determine whether it is formally recorded, which, in turn, will have fundamental implications for the individual concerned. If the work is done informally this does not, of course, put it in any separate informal economy but it should be described as shadow or hidden wage-labour to distinguish it from the formally recognized and recorded form.

The woman could be preparing the garment for sale but she may own the material and the iron; she may have dyed the cloth, designed the style, or decorated the garment in some distinctive way. She may have her own stall or boutique or she may be selling by contract to specific retail outlets. Whatever the details, she is a self-employed worker engaged in petty-commodity production. She is responsible for her own pace of work and the quality of what she produces. She may employ others, who may or may not be members of her family. If the latter she may be engaged in family capitalism with its own distinctive sets of social relations. Again, her activities may be more or less officially recognized and she may prefer to defraud the tax authorities, despite the risks involved. This may involve the simple under-declaring of profits or it may be coupled with paying other people in cash, so that she has no contractual obligations towards them.

So far the women at the ironing board has been viewed as an income-generating agent. We know nothing about her age, marital status, race, or subjective preconceptions and attitudes. She could be married or single, and in both cases she may or may not have a child. Let us assume that she is ironing the garment for another member of the household in which she lives. What kind of work would that be? Again we need to know more about the nature of the social relations in which the task is embedded. This time we are not concerned with the social relations of capitalist production but with the familial or patriarchal relations, and these may get very complex. There is a great range of possibilities. The woman may be ironing a shirt for her lover. Her mind is full of loving or erotic thoughts so that the task is highly charged emotionally and provides substantial pleasure as she, perhaps, fantasizes about the person as she irons the various parts of the garment. She may have offered to do the task as an act of love, knowing that her lover was willing and able to do the task himself and, indeed, in the past has done the same for her. The work is thus symbolic: it is work with a purpose, done for love and is similar to the toil of monks or nuns who work, literally, for love as a means of self-expression. The distinction between this kind of work and play is that, in the latter case, the pleasure would be solely in the activity of ironing. It would not matter for whom the shirt was being ironed: the important activity would be the ironing itself and the pleasure would be similar to that experienced by those who play tennis or go fishing as a recreational activity.

However, the woman may have been married for many years to a man she barely tolerates. He insists on a clean, well-ironed shirt every day. He may hit her if she fails in what he claims is her duty. She resignedly goes about her task heavily dominated by patriarchal social relations. The task is a burden and brings no pleasure: she feels constrained, oppressed and resentful. She is but one example of the oppression of women and she may be brooding on the unfairness and injustice of her situation. Even if she is ironing her children's garments the resentment may be much the same if she feels constrained by her domestic role and the social relations established by the power of her spouse.

If the woman is ironing her own blouse then much will depend on the context in which she is to wear it. If, on the following day she has to wear the garment at the office then she is, as it were, working to reproduce herself as a smart worker. She knows that the way she presents herself is part of the way she is able to demonstrate her effectiveness as a worker. She has internalized the expectations of employers and colleagues – whether male or female – and thus feels constrained to dress in a given way. She is thus working for her employer in her own time but, of course, she is also reproducing herself as a worker when she is cleaning her teeth or eating muesli. However, she would do these things even if she were not in employment. Hence, the task of ironing her blouse is more directly related to her employment and she would not do the task if she was on holiday. Some occupations require specific uniforms or work clothes that are provided and maintained by the employer. Other jobs make no demands on their incumbents and the workers may wear what they like. By exploring the task in this way we can see that some women do have extra employment-related work to carry out in their own time. Unmarried men may have the same burden; married men typically pass on the burden to their wives.

It may be that the woman is ironing her elderly mother-in-law's blouse. A combination of social pressures have put her in the position of being responsible for the care of someone who is unable to care for herself. She may be engaged in what is euphemistically termed 'community care'. She is an unpaid community worker and the obligation she is made to feel to care for her husband's mother may prevent her from engaging in paid employment. Such burdens of family and kin are highly gender-specific. Men would not be expected to care for the elderly in the same way and in the case of an unemployed single man with a dependent relative the social services would provide support that would not be available to a woman in the same position. The social relations of family obligation are sharply divided by gender.

Let us now turn away from the labour market and the ageist or sexist domination of the household and consider the situations where the woman is ironing for someone who is not a household member. She might be doing a little casual work as a domestic cleaner and getting extra cash for doing the ironing at home. She would be sharing in the social relations of the casualized lumpenproletariat, however sweetly her employer asked her to do the work. The more likely situation, however, is that she is doing the ironing for a non-household-member without receiving payment. She may be a member of the local dramatic society and the producer has flattered her into pressing the costumes of the leading actors. She may have agreed to do the work calculating that her willingness will put her, as it were, into credit with the producer – she has entered into a relationship based on the norm of reciprocity. Her reasonable assumption is that by giving her time and effort in doing the ironing she will be repaid with a comparable favour in the future. She may be wanting a part in a play; she may hope that the producer will be stimulated by his appreciation of what she has done to notice other more personal qualities; she may want the esteem and support of other members of the dramatic society. Whatever the reward for which she hopes, she will perceive the task as an investment: she is banking reciprocity and she may expect to get her return in due course. If, on the other hand, the producer has looked round the room and simply cajoled or flattered the nearest woman to do a tedious chore, then she has suffered the effects of normative patriarchal oppression (assuming that the producer does not equally victimize men to stay behind to move scenery or to paint the theatre). The woman could, of course, volunteer to iron the garments solely and simply because she enjoys the chance of helping the group. The task is a pleasing relaxation, perhaps, from a mentally exhausting job and she enjoys the chance to share in the collegial style of the amateur dramatic group. She may not care whether or not she is socially rewarded with thanks and gratitude. The activity is genuinely a pleasure and would not, therefore, be classed as work. However, it would cease to be play if, after offering to do the task a number of times, the group started to assume that it was her job and began to apply the pressures of collective domination to trap her into regular labour.

This is not meant to be an exhaustive survey of all the possible patterns of social relations in which the task of ironing could be embedded. It is simply a way of exploring the various structures of constraint that are created by social relations in which wage-labour, domestic labour and communal labour are embedded. It would clearly be quite wrong to say that our busy ironing woman was not working when she was not engaging in wage-labour. However, it is important to recognize that her orientation to the task substantially altered the form of work in which she was engaged. It matters a great deal whether she is a subordinated, physically and economically powerless person living with a domineering husband or someone living with a man in a spirit of partnership. In the former case it could be claimed that she is living in a situation of patriarchal domination, whereas, in the latter case, the lifting of the dominating structure of social relations changes the nature of the task. This point is important. It is not always necessary to change the nature of the task in order to reduce the burden of work but rather, more significantly, it may be more effective to change the nature of the social relations in which the task is embedded. Thus the dramatic society could turn the pleasurable task into work by taking the activity too readily for granted. Similarly, the woman who was producing her own garments for sale on her stall could make some to give to friends or to exchange for their craft products. In such a case principles of altruism and reciprocity would transform a product aimed at the exchange values of the market to something produced solely for its use value to a friend or relative. It is not the nature of the task that determines whether use values or exchange values are being produced: it is a combination of the social relations and the social orientations in which the task is embedded that defines the form of the work. The meanings that individuals bring with themselves as they face a given task are critical. Throughout our example we have been thinking about a woman doing the task. If the example had referred throughout to 'the person' many readers would still assume that it was a woman doing the work. The tyrannies of custom and convention may create work as much as the economic relations of production.

Regulation, deregulation and the uneven distribution of all forms of work

I have suggested that the term 'informal economy' is not a very meaningful category for comparative analysis but that the notion of forms of work might provide a sharper analytical framework. This implies a shift from an economistic or managerialist perspective which is simply concerned with measuring or controlling 'the hidden economy', often to achieve more effective taxation, to one that is more sociologically sensitive. It may now be objected that focusing on forms of work makes the task of cross-national research no less difficult – the principle of plural causation remains even more salient. Petty commodity production may be increasing in Ghana, Hungary and Britain, perhaps even at a similar rate, but correlation evidently does not imply causation. However, there *are* common global processes of causation and these must underpin comparative analysis.

First, and most obviously, there are the latest developments in the endless battle between capital and labour now being played out in a global arena. The restructuring of manufacturing industry in the developed societies has led to an expansion of labour-intensive services, based very often on female, part-time and subcontracted labour and the official encouragement of small businesses (Hakim 1987a, 1987b; Scase and Goffee, 1987; Goffee and Scase, 1987). The UK government's reluctance to regulate the relationships between employer and employee means that work that was once in the informal economy is now perfectly legal. Unlike most other countries in the European Community the UK government is not prepared to support an EC Directive on minimum rights for part-time workers (Labour Research Department, 1986). Significantly, it is also the pressure from above that is leading to the extraordinarily rapid expansion of VGMs – the enterprise business work partnerships – in Hungary. In order to reduce the effects of uncertainties from the bureaucratic environment, managers in the socialist firm depend on workers' co-operation at crucial moments and in key aspects of the production process (Stark, 1986, p. 495). This provides an excellent example of plural causality: distinctive forms of work emerge from quite different causes. As Stark (1986, p. 497) puts its:

> Cast in the language of dual labour market theory, whereas in the capitalist economy, occupants on the internal job ladders of the 'primary' sector differ from their counterparts in the 'secondary' sector in the degree to which they are *protected from the market*, dualism in the socialist economy is structured round differential opportunities for *participation in the market* (original emphasis).

Thus the fluctuation in the formal/informal divide is determined by the changing forms and styles of regulation and deregulation in an uncertain economic environment.

The second main element in the new mix of diferent forms of work flows from the first. The processes that produce more marginal and peripheral workers also, paradoxically, produce more protected 'core' workers whose privileged position allows them to accumulate even more privilege by engaging in other forms of work as well. Such privileged workers are best seen in the context of their *households*. The growth of multiple-earner households has been most dramatic amongst skilled manual workers. My own detailed research on the Isle of Sheppey in Kent has demonstrated the ways in which such households accumulate more resources and income by engaging in various forms of informal work, moonlighting and other forms of reciprocal and communal work. Those best placed to gain income in employment are also well placed to get extra income informally in employment and in work outside employment (Pahl, 1984, 1988b; Pahl and Wallace, 1985). The net result is a form of social polarization with work-rich households at one extreme and work-starved households at the other. This process has also been carefully documented in the FRG (Glatzer and Berger, 1985).

This recent analysis in Britain and Germany makes clear that patterns of self-provisioning and other forms of informal work, far from reducing or compensating for patterns of structured inequality, actually add to it in a cruelly regressive way.[8] This produces the so-called 'Matthew effect' – to those that hath more shall be given (whereas those that have little even that which they have is taken away) – and evidence is growing that such a process is, indeed, taking place in Britain. However, it would be wrong to assume that this cumulation of forms of work is a universal phenomenon. In some cases compensation is allowed and in other cases it is not. This point can be made clear with an example. In Britain if a man is unemployed but his wife has a job, her earnings are set against his unemployment benefit. Hence, if she is low paid or a part-time worker, the household may be no worse off if she, too, ceases to be formally employed. If, however, she takes employment and does not declare her income – even though the actual money is below the tax threshold – she is still liable to be prosecuted, since the extra earnings would reduce her husband's unemployment benefit. Thus there are strong incentives for partners of unemployed people also to become unemployed. This, however, is not the pattern in other European countries such as Spain or Italy where the state support system (in so far as it exists) provides incentives rather than disincentives for informal work.

Recent developments in labour market organization and changes in internal company flexibility are creating new divisions between core workers and peripheral workers, between men and women, between younger and older workers, and between minority racial and ethnic groups and the dominant majority. The industrial restructuring and the economic recession of the last decade led to more companies attempting to produce the same or greater output with fewer employees. This helped to produce the 'shake-out' and higher unemployment in OECD countries. Once this had been achieved, firms became increasingly wary about increasing the size of their permanent workforce. This so-called 'flexibilization' of labour, often wrapped up in euphemisms such as 'human resource management', is aimed at producing neo-feudal docility from the permanent and pampered core workers, who receive a variety of benefits in relation to health and occupational insurance, access to housing and so forth. The peripheral workforce, by contrast, is likely to be temporary, on short-term contracts, and may not be eligible for much of the support of employment protection legislation. Subcontracting ensures that the fixed costs for which the company itself is responsible, whatever the demand for its products, are kept to the minimum. All the risk is passed on to the subcontractor, who in turn is reluctant to employ a large and inflexible workforce. Furthermore, more work is arranged in a pattern more typical of eighteenth-century Yorkshire where individual workers work in their own time, in their own homes, heated and maintained without any subsidy from the firm that supplies their materials. This outwork or homework is developing in Spain, Italy and Britain and is likely to continue to expand in OECD countries as the charm of increased flexibility is impressed upon employers. As a report from the European Trade Union Institute concluded in 1985:

> It is clear that many European countries have seen a growth of 'insecure' employment over the last five years and a proliferation of different types of employment contract. Besides workers on standard employment contracts, there now exists growing numbers of part-time workers, temporary workers or workers on fixed-term contracts, out workers and freelance workers of various kinds.
>
> (p. 103)

The same report gives examples of a Belgian company that dismissed women workers for refusing to change over from full-time to part-time work. This forced reduction of working hours was directed only against women. The desire by employers to reduce short-term labour costs and to make the labour force act as a buffer to protect firms from fluctuations in demand is reinforcing the tendencies towards a secondary labour market. These newly

114

created peripheral workers have, on average, lower hourly rates of pay than full-time workers. They are likely to work both fewer hours and receive a lower rate per hour.

This strategy by many companies to pass on the costs of an uncertain economic environment on to the workforce is sometimes defended on the grounds that these peripheral workers are disproportionately women who would otherwise not be employed. In 1981 women comprised 86 per cent of part-time workers in Belgium, 85 per cent in France and 94 per cent in both the UK and West Germany. To give some indication of orders of magnitude, there were, in the UK in 1986, 21 million employed workers. Of this total 55 per cent were males and 45 per cent females. But of the 9.4 million female workers 42 per cent were employed part-time. In all, 23 per cent, nearly a quarter of all employed workers, were hired part-time. The most recent statistics also show a new tendency for the growth of male part-time workers (Department of Employment, 1987a and b).

Now whereas there may be an argument about the level of wages and household poverty there is no dispute that those paid on a part-time basis cannot support themselves or their dependants without supplementation. Curiously, the social security system in Britain makes it impossible for earnings from part-time work to be offset against unemployment benefits, since the assumption is that those who are unemployed must be available for full-time employment. A part-time chief earner may be eligible for Family Income Supplement under certain circumstances but those same circumstances may produce much the same household income by relying entirely on Supplementary Benefits payments, without the added burden of taking on employment. The consequences of this and other factors is that most peripheral workers, whether temporary, part-time, or short-term contract, who are paid *component wages* that are inadequate to support themselves, live in households in which there is a full-time, generally male, worker. Hence, rather than there being new conflicts and divisions between core workers and peripheral workers, which might be initially expected, core and periphery workers have a lot in common. They are likely to share the same house, and indeed, the same bed. The growth of component wage earners has resulted in new divisions to be sure, but these are most likely between employment-rich households, with multiple earners and employment-poor households in which there are no earners. This *polarization between households* is growing in West European societies where the single-earner household is becoming a statistical rarity, limited to a very short period of the life cycle when women decide not to be economically active in order to become full-time working mothers in the home.

Typically the work-rich households can become cumulatively advantaged by engaging in other forms of work outside employment, such as various forms of self-provisioning in and around the home (Pahl, 1984). Even lower-paid manual workers can enhance their household income with component wages and, by buying their dwelling from their local authority on favourable terms, can work to make their life-style more comfortable by improving their domestic living conditions through improvements such as double-glazing, extended kitchens, or living areas. By using their own labour, skills and tools they can make substantial savings and often do a better job for themselves. They are also working towards the capital appreciation of their most expensive asset – their own home (Pahl, 1984).

Evidence for these tendencies is not limited to Britain. A report of a representative survey of the adult West German population revealed that 30 per cent of all home owners built the actual shell of the house themselves and 37 per cent carried out most of the interior design work themselves. The authors of this study emphasize that it is *household composition* that is most significantly correlated with this informal work outside employment:

> The lowest degree of self-support can be found in one-person households. Incomplete families are in general below the average level. By contrast, complete families and especially extended families show a high amount of self-support. The differences remain significant if income level, social class and age of the head of household are controlled . . . [these factors] have some influence on household production but not in each area, and generally not as strong as has household composition.
> (Glatzer and Berger, 1988, pp. 517–18)

Although it is certainly true that women and young people are in the disadvantaged situation in the labour market, being more likely to receive component wages, it does not follow that as individual members of households they are disadvantaged in terms of access to consumption. This is because, as explained above, their component wages are combined in a collective household income. Furthermore, those working part-time or in temporary and casual employment may well have the time and also the social contacts to find a second job. These moonlighters, second-job holders, are in a position to enhance still further their collective household income. Certainly, there may be a proportion of chief earners who support themselves and dependants through multiple part-time jobs, so that two or three component wages are aggregated into an adequate income. Some actors, musicians and artists are obliged to operate in this way when they do not get enough of their preferred work to provide an adequate income. The tendency of work-rich households to accumulate further resources is being documented in a number of countries, particularly those in which the core–periphery distinction in the workforce is growing. This distinction cuts across traditional class divisions so that, for example, craftsmen may be in the core and draughtsmen in the periphery. The distinction will vary between one firm and another. The skills of the core workers are increasingly firm-specific and are not easily transferable or brought in from other firms.

It must be stressed that the growth of component wage earners, working part-time or as contract workers, are overwhelmingly in the service sector where there are fewer core workers. Thus, in Britain, out of just over 6 million employees in health, education and other public services (Standard Industrial Classification Division 9) over a third of these workers were part-time in 1984. The proportion rises to 41 per cent in retail distribution (Department of Employment, 1987a and b). More recently Hakim has provided a detailed industrial and occupational breakdown of the flexible workforce showing that health, education and other public service industries had 42 per cent of *all* workers in the non-core sector (Hakim, 1987). Hence, this polarization between households is likely to reflect urban and regional variations in the distribution of industry and the occupational shifts within industries. Households in the areas of declining 'smokestack' industries are likely to be hardest hit with few alternative opportunities in the service occupations to provide income for other household members (Harris, 1987). Hence those regions with declining heavy manufacturing industry have high levels of unemployment and few opportunities for getting and doing extra work whether as moonlighting or self-provisioning. Those in employment get most opportunities to get more work; those who are unemployed get least opportunities. The self-employed have most opportunity in organizing their income tax to suit themselves best.

Clearly European governments are concerned about the consequences of these different patterns of regulation or deregulation on labour market behaviour, income inequalities and the possibility of the creation of pools of cheap labour. Different political policies and programmes produce different social and economic consequences. It would clearly be a mistake to bring all these activities under the umbrella of 'the informal economy', with the implication that it is an autonomous entity with a life of its own, which the state has to control or to manipulate in some way.

Conclusion

Sociologists should, perhaps, have recognized more readily the dangers of turning their backs to the fire while watching the flickering shadows on the wall. The pattern on the wall is elusive and constantly changing. If those concerned with cross-national studies of the informal economy or, as I would prefer, *forms of informal work*, focused more on the power of established political and economic institutions, the variations in the empirical reality of informal work would become more intelligible. O'Higgins (1985, p. 140) concluded his heroic attempt to explore the relationship between the formal and hidden economies in four countries by remarking: 'the results emphasize the diversity of national experiences and, therefore, the weakness of generalized assumptions based on the experience of any country'. He did, however, suggest that there were positive links between the hidden economy and structural changes in the measured economy. The fire is being fanned by global processes of capital accumulation and by the state through its pattern of regulation or deregulation. Sociologists and anthropologists, who have provided so many interesting detailed case studies of forms of informal work and so many *ad hoc* explanatory accounts, need to turn round from the wall and face the fire.

My argument is that informal work and the informal sector are largely the creations of the policies and the actions of governments, employers or, in the case of socialist societies, bureaucratic controllers. The results can be very diverse and social scientists have in general done more to document the consequences than to focus on the causes. Employers' strategies, the growth of entrepreneuring and governmental patterns of regulation or deregulation are the crucial determinants of patterns of informal work in households, often mediated through the social uses of new technology.

118

Acknowledgements

This paper was written as part of a programme of work financed by the Joseph Rowntree Memorial Trust. An earlier, much shorter, version was presented to a thematic session on Comparative Urban Sociology at the American Sociological Association Annual Convention, Chicago, 17 August 1987.

Notes

1 For example, Consiglio Italiano per le Scienze Sociale: The Informal Economy, Social Conflicts and the Future of Industrial Society, International Conference at Villa Tuscalona, Frascati (Rome) November 1982, and the conference whose papers appeared in Gaertner and Wenig (1985). However, 1986 was the best vintage so far: international conferences were held in Messina (Sicily) in May, Bielefeld (FGR) in September and Harper's Ferry (West Virginia) in October. There were certainly others in addition.
2 See, in particular, OECD, 1986b, pp. 66–79 and the references cited therein. More recently the European Commission in Brussels (DGv) has attempted a review of '*le travail noir*' in its member states, which is likely to be published in 1989.
3 A lively and well-researched popular account is by Mattera, 1985. For sceptical and well-informed critiques of the work of economists, especially in the United States and Britain, see Smith, 1986, and Thomas, 1988.
4 There are indications that this distinction between the state public system and the private market system is endorsed by Mr Gorbachev (if not by all of his colleagues).
5 See Gorz, 1982; Robertson, 1985; and the international network organized by James Robertson and Alison Pritchard from the Old Bakehouse, Cholsey, Near Wallingford, Oxfordshire, OX10 9NV. Pamphlets and a newsletter are available. Links appear to be strongest with others in Canada, the USA, FRG, Scandinavia, Britain and the Netherlands – see Robertson's references.
6 The literature on 'flexibility' and 'restructuring' is large and mostly ephemeral. A useful introduction is OECD, 1986a; see also Piore and Sabel, 1985; and the now classic Bagnesco, 1977.
7 This example is taken from Pahl, 1988b.
8 Pahl, 1987; Klein *et al.*, 1986. Astonishingly similar results were also found in Naples! See the most interesting results in Serpieri and Spano, 1986.

5

Economic Recession and Gender Divisions in Western Capitalism

SHEILA ALLEN

Introduction

The purpose of this chapter is to examine the relationship between gender divisions and the recession in Western capitalist societies. This must be regarded as a tentative exercise, for although gender divisions are an integral part of capitalist societies they have until recently been little researched and still do not appear in much sociological discourse.[1] Recession, too, is no novelty in the two hundred years of capitalism and has been extensively studied by economic historians and economists but it was not until the late 1920s and 1930s that the depression, as it was then termed, was subjected to sociological enquiry. This work was mainly concerned with the impact of unemployment (Bakke, 1933; Jahoda *et al.*, 1933; Jones, 1934; Eisenberg and Lazarsfeld, 1938) and most of it investigated or reported only on men (Hurstfield, 1986).

In this paper I shall consider how gender divisions are relevant to our understanding of the current recession as well as how the recession is affecting men and women. I shall focus on work as a gendered terrain, drawing on some of the major debates of the 1970s and 1980s and relating them to those aspects of the recession which are, or are construed as, gender-related or gender-specific; in particular, those of unemployment and economic restructuring. This involves exploring the interrelations of the household and the economy which the perspectives developed in feminist writings have done much to demystify, but which were for several generations separated in sociological discourses into the sociology of the family, a private and personal sphere, and the sociology of industry or industrialization, a public sphere peopled only by men.

First, I shall outline some of the issues which arise both with gender and recession. Then I shall examine some of the literature and the empirical evidence on gender and work, employment and unemployment, drawing from recent sociological work as well as official data. Finally, I shall discuss how the recession is relevant to our understanding of gender divisions.

Gender and recession

Whatever the merits of claims of 'a feminist revolution' in knowledge (Spender, 1987) or 'that taking women seriously has led to a revolution in sociology and to a lesser extent in economics' (Dex, 1985), I would argue that given the gender-blind or gender-biased assumptions found in much mainstream sociology, most officially produced information, as well as in popular treatments of the subject, it is still inordinately difficult to interpret or even to relate in any systematic way the differential impact of the recession in terms of gender. In part such difficulties arise because the social relations between men and women are not a special, discrete area which can be cordoned off into a narrowly defined private or domestic sphere but are directly or indirectly enmeshed in the whole range of social, economic, political and cultural relations and therefore go to the roots of theorizing about how capitalist societies developed, persist and change. Gender divisions cannot be excluded any more than the other major social divisions, particularly those of class and race, which characterize Western capitalist societies. On the contrary the interrelation of these divisions constitutes one of the most important, and as yet unresolved, theoretical issues in contemporary sociology (Allen, 1987).

Questions about gender relations, dormant for decades, were raised in the 1960s and 1970s and in most branches of social science a considerable literature exists which seeks to redress the former neglect and/or to reformulate the basic conceptual vocabularies to analyse gendered social relations and processes.[2] For instance, the gendered division of labour has played a crucial role in the processes of industrialization, and in recessionary periods it is particularly significant as a barometer of change. Whether, when and where the relations between historically constructed male subjects and female subjects constitute *the* major division requires to be treated as an open theoretical and political question. Nevertheless, the perspectives developed over the past two decades and the work resulting from these are integral to the analysis of the current restructuring of economic activities, the effects of the recession, and associated political and cultural changes in the 1980s.

We know, or have rediscovered, much more than we did only a decade ago about the structuring of economic, political and cultural differences between men and women, and some patterns of sexual inequality are now more clearly documented. There is much, however, that is neither understood nor explained. There are still wide areas of disagreement on the significance or salience of gender in both theoretical and political discussions about capitalist social relations. The ways in which gender divisions have constrained or facilitated economic and political policy options in recessionary periods in capitalist societies remains relatively uninvestigated. Furthermore, while much of the data from official or social-scientific research still either relate only to men or are undifferentiated by gender, some relate only to women. Thus, their use in specifying the gendered impact of economic recession remains problematic.

It is not possible to do justice to all aspects of the theoretical and empirical work carried out over the past decade by social scientists who have taken gender seriously. Nor can one short chapter cover either many of the criticisms advanced by those who remain unconvinced that gender is a major and enduring division in capitalist societies or those very different arguments which rest on an assumption that the relations of men and women constitute in capitalism and all other societies and systems, the major form of oppression and exploitation. Each of these is well represented in the literature.[3]

In reviewing some of the key issues and problems of gender divisions and the recession I shall develop an argument put forward more than a decade ago that gender relates centrally to the theories and methodologies of sociological enquiry and its neglect is deleterious to our understanding of social structures, processes and change (Barker and Allen, 1976a, 1976b). This argument has two aspects which though interrelated can be usefully separated for ease of clarification. The first is concerned with the redressing of the balance in the sense that although women make up more than half the world's population and according to United Nations calculations do two-thirds of the world's work, own 1 per cent of the world's assets, and receive between 5 and 10 per cent of the income, in much social science and in many areas of social life their activities, beliefs and experiences are marginalized in theory and common sense, and by institutionalized sexism. Redressing this combination of invisibility and marginalization would be an immense improvement on present practice.[4]

The second aspect of the argument is more challenging. Put simply it is that gender-blind or genderless sociology not only fails to take account of women's lives, but cannot describe or theorize the social relations of men adequately. It is therefore at best limited and at worst absurd, both in terms of its descriptive and explanatory powers. Moreover, its potential for distortion of everyday life and the terms of wider political debate appears to be endless. To explore the relations between men and men, between women and men, and between women and women requires approaches which explicitly recognize gender as part of the problematic and which develop theories and methods appropriate to addressing all these relations. Until this becomes a commonplace of sociological practice we cannot know how far the argument that 'the value of feminist critiques to the discipline of sociology lies in the accumulating evidence that gender is not a good index to understand the social world' (Matthews, 1982) has a general validity or relates more specifically to some situations, periods, or social formations. Rowbotham (1979) suggests, for instance, that 'There are times when class or race solidarity are much stronger than sex-gender conflict' which indicates not only that at other times gender carries more force, but that unless all three are analysed together as one reality, sociological investigation of contemporary capitalist societies is fundamentally flawed (Joseph and Lewis, 1981; Davis, 1982).

The term 'recession' is in everyday use in the 1980s. Its meaning and import are, however, far from clear both in social science and in popular usage. On the one hand it carries general connotations which contextualize all manner of events and direct and indirect experiences of political, social and cultural life, and on the other it relates more specifically to the economy or some particular part of it. When it started, what caused it, how it is to be measured, what its effects are, how and when it will end, are all matters which remain marked by a diversity of views (Kilpatrick and Lawson, 1980; Cooke, 1982; Hesselman, 1983; Fine and Harris, 1985). Furthermore, interpreting which aspects of social life can be said to be recession-related and which are simply associated with it temporally is by no means straightforward. The term 'recession', moreover, by indicating a temporary phase after which a former state of affairs will be resumed, albeit in a moderated form, does not convey a sense of structural change. It is, however, to be found increasingly treated within a context of economic restructuring which does presume changes, propelled in part by technology, but reflecting longer-term trends in the organization of production relations, in the terms and conditions under which buyers and sellers of labour operate, and the ways in which goods and services are produced and consumed (Purcell *et al.*, 1986). Kumar (1977) raised the issues more broadly. His discussion involved questions about the adequacy of sociological conceptualizations, derived from nineteenth-century characterizations of industrialism, for analysing social, economic and political realities of industrial societies in the late twentieth century. He argued that 'At the objective level, industrialism has run into the ground'. The premisses on which it was based for two centuries 'are clearly revealed as shaky' and the need now 'as a matter of sheer survival, is to restructure those institutions and technologies to meet the new situation' (pp. 41–2). The issue of the continuing viability of the dominant form of industrialism cannot be pursued in further detail here. It nevertheless affects understandings of the present recession and restructuring.

It is not necessary to accept Kumar's arguments in every particular to recognize the general force of his case for rethinking. His portrayal of the failures of industrialism to provide the basis for the material and cultural well-being of increasing sectors of those in advanced industrial societies is confirmed by much subsequent experience. The evidence of increasing internal polarization between the few who amass considerable wealth in some Third World societies and the precarious livelihood of the urban and rural poor in these societies, and of external indebtedness cannot adequately be explained by the concept of recession or on the basis of the sociological assumptions of rationalization or bureaucratization (Bromley and Gerry, 1979). The following discussion of gender divisions in the recession, is necessarily restricted in scope. The context is one, however, of heightened competition, resulting from the continual search for profit in a situation of declining effective demand. The consequent relocation of production and the internationalization of capital has led not only to unemployment, but to an intensification of labour. The relevance of these to gender divisions will be discussed below.

Gender and work

For much of the twentieth century man as bread-winner and woman as housewife and mother was constructed as the norm within social science and in everyday life in Western capitalist societies. This social construction has been so pervasive that for long periods questions about gender divisions went unasked. They were just normal, indeed natural. One of the most fruitful developments in sociology over the past decade has been in relation to work. While the term still creates problems for those who look for precise definitions it is true to say that work is no longer simply equated with full-time, permanent, regular employ-ment, carried on outside the home and recorded in official statistics. Much of the initial impetus for this development came from those who raised questions about unpaid domestic labour, that is, work carried out largely by women in and for the domestic unit. One issue in the debate was how the family–society relationship was to be theorized. This centred specifically on the relations of productive and reproductive labour (Seccombe, 1974; Coulson et al., 1975; Gardiner, 1976). This shifted the debate away from the plight of the 'housewife', characterized as isolated, increasingly functionless, prone to depression, in short a problem to herself, her children and her spouse, to that of the political economy of the household, the industrial sociology of housework and the relation of unpaid to paid work. Moreover it challenged the approach of structural functionalism which had dominated family sociology for more than a quarter of a century. This had portrayed the nuclear family as functional for industrialism through its role segregation and specialization with only one adult member (the husband) employed outside the home and the other adult (the wife) engaged in bearing and rearing the children and attending to the needs of the working husband (Parsons, 1943). This was not a description of each and every family, but a theory of the dominant trend of the relation between kinship and economy. While not espousing this approach, nor wishing to diminish the strait-jacketed intellectual tradition developed from it by those who erected snippets of this theoretical exposition into a dominant orthodoxy of role segregation and mechanistic gender socialization, we need to recognize that this approach still informs large areas of work on gender relations by feminists as well as others. I would argue that this is because it fits so well into the voluntaristic, individualistic portrayal of the development of Western industrialism shared by some North American and other feminist writers in the 1970s. The criticism was not of the theoretical approach, but that women had not shared in the escape from family control offered by industrialism equally with men. The challenge from those engaged in relating reproductive and productive labour in the structuring of both households and markets directed attention towards patterns of exploitation rather than socialization and helped to develop a new approach to work in all its forms.

A second influence on the way work is conceptualized came from attempts to theorize the informal sector in the Third World (Moser, 1978; Bromley and Gerry, 1979). Debates in the West on the informal sector developed with the decline in many basic industries – shipbuilding, steel, coal and textiles – and as the growth in the service sector slowed down. The recession in the 1970s accelerated by economic policies to reduce inflation after 1979, particularly in Britain, brought large-scale unemployment and interest in the informal sector was prompted in part by the belief that unemployment could be reduced by a shift to informal-sector working (Gershuny and Pahl, 1979/80). Theorizing the relation of the formal and informal sectors proved as problematical in Western capitalism as it was in the Third World. Classification was attempted to cover all forms of work and in some cases to deal with the different phases and social formations in industrialism (Mingione, 1985). These included subsistence work (for self- or household provisioning), reciprocal work between kin, friends and neighbours ranging from caring work to repair and main-tenance tasks; self-employment, second jobs, informal or formal, as well as regulated and recorded formal employment (in relation to women see Allen, 1982; Pahl, 1984). While raising many as yet unresolved theoretical issues, interest in the informal sector shifted the sociological perspectives on work and employment, opening up for investigation a range of economic activities formerly ignored or marginalized by industrial sociology and economics. In particular the gendered divisions of labour became more central and those theoretical approaches which were predicated on the separation of home and work and of market relations from relations between kin came under critical scrutiny. Essentially it was argued that household divisions of labour, market relations and processes of capital accumulation are integral parts of one system to be analysed as a totality (Redclift and Mingione, 1985; Mies, 1986).

An example of these influences was the development of analyses of homeworking. Portrayed in the 1970s as a pre-industrial relic, as 'spare-time' work, as not a real job, as predominantly an ethnic minority activity, or as a convenient option willingly undertaken by women 'trapped' in their homes, subsequent investigations and analyses have demonstrated not only how persistent and widespread this form of paid labour is in Western societies, but how the terms and conditions under which it operates are explicable only within a context of the sexual division of labour in the household and the segregated and segmented labour markets of patriarchal capitalism (Brown, 1974; Hope *et al.*, 1976; Allen and Wolkowitz, 1987; Boris and Daniels, 1988).

The casualized employment relations which are such a marked feature of homeworking are relevant to the current debates on the restructuring of work. The implications of new technology and its potential for the growth in home-based employment are in many discussions of the 'future of work' predicated on unrealistic assumptions both of power relations in households and between those who produce goods and services and those who control the markets for them. Homeworkers are disguised wage-workers, lacking the protection of legal rights and benefits and of trade-union organization. In the restructuring of capital and as part of the recession the range of those now entering their ranks may be widening and their numbers growing, but their relations with capital remain objectively those of exploitation in which their labour time and skills produce relatively high levels of surplus value. Subjectively, particularly among those new to this form of work an individualistic approach to work may be adopted akin to that associated with self-employment and small enterprises more generally (Gerry, 1985). Whereas a decade ago homeworking along with those who did it was written off as economically marginal, recession and restructuring have brought home-based economic activity, self-employment and small enterprise to the centre of political strategies not only for economic recovery but for the 'future of work'.

Gender and employment

The developments in studies of the labour market over the decade up to the mid-1980s provide further indications of the structuring of paid work along gender lines. Race, not gender, had prompted an interest in overcoming the obvious shortcomings of neo-classical approaches in economics and an undue emphasis on occupational choice or individual characteristics in sociology (Doeringer and Bosanquet, 1973; Allen and Smith, 1975). The neo-classical approach of labour economists had worked with the notion of the individual rational man as the unit of analysis and had based the models of labour supply on assumptions about individual wages, unearned income, levels of taxation and individual preferences for income or for leisure. This approach was applied to women as well as to men despite its limitations. Industrial sociologists studied a variety of aspects of labour supply in terms of attitudes or orientations to work, but for the most part these were concerned either solely with men or portrayed those employed as genderless. (See Dex, 1985 for a critical summary of these approaches.)

It was through the dual labour-market approach, followed by the elaborations of segmented and segregated models that first women and then gender began to feature more seriously in labour-market studies (Piore, 1975; Edwards *et al.*, 1975; Barron and Norris, 1976; Wilkinson, 1981). Much of this work was descriptive but it served to order empirical data in such a way that the high concentration of employed women within a narrow range of industries and occupations marked in the main by low wages, poor working conditions, irregularity of employment and little or no prospect of promotion became abundantly clear. The approach frequently failed, however, to provide explanations for these gendered divisions of employment (Beechey, 1978).

For this we must turn to studies which in various ways took up the issue of women's work and employment as a central problematic (West, 1982; Gamarnikow *et al.*, 1983). One of the most fruitful advances came from those who challenged the unproblematic concept of skill inherent in much labour-market analysis and the consistent undervaluing of women's skills (Phillips and Taylor, 1980; Coyle, 1982) and studies such as Wray (1986) and Bradley (1987) of the hosiery and knitwear industry discussed segmentation in the context of employers' strategies and divisions of labour in the family. These demonstrate the need for critical empirical grounding if labour-market segmentation is to provide anything more than a simple description of the different profiles of men's and women's employment. In discussing the impact of new technologies on gender divisions of labour it has been argued that 'the relations of technology and technological careers are profoundly gendered' (Cockburn, 1986, pp. 184–5). Therefore the displacement of men by women is unlikely. Cockburn observes that 'these jobs [those exhibiting technical competence] are not neutral, waiting innocently to be filled by either men or women. They are deeply into partitioned gendered terrain' (1986, pp. 184–5). Segmentation with women in 'unskilled' and men in 'skilled' jobs is not a feature only of yesterday's technology. Pearson (1986, p. 84) using material from the First and the Third Worlds demonstrates how labour is constituted by the careful cultivation of pre-existing sexual divisions of labour. In the case of 'women workers in advanced industrial countries [they] have also been targeted by management to provide, for given production tasks, a category of labour power which can be differentiated from the male labour force and utilised under specific conditions to provide a highly efficient and cost effective labour force'. She goes further by pointing out that 'Far from seeking a homogeneous workforce which spontaneously delivers the desired qualities of docility and high productivity, management is actively using the differences between different women – age, class, cultural attributes – to aid its objective of developing the internally applied discipline it requires in order to achieve a highly productive and flexible workforce, a strategy which not only includes scientific management techniques such as quality control, but also direct and paternalistic forms of management–employee relations' (1986, p. 90). It is studies such as these which enable us to see how gendered labour markets incorporate and reproduce the processes and relationships of power which benefit employers and some male workers while consistently disadvantaging the majority of women in times of recession and restructuring as well as in times of 'full employment' (see Glucksman, 1986 for comparison with the 1920s and 1930s).

One of the most frequently remarked upon aspects of economic activity is the increased participation of women, particularly married women, in the recorded labour force. This increase is extensively documented (Economic Commission for Europe, 1985) and has been subjected to various interpretations. These can be grouped roughly according to whether circumstances associated with the family or the conditions of the labour market are stressed. The 'reserve army' thesis, a demand-side interpretation, for instance, emphasizes the labour market, as do many explanations relating to the restructuring and relocation of employment within a context of de-industrialization (Beechey, 1978; Bruegel, 1979; Anthias, 1980; Massey, 1983, 1984). Other interpretations, on the supply side, stress factors such as the decrease in family size, the increase in female-headed households, the reduction in household work, the need for two incomes to maintain or acquire an appropriate standard of living, or the development of a more democratic relationship between husband and wife.[5] These interpretations are not necessarily at odds with each other. In fact to explain the increase in women's participation in employment without considering the influence of both family and labour market is to separate artificially spheres of women's existence which are inextricably intertwined.

The statistics for Britain show women as 30 per cent of the labour force in 1961, 37 per cent by 1975, 49 per cent in 1980 and 40 per cent in 1984. The number of women employed has not increased consistently. There were more women employed in 1964, for instance, than in 1982. As a proportion of the recorded labour force, the increase is related to the decrease in male participation. The loss of employment in manufacturing and in extractive industries reduced male participation, while the expansion of service industries accounts for most of the increase in women's participation.

It is frequently argued that in manufacturing the shift in demand for labour has been from male manual workers defined as skilled to female workers classified as semi-skilled or unskilled. Jobs performed by women in manufacturing industries have rarely been regarded as skilled, partly through the closure of the apprenticeship system and other forms of industrial training to women, but also through the ideological elements in definitions of skill (Phillips and Taylor, 1980). Manufacturing industries, of course, show wide variations in their organizational structures, but in the majority of cases have engaged large numbers of semi- and unskilled men as well as women. It is therefore the loss of skilled jobs which has affected men, while women remain, as they always were, concentrated in the semi- or unskilled grades. Since the 1960s, however, manufacturing has employed a minority of the labour force and by the 1980s was employing less than 30 per cent of Britain's labour force. Similar proportionate declines are found in Belgium, Denmark, Holland, the United States and Sweden (Brown and Sheriff, 1979).

The statistical data on the differential modes of integration of men and women in terms of economic activity relate to recorded employment and self-employment. These are based on assumptions which preclude notice being taken of many kinds of work and working patterns (Hyman and Price, 1979; Oakley and Oakley, 1979; Hunt, 1980). First we need to note that when using such statistics we are dealing with a socially constructed economic activity which reflects ideologies of gender and of work. Hunt

(1980) argues that 'the paucity of collected data results in too rosy a picture being presented of the position of working women in Britain because the majority of those who do not appear are the most disadvantaged, the low paid workers, homeworkers and the unemployed'. Secondly, however, we need to keep in mind that women with responsibilities for caring for the young, the sick and handicapped and for the elderly are unlikely to be integrated into economic activity in the same way as adult men who do not carry such responsibilities and whose economic integration is predicated on unwaged servicing by adult women. This difference is indirectly illustrated by the way in which 'motherless' and 'fatherless' families provide economic support for their children. While for 'motherless' families 78 per cent of income derives from parental earnings, only 31 per cent of the income of 'fatherless' families comes from this source. Fifty-one per cent of lone mothers' income is from the state while for lone fathers the figure is 14 per cent (Leonard and Speakman, 1986). Men, even lone fathers, are expected to be in employment, lone mothers are not. Furthermore the probability of men being able to earn sufficient for support is very much greater than it is for women, given the pattern of differential earnings.

Statistics on employment are a relatively poor guide to women's economic activity. While it may be that 'they are indispensable for understanding the overall patterns of women's employment; changes in women's participation rate in the world of paid work; the distribution of women across industries and occupations; and evidence about rates of pay, hours of work and so on' (Beechey, 1986), I would argue that unless handled with extreme care their use distorts analyses of women's paid work, their hours of work and their rates of pay. The increased participation of women in the recorded labour force is put into context by Pahl: 'What *is* new is the large-scale employment of married women from all social classes for most of their married lives on a full-time basis. There is certainly no historical precedent for that' (Pahl, 1984, p. 85). However, what he also maintains is that 'Historically, women have been the most flexible in engaging in all forms of work: the likelihood is that, too, will be the pattern for the future' (Pahl, 1984, p. 85). Sociologically, then, this increase in women's (including married women's) economic participation may be more apparent than real, whether we are considering the past or projecting future trends.

Statistically much of the increase in women's recorded employment has been in part-time jobs, and part-time employment is predominantly a feature of women's lives (Martin and Roberts, 1984; Dex and Shaw, 1986). In most capitalist societies part-time employment is relatively insignificant for men. Over 90 per cent of part-time employment in Denmark, West Germany and the United Kingdom is done by women and over 80 per cent in Belgium, Finland, France and Norway. The actual proportion of women employed on a part-time basis has been increasing in recent years and is highest in Norway where it is about one in two women workers and lowest in Finland with only 8 per cent of women workers being part-time. In Britain around 4 out of 10 women fall into this category compared with 3 out of 10 in 1971 and the official definition of part-time employment varies according to separate pieces of legislation. For taxation or national insurance purposes and employment rights, for instance, notice of dismissal, maternity rights, rates of pay, holidays and pensions different rules apply. Some of these have hours per week attached to them. The overall definition is, however, officially, that part-time work equals less than 30 hours per week. But one of the problems with aggregate statistics is that they do not indicate the hours of work involved, which can range from a few hours a week to almost full-time. In Britain full-time working varies with industry and occupation, but in general full-time for manual workers is longer than for non-manual workers. For instance, office workers may be full-time if they work 35 or 36 hours, but in many jobs where full-time working hours for manual workers are 40 per week these hours count as part-time. Where annual contracts apply in schools, colleges, or university teaching, part-time is calculated as anything less than a normal full-time term or year. In Britain, then, the meaning of part-time employment varies with context amounting overall to no more than something less than full-time for the job, grade, or contract normal in the workplace, the industry, or the occupation. As such it is applied very differentially to different levels of work. 'We part-timers are treated as though we are some form of industrial leper, often poorly paid and always expendable in a redundancy situation. It makes you feel different from everyone else' (Gill and Whitty, 1983).

Part-time consultants in the National Health Service are rarely, if ever, regarded as part-time workers and do not enter statistical records of part-time work. Even more rarely are part-time directors considered in this way. For the most part these part-timers are men and if we were to consider them we would quickly recognize that their part-timing is not to be explained by their domestic

responsibilities. Yet part-time work of women is not only assumed
to relate to their domestic, family responsibilities but is regarded
as both convenient and appropriate to them. This assumption has
some force but has to be set against much evidence that women
take part-time employment because full-time jobs are not available
and may take on more than one part-time job. For instance, one
woman may be an office cleaner, a school meals assistant, work in
a bar and be a child minder and homeworker (Allen, 1983). She
can be working an 18-hour day in paid work but in the statistics
she appears as three part-time workers because she has different
employers and her other two jobs will be invisible. She will fit her
domestic responsibilities around her paid work.

Unemployment

It is taken more-or-less for granted that economic recessions are
global in their impact but in comparing capitalist societies, while
there are similarities, there are also marked differences between
them on the indices used to measure recessions. One of these is
the level of unemployment. Comparisons based on official counts
show that while all have experienced a growth in unemployment
there is considerable variation in the rate (see Table 5.1). General
economic factors such as the declining rate of profit, the fall in
investment, changes in the relationship of employment and
output, the international movement of capital and international
trade have differential impacts on individual economies
(Edwards, 1979; Glyn and Harrison, 1980; Littler and Salaman,
1984). It has been argued, for instance, that in Britain finance
capital has secured a uniquely independent and flexible role with
regard to industrial capital and the state which, in part, explains
the inability of Britain to restructure its economy to prevent further
decline in the manufacturing sector and for the state to intervene
effectively to reduce unemployment or maintain the levels of
public expenditure on social welfare services (Fine and Harris,
1985). Nevertheless the variations in the levels of unemployment
are to some extent related to political responses to the phenomenon
of unemployment and the policies devised to deal with it (Ashton,
1986).

These policies include different kinds of measures. Those which
aim to reduce unemployment involve, on the one hand, strategies
for investment by the state in the physical and social infrastructure, in communications, construction of housing, schools

Table 5.1 International Comparison of Unemployment Rates

Unemployment rate (%), approximating US concepts

	United States	Canada	Australia	Japan	France	West Germany	Britain	Italy	Netherlands	Sweden
1975	8.3	6.9	4.8	1.9	4.1	3.3	4.5	3.0	5.1	1.6
1976	7.6	7.1	4.7	2.0	4.5	3.4	5.9	3.4	5.2	1.6
1977	6.9	8.0	5.6	2.0	4.8	3.4	6.2	3.5	5.0	1.8
1978	6.0	8.3	6.2	2.3	5.2	3.3	6.1	3.6	5.1	2.2
1979	5.8	7.4	6.2	2.1	6.0	2.9	5.5	3.8	5.2	2.0
1980	7.0	7.4	6.0	2.0	6.3	2.8	6.9	3.8	5.9	2.0
1981	7.5	7.5	5.7	2.2	7.5	4.0	10.4	4.2	8.8	2.5
1982	9.5	10.9	7.1	2.4	8.5	5.8	12.0	4.7	12.0	3.1
1983	9.6	11.8	9.9	2.7	8.6	7.2	13.2	5.1	17.1	3.4

Source: Ashton, 1986, p. 9.

and in health and education or directly by subsidies, tax incentives to industries. On the other hand measures may be designed to remove people from the labour force by, for instance, changing the age of retirement or lengthening the period of education and training. It is argued that much of the difference in youth unemployment between West Germany and Britain is explained by the latter. Rather different steps are those which remove from the unemployment figures those who can by various means be portrayed as not genuinely unemployed. The difference between the rate of women's unemployment in Belgium compared to Britain may well be a case in point.

Some measures which do not increase the number of jobs, seek to reallocate workers, for instance, from areas of high unemployment to where vacancies exist. Success is dependent on a large number of factors including housing and skill matching and for adult women, it is usually even less of an option than for men. A wide range of job-sharing or splitting arrangements may be used by substituting part-time working for full-time jobs. Reductions in overtime or full-time hours to share out employment, though frequently advocated in Britain, have rarely proved achievable. Part-time, temporary and casualized employment is an increasing feature of many economies in the 1970s and 1980s. Whether this is a response to the recession or, together with the growth in self-employment, it signals a strategy of flexible manning as part of the restructuring of employment and economic activity more generally is debatable (Allen and Wolkowitz, 1987). Rates of unemployment as officially recorded do not normally take account of hidden unemployment or underemployment and these, though not confined to women, assume a particular importance when attempting to compare women's and men's unemployment.

The data collected by the OECD allows broad comparisons to be made between Western Europe, Australasia, North America and Japan of both unemployment rates and employment trends in terms of gender over a period of several decades (Paukert, 1984; OECD, 1985). The differential contribution made by men and women to labour force changes between 1950 and 1980 is shown below (see Table 5.2). Since the 1960s the unemployment rates of women have been rising faster than those of men and disproportionately to their share of the labour force in all but a few of the countries, at the same time as employment of women increased (see Table 5.3).

The unemployment rates for men and women, the percentages of women unemployed compared to their labour force participation

Table 5.2 Trends and Structure of Labour Force Changes by Sex in OECD Countries, 1950–1980

		1950–60		1960–70		1970–81	
		Percentage change	Contribution of M+F to change	Percentage change	Contribution of M+F to change	Percentage change	Contribution of M+F to change
OECD total	T	11.2	100.0	11.0	100.0	15.6	100.0
	M	7.9	48.3	8.0	48.8	8.7	36.2
	F	18.5	51.7	16.8	51.2	28.2	63.8
North	T	13.5	100.0	20.0	100.0	30.9	100.0
America	M	8.0	42.9	11.7	39.9	19.7	40.2
	F	27.3	57.1	37.9	60.1	50.1	59.8
OECD	T	7.8	100.0	4.8	100.0	6.7	100.0
Europe	M	5.9	52.3	3.5	49.6	0.4	3.6
	F	11.9	47.7	7.4	50.4	19.4	96.4
Australia	T	19.2	100.0	32.0	100.0	22.5	100.0
and New	M	16.4	66.1	19.5	45.9	14.2	43.2
Zealand	F	28.7	33.9	70.8	54.1	40.0	56.8
Japan	T	18.8	100.0	13.3	100.0	10.8	100.0
	M	14.4	47.2	16.1	71.7	11.8	66.6
	F	25.8	52.8	9.3	28.3	9.1	33.4

T: total; M: male; F: female
Source: Paukert, 1984, p. 11.

and the ratio of female to male unemployment are shown for twenty countries for 1975 and 1984 in Tables 5.4 and 5.5. In 1975 all but six, and in 1984 all but five, had higher rates of unemployment for women, despite the argument that male unemployment tends to rise more than women's during recessions. By 1984, five had rates of over 10 per cent unemployment for both men and women; in a further seven, women reached this level and in one (Britain) men exceeded the 10 per cent rate while the women's rate fell below it. The favourable unemployment rate for women in Britain compared to that of many European societies is explained by the greater proportion of women in part-time employment and the poorer conditions of part-time workers compared to West Germany and the Netherlands (van Ginneken and Garzuel, 1983; Walby, 1983).

Rates vary with age for both men and women and as in many societies the average age of women in the recorded labour force is lower than that of men it is argued that this disproportionately affects the overall rate of women where there is high youth unemployment (Paukert, 1984). The unemployment rates for those under 25 years of age are shown in Table 5.6. This illustrates the general phenomenon of higher – in some cases very much

Table 5.3 Average Annual Rates of Change of Labour Force, Employment and Unemployment in OECD Countries, 1960–1981*

	Labour force			Employment			Unemployment		
	Total	Male	Female	Total	Male	Female	Total	Male	Female
1960–70									
OECD total	1.0	0.7	1.6	1.0	0.8	1.5	1.0	-0.4	3.5
North America	1.8	1.1	3.3	1.9	1.2	3.3	0.6	-1.2	3.5
OECD Europe	0.4	0.2	0.7	0.3	0.2	0.6	1.5	-0.1	4.6
Australia and New Zealand	2.8	1.8	5.5	2.8	1.8	5.5	5.2	5.1	5.3
Japan	1.3	1.5	0.9	1.3	1.5	0.9	1.7	4.3	-1.7
1970–80									
OECD total	1.2	0.6	2.3	0.9	0.3	2.0	8.7	8.1	9.5
North America	2.3	1.3	3.8	2.0	1.0	3.7	6.4	6.4	6.4
OECD Europe	0.5	-0.1	1.7	0.1	-0.4	1.2	11.5	10.1	13.3
Australia and New Zealand	1.9	1.3	3.2	1.5	0.9	2.6	18.3	19.6	17.1
Japan	0.9	1.0	0.8	0.8	0.9	0.7	6.8	6.4	7.4
1980									
OECD total	1.2	0.7	1.9	0.4	-0.2	1.5	14.9	20.4	8.8
North America	1.8	1.1	2.9	0.6	-0.7	2.4	22.3	33.6	10.4
OECD Europe	0.6	0.4	2.9	0.6	-0.3	0.6	11.5	14.4	8.2
Australia and New Zealand	2.8	1.8	4.7	2.9	1.8	5.0	1.3	1.4	1.1
Japan	1.0	0.8	1.2	1.0	1.0	1.2	-2.6	-4.1	0.0
1981									
OECD total	1.2	0.7	1.9	0.1	-0.4	0.9	18.3	12.1	15.3
North America	1.7	0.9	2.8	1.3	0.5	2.3	7.8	6.9	9.0
OECD Europe	0.7	0.4	1.3	-1.1	-1.5	-0.4	30.7	37.6	22.8
Australia and New Zealand	1.5	1.3	1.9	1.6	1.3	2.0	1.4	1.8	1.0
Japan	1.0	1.0	1.1	0.8	0.7	0.9	10.5	11.2	9.3

* Excluding Iceland and Turkey
Source: Paukert, 1984, p. 15.

Table 5.4 Unemployment Rates, by Sex, 1975 and 1984 (Percentages)

	1975			1984		
Region and country	Both sexes	Males	Females	Both sexes	Males	Females
Western Europe						
Austria	1.7	1.3	2.3	3.9	4.1	3.7
Belgium	4.2	3.1	6.3	13.0	9.4	18.8
Denmark	4.9	4.7	5.1	10.2	8.8	12.0
Finland	2.2	2.4	2.1	6.1	6.0	6.2
France	4.1	2.8	6.3	9.1	6.7	12.8
Germany, Federal Republic of	4.0	3.7	4.5	8.3	7.6	9.4
Ireland	6.0	6.6	4.3	16.2	17.5	13.0
Italy	5.8	3.7	10.5	10.7	7.3	17.2
Netherlands	4.5	4.9	3.5	13.7	14.3	12.7
Norway	2.3	1.9	1.9	3.0	2.8	3.2
Sweden	1.6	1.3	2.1	3.1	3.0	3.3
Switzerland	0.3	0.4	0.2	1.2	1.1	1.3
United Kingdom	3.1	3.6	2.1	11.6	13.5	8.8
North America						
Canada	6.9	6.1	8.1	11.2	11.1	11.4
United States	8.3	7.6	9.3	7.2	7.0	7.4
Southern Europe						
Greece	1.8	1.2	3.0	8.3	6.9	11.3
Portugal	5.5	5.1	6.1	10.8	6.4	15.3
Spain	5.0	4.8	5.7	20.4	19.3	23.1
Turkey	12.9	15.2	8.9	21.0	26.3	11.0
Yugoslavia	1.2	4.6	8.8	9.5	6.7	13.9

Source: Economic Commission for Europe, 1985, p. 28.

higher – rates of unemployment of young people compared to all age groups with Group A showing those (8) with higher rates for women under 25 than for men of equivalent age and Group B where the opposite holds (6).

The distribution of unemployment between occupational groups is generally unevenly spread and for the most part those in lower grades have the highest levels of unemployment in relation to the proportion employed (Ashton, 1986). Similarly unemployment levels in multiracial societies are in general greater for those defined as racial minorities, whether of indigenous or immigrant status. Statistical data on gender differences in terms of both these are becoming available for individual countries but comparisons within and across societies still remain difficult.

Table 5.7 indicates the relation between unemployment and occupation, ethnic groups and gender in Britain in 1984.[6] For both men and women the overall rates for whites are half those for

Table 5.5 Female Shares in Unemployment and Ratio of Female to Male Unemployed, 1975–1984

| | Women as a percentage of | | | | Female/male unemployment ratio | |
| | Labour force | | Unemployed | | | |
Region and country	1975	1984	1975	1984	1975	1984
Western Europe						
Austria	40	41	54	38	65	62
Belgium	34	38	52	55	51	124
Denmark	41	45	43	53	70	112
Finland	47	48	43	48	88	94
France	37	39	57	56	56	125
Germany, (Fed. Rep.)	37	39	42	44	59	77
Ireland	27	29	19	24	37	31
Italy	30	35	55	56	40	125
Netherlands	28	35	22	33	40	48
Norway	38	43	48	46	60	85
Sweden	43	47	54	49	73	97
Switzerland	34	35	20	40	52	67
United Kingdom	38	40	26	31	61	44
North America						
Canada	37	42	43	44	57	74
United States	39	43	44	45	63	80
Southern Europe						
Greece	30	31	50	42	41	73
Portugal	38	43	42	62	61	164
Spain	21	30	25	34	27	52
Turkey	36	35	25	18	61	22
Yugoslavia	38	39	54	57	58	133

Source: Economic Commission for Europe, 1985, p. 27.

Table 5.6 Unemployment Rates of Women and Men under 25 (Percentages)

| | | | 15–19 | | 20–24 | | Total all age groups | |
			Men	Women	Men	Women	Men	Women
A	Denmark	(1981)	6	10	16	17	8.3	8.5
	France	(1982)	22	44	14	21	5.8	10.5
	Germany (FR)	(1981)	6	9	6	8	3.7	6.2
	Italy	(1981)	28	42	19	27	5.4	14.4
	Norway	(1981)	8	9	4	4	1.4	2.7
	Portugal	(1981)	10	28	6	22	3.5	12.2
	Spain	(1982)	44	53	27	37	15.1	19.9
	Sweden	(1982)	10	12	6	6	3.0	3.4
B	Canada	(1982)	25	19	19	14	11.1	10.8
	Finland	(1982)	20	18	10	9	6.3	6.0
	Netherlands	(1981)	13	11*	–	–	6.1	6.1
	Turkey	(1980)	11	6	8	4	5.4	2.4
	United Kingdom	(1981)	26	24	18	13	12.5	8.0
	United States	(1982)	23	22	15	13	9.6	9.4

* 15–24.
Source: Economic Commission for Europe, 1985, p. 29.

Table 5.7 Economically Active Persons 16+ by Occupational Group, Sex and Ethnic Group: Britain, Spring, 1984

	Males				Females			
	White		Ethnic minority		White		Ethnic minority	
	Number economically active	Percentage unemployed	Number economically active	Percentage unemployed	Number economically active	Percentage unemployed	Number economically active	Percentage unemployed
Professional and related – management and administrative	923	2	23	5	259	3	7	0
Professional and related – education etc.	673	2	37	8	1,320	4	67	5
Literary, artistic and sport	162	9	5	–	105	7	2	–
Professional and related – science etc.	942	3	24	8	97	5	2	–
Managerial	1,710	4	86	7	554	4	19	0
Clerical and related	883	4	35	7	2,911	6	83	10
Selling	642	9	23	18	1,005	9	29	10
Security etc.	375	6	6	18	41	2	–	–
Catering, cleaning etc.	556	13	47	14	2,313	7	74	9
Farming, fishing and related	386	10	2	–	75	7	0	–
Processing etc. (excluding metals and electrical)	1,153	9	63	20	507	10	31	8
Printing, assembling etc.	531	12	31	14	379	12	23	13
Construction, mining etc.	954	14	17	21	6	13	0	–
Transport operating etc.	1,336	10	42	14	75	12	3	–
Miscellaneous	392	18	16	36	26	15	2	–
All occupations groups	14,613	11	637	21	10,229	10	402	19

Source: Barber, 1985, p. 474.

blacks but the highest ratios of black to white unemployment are found for men in the professional and related occupations in education and science and in security, whereas for women the highest is in clerical and related jobs. In four occupations black women had lower rates than white.

Unemployment by socioeconomic group is concentrated in semi-skilled or unskilled manual occupations for both men and women. Whereas only 18 per cent of employed males and 30 per cent of employed females were in this group 39 per cent of those unemployed were in 1984. However, some two-fifths of unemployed women and one-third of unemployed men were excluded because they had never had a job or had been unemployed for longer than 3 years (Central Statistical Office, 1986, p. 73).

Occupational segregation between men and women, and the different concepts of race and ethnicity employed require cautious interpretation of officially collected data. Investigations by social scientists confined to particular occupations, labour markets, and carefully defined racial/ethnic/migrant/indigenous groups, though more limited, are more likely to provide reliable data on the inter-relation of gender, race and class with unemployment rates.

As Hurstfield (1986) has shown for Britain in the 1930s and in the 1980s the underrecording of women's unemployment, arising from conventional assumptions about women's economic activity and the methods of counting the unemployed, is a major problem in making comparisons between men and women. The problems of measurement and comparison are not confined to Britain. OECD countries where the unemployment rate of women is recorded as lower than that of men use a system of counting as unemployed only those who register at an unemployment office (OECD, 1980). In Britain, for instance, the official figures reflect only those eligible for unemployment benefit or social security, both of which more often exclude women, particularly married women (Sinfield, 1981). If all those actively seeking a job and those who would take one if it were readily available were included in the unemployment rate then not only would it be higher overall, but the women's rate would rise more than that of men. The phenomenon of hidden unemployment is not only a matter of the specifics of counting, but as research has increasingly shown, an aspect of the gendered division of labour in the household and the labour market which can be understood only through conceptual-izing work, employment and unemployment with reference to both men and women.

141

Concluding remarks

The impact of the recession is seen largely in terms of male unemployment, and wide currency is given to the view that near full employment is no longer achievable in Western capitalist economies, so that for many, self-employment or small-business enterprise will provide the means of material existence. Neither of these pay serious attention to the gendered nature of social relationships. The first not only marginalizes the impact of unemployment on women as workers, but ignores the intensification of unpaid work in the households of the unemployed. The second is based on models of self-employment and small-business enterprise which by and large apply only to work patterns and life-styles of men.

Most sociological studies of the recession have focused on the impact of unemployment on those made redundant in major industries or on groups of young people who have never been in employment. Although the bias towards men remains, some studies of women's experience of redundancy and of never-employed young women have been undertaken (Coyle, 1984; Martin and Roberts, 1984; Martin and Wallace, 1984; Coles, 1986). Other studies of households with unemployed members have examined the impact on relations between spouses and between parents and children, and in the case of the young unemployed between them and friends, siblings and parents (Allatt and Yeandle, 1986; Brah, 1986; McKee and Bell, 1986; Wallace and Pahl, 1986).

Studies of restructuring have mainly related to employment, of which unemployment is one aspect but the fragmentation of production and the centralization of control are others. Investigations of patterns of workplace organization, management–labour relations and the impact of new technologies on the labour process, have reported a variety of findings but in so far as they treat employees (and managers) as genderless, which many do, these are difficult to interpret for the purposes of this paper. The occupational segregation of men and women has much to do with this, and women tend to appear only in investigations where they form the bulk of the employees (Huws, 1982; Cunnison, 1986; Webster, 1986). Cockburn's study of the relations of technology is exceptional, both because it compares workplaces with unchanged as well as those with new technology, spread over manufacturing, distribution and public-sector establishments, and includes both men and women (Cockburn, 1986).

A different kind of investigation has examined the way in which large organizations have attempted to reduce or externalize labour and other costs through various methods, subcontracting being one, flexible manning another (Atkinson, 1984; Schutt and Wittington, 1984; Fevre, 1986). Most of these affect both men and women but how far their impact is similar or different according to gender has featured in few analyses (Murray, 1983; Mitter, 1986; Allen and Wolkowitz, 1987). Between 1979 and 1985 the self-employed in Britain rose from 7.4 per cent of the labour force to 10.6 per cent and the proportion of women among these rose from 20 per cent in 1979 to 25 per cent in 1985. Much of the growth since 1981 was in single-person businesses and in 1985 self-employment was concentrated in the distribution, hotels, catering and repairs industries; construction and 'other' services (Central Statistical Office, 1987). Almost half of the women classified in 1981 as self-employed without employees work at or from home and 25 per cent of these worked for an outside firm or organization (Pugh, 1984). For men in the construction industry self-employment covers those who sell their labour to contractors, estimated at one-third of the total in the early 1980s, as well as those who have their own businesses. The label 'self-employed' is attached to quite different kinds of relationships. Those who are disguised wage-workers bear all the costs of employment and receive none of the protection of employee status, and their numbers appear to be increasing and the range of work they undertake widening (Huws, 1984; Allen and Wolkowitz, 1987). Others are part-time workers or the disguised unemployed, unable to earn sufficient to live on, but using their skills to produce goods or services (Hogg, 1985).

The growth in self-employment and in micro-enterprise relates both to the increase in unemployment and to the outsourcing and decentralizing of production by large corporations. The formally independent units (small firms and individuals) are dependent on the large enterprises (including the state) for work and for their markets and compete with each other to gain them. They absorb the costs of production either by passing them on to their employees or by high levels of self- or family exploitation. These forms of restructuring have many historical precedents and their social and distributional effects were the source not only of academic debate but of organized political resistance in the nineteenth and early twentieth centuries. In the current situation they pose several analytical problems which would benefit from a closer scrutiny of women's economic activity in waged, income-generating and subsistence work and the costs they have carried as ideologically marginalized, casualized and flexible workers.

The contradictions in their situation are well illustrated in some of the studies of unemployment. The reproductive and servicing work not only continues but is intensified where their daughters, sons, or spouse are unemployed. They are then called upon to manage many of the consequences of unemployment for the household. These include not simply the material aspects of a reduced income, but the physical and emotional stress through the loss of status experienced by men deprived of their bread-winner position and by sons and daughters who fail to find jobs on which their transition to adulthood depends. The woman's own unemployment may go unrecognized since she remains responsible for the management of the household and little significance attaches to her paid job, particularly where it is part-time and low paid. Indeed she may withdraw from paid work altogether because the regulations about unemployment benefit make it uneconomic for her to continue or because she gives priority to her spouse's feelings.

The evidence now available does not indicate that unemployment is worse for men than women psychologically or otherwise (Jahoda, 1982) but that differences may exist in terms of position in and identification with the labour market, the actual or expected divisions of labour within the family and household, and the more general attitudes about men's and women's place in society. For instance, the relation between unemployment, ill health and attempted suicide has been the subject of much debate (Platt, 1986). However, so far research has been confined to men because of the difficulty of deciding who among women are unemployed. Such difficulties are both a creation of official accounting and of an ideology which prioritizes the man's unemployment over the woman's. Not surprisingly, many women share this ideology. Coyle's research and that of others showed, however, that women expect to undertake paid work, and unemployment removes from them their income, personal autonomy and ability to contribute to the financial support of dependants as well as reducing their confidence and self-esteem (Coyle, 1984). The recession intensifies unpaid labour in the household through unemployment or the threat of it and through the reduction of support services for those caring for the elderly, the sick and handicapped and young children while at the same time restructuring increases the likelihood that paid labour will be in unregulated, temporary, part-time jobs. It is women who are especially hit by these changes. The discussion in this paper on the differences between men and women is not intended to minimize the differences between men or those between women in terms of class, age and race but to develop an approach in which the gendered structures of work, employment and unemployment are accorded sufficient attention to allow the consequences of recession and restructuring to be analysed more adequately.

Notes

1 I am using gender as a category which is constructed by and part of social, political and economic relations. See Morgan, 1986, for a summary of the sex/gender discussion in the sociological literature and Rose *et al.*, 1984, for an extended discussion and critique of biological reductionism and determinism.

2 A detailed bibliography is beyond the scope of this paper. See Burton, 1985, for a discussion of socialist feminist ideas in the 1970s; Mitchell and Oakley, 1986, for a reappraisal of two decades of feminist work; Oakley, 1981, for an overview of work on women; Mies, 1986, for a comprehensive discussion of patriarchy from an international perspective and Roberts, 1981, and Bell and Roberts, 1984, on methodological issues. The thrust for transcending the limitations integral to theoretical and empirical sociology came out of a vocabulary and consciousness developed in the struggle against many forms of oppression and exploitation associated with the general subordination of women by men. Much of the re-thinking about some of the inadequacies of sociological explanations was prompted initially by work outside accepted social science circles. See for instance, Dalla Costa, 1972; Allen *et al.*, 1974; Comer, 1974; Hewitt, 1975; James, 1975.

3 See, for example, Millett, 1971; Game and Pringle, 1983; Goldthorpe, 1983, 1984; Delphy, 1984; Eisenstein, 1984; Matthews, 1984; Lockwood, 1986.

4 This aspect is often seen as a special concern of and for women both inside and outside academic institutions. While it may be argued that women have a particular interest in ensuring that practice is changed I do not think that only women have a responsibility for changing it.

5 The stress on the family/household includes both traditional approaches which assume that wife/mother duties take precedence and the more radical treatment in terms of material needs (see, for instance, Myrdal and Klein, 1968, and Land, 1976).

6 Ethnic group is determined by those interviewed in the Labour Force Survey on behalf of themselves and others in their household. The categories presented are White, West Indian or Guyanese, Indian, Pakistani, Bangladeshi, Chinese, African, Arab, Mixed Origin, Other. Ethnic minorities include all categories, except white, plus those in the 'Other' category. Since the official differentiation is made on grounds of colour rather than ethnicity I use the term 'black' in the text to refer to all those not classified as white when general comparisons are made. Unfortunately ethnic differentiation between whites is not possible because of the definitions used, though sociologically ethnicity may be an important differentiator of labour-market experiences (including unemployment). (See Allen, 1987, for further comments on this kind of definition.) Only the total figures include those who have been unemployed for longer than 3 years.

6

Ethnic Divisions and Class in Western Europe

ROBERT MOORE

Introduction

It is rarely necessary for writers to read what they wrote a decade or more ago and most would prefer not to do so. Society and sociology change and we do not relish encounters with our lack of foresight. Reading 'Migrants and the class structure of Western Europe' (Moore, 1977a) was not entirely dispiriting, however. The first reaction is bound to be that while Europe has changed for the worse, sociology has changed for the better.

The changes in sociology have been both theoretical and empirical. In other words, compared with the mid-1970s, we have a lot more data on Europe and are better equipped to interpret them. I attempted to address the question of a *European* system of social stratification, or a *European* class system. The problem arose from sociologists' unquestioned acceptance of the boundaries of nation states as bounding a unit of analysis called 'society'. This issue has still not been adequately addressed except in the literature of the sociology of development where nation states are treated as actors (and often quite minor actors) in the powerplay of transnational corporations. Johann Galtung (1973) made an interesting analysis of Europe as a superpower in the context of the development of Third World nations, but no one since has attempted a sociology of Europe in spite of the existence of important supra-national political institutions whose decisions affect daily lives throughout Europe. Perhaps the most significant theoretical development has taken place largely through the efforts of women in the profession of sociology. We will see some examples below but, of particular importance has been the analysis of the position of women in the labour market and the means by which the social construction of gender has disadvantaged women (see, for example, Barrett and McIntosh, 1982). The neglect of women by sociologists had always been an especially disabling aspect of the analysis of both the position of minorities in Europe and the stratification of European society. Women are now taken seriously in sociology and the 'new visibility' of women will be apparent in what follows.

In 1977 I tried to break out of the narrow 'race relations' perspective within which in each European nation the presence of people from abroad was seen as a 'problem' unique to them. Migration was a European (indeed, worldwide) phenomenon and had to be understood in a European rather than British (or English) context. The pathfinding work was Castles and Kosack's *Immigrant Workers and Class Structure in Western Europe* which was published in 1973. Since that book was written, migration to Europe, as we then understood it, has virtually ceased. Castles *et al.* (1984) in his more recent *Here for Good* has pointed to the emergence of new ethnic communities in Europe. Whereas migration was seen as a temporary phenomenon by politicians, the fact is that we now have large ethnic communities, with a rising proportion actually born in Europe. This suggests, as we will see below, that a race relations perspective may have a renewed relevance in that each country now has a permanent black population.

The political context has changed markedly since 1977. Then, social scientists, policy makers and migrants defined 'the problem' largely in terms of settlement and integration into a host society. The presence of migrants of ethnic minority status has, from the mid-1970s, however, been redefined as a problem of social control, part of the 'law and order' problem of modern European countries. Meanwhile the children of settled migrants try to enter, and to a very significant degree are excluded from, an increasingly competitive labour market.

In the early 1970s it was possible to argue that migrant workers (whether or not they saw themselves as potential permanent settlers) were to a large extent encapsulated by the labour market. They did not fully share the interests of the indigenous working class in the quality of housing (they were temporary and made their own arrangements), in educational provision (they had no children here), or in, say, the health service (they were young and healthy). But now, as permanent residents with families growing up or grown up in Europe they are vitally interested in housing, education and the social services. In their increased demands upon these services, there is a new potential for conflict over resources (how much is delivered) and culture (how the service is delivered). Indeed, the most dramatic changes in Europe since the early 1970s have been in the labour market itself and in the strategies of capital and the state.

Ten years' retrospect

By 1977 it was possible to look back over a long period of economic growth and not to appreciate that the early 1970s' recession, apparently precipitated by the sudden rise in the price of oil, was more than temporary. I wrote, therefore, of the shortage of labour caused by economic growth and the rising expectations of native workers. The policy options open to governments who wished both to fill the gaps in the labour force and resist inflationary pressures were:

(1)   to reverse growth policies and create unemployment,
(2)   to pay the economic rate for undesirable jobs,
(3)   to import foreign labour,
(4)   to recruit more women to the labour force (Moore, 1977a, p. 138).

I mentioned also a fifth possibility of lowering the school-leaving age to enable employers to hire younger (and in the United Kingdom, cheaper) labour. The first two were politically unacceptable, not least because paying the rate for the job was seen also as potentially inflationary. The import of foreign labour was a preferred method, especially as labour shortages were seen as essentially short-term. The 'internal migration' of women into the labour market had been under way since the Second World War, so the fourth option had already been adopted to an extent.

In 1987, in the United Kingdom at least, the creation of unemployment is no longer a politically unacceptable option and, indeed, 1.6 million jobs have been lost between 1979 and 1986 and unemployment risen to about 4 million. In manufacturing and construction, there has been a drop of 28 per cent in the United Kingdom, 8.5 per cent in West Germany and 9.4 per cent in Italy. In seven nations of the Europe of Nine, unemployment is above 10 per cent. It might also be argued that in Britain the fifth possibility of using youth labour has been realized not through lowering the school-leaving age but by introducing special work schemes for otherwise unemployed school-leavers.

The loss of jobs in Europe does not necessarily mean that the jobs are no longer being done. There is *both* technological unemployment as machines take over the tasks of workers *and* the export of jobs to Third World countries. The most systematic analysis of this latter phenomenon is to be found in the work of Frobel *et al.* in their *The New International Division of Labour* (1980). They show, for example, that there were a million fewer jobs in manufacturing in West Germany in 1976 than in 1973. Yet, by 1974, nearly 40 per cent of the employment in the 87 companies surveyed by Frobel *et al.* was employment abroad or foreign workers employed in West Germany (1980, p. 285). 'Thus, a conservative estimate of the *foreign employment of Federal German productive industry* is 1.5 to 1.6 million workers for 1975' (pp. 200–1, original emphasis).

The consequences of these changes for the Third World countries in which migrant corporations locate are far-reaching, but not the topic of this chapter. For Europe it means that native workers are now in competition with Third World workers. For some workers, the implications of this are clear: to compete, we must be a low-wage economy, hence, the constant exhortations to British workers not to 'price themselves out of a job'. Furthermore, wages can be reduced by removing legislative protection against low wages, by holding down the incomes of public employees and by introducing competition from young workers. In addition, the power of organized labour has to be substantially reduced. All of these have been tried in the United Kingdom. One British minister identified the fast-food industry as a typical industry of the future. What it typifies is the low-wage economy: young, non-unionized workers, working under continuous pressure, their performance measured daily by the cash register and their labour turnover extremely high.

But although manufacturing and assembly may be exported, services are harder to send abroad. Here, the effects of high technology are beginning to be felt, especially in banking and financial services, where a wide range of technical devices is reducing the need for labour, which can be shed by natural wastage. It is here that women suffer, having for some time been protected from the heavy job losses in the traditional industries in which they were underrepresented. The secretary who loses her job in Bradford (or perhaps her daughter who fails to find a job) has been replaced by microprocessors assembled by a young woman in Taiwan. In addition, in the public sector, wages have been to some extent kept down by direct government action and the wages bill reduced through a reduction in services, but here, too, the effects of new technology, and the new management methods it makes possible, are being felt. The effects of the internationalization of the labour force are, therefore, not confined to manufacturing alone. The need to recognize the international nature of the labour market and the strategies of capital is, therefore, as essential as it was in 1977, but it is today much more transparent and more publicly discussed than a decade ago.

What hardly needs to be stated is that the immigration of labour to north-western Europe on the scale of the 1960s has now ceased. Migration to Europe stopped in 1973–4 and the 'guestworker' system is dead (Castles *et al.*, 1984, ch. 2). In the United Kingdom, migration from the Commonwealth was reduced from 1962 onwards. By 1971 the status of Commonwealth immigrants had been virtually reduced to that of guestworkers, and primary immigration for work and settlement was at an end. Throughout the 1970s, the majority of Commonwealth people admitted for settlement were dependants of those already here. In 1982, 90 per cent of those admitted to settle in the United Kingdom were dependants. Minority populations are given in Table 6.1. Roughly speaking, 38 per cent of migrants are non-European and 38 per cent 'other European' (including Ireland, Italy, Greece and Finland) and about 8 per cent from other European Community countries (Castles *et al.*, 1984, Table 3.11).

In 1977 (Moore, 1977a) I tried to identify the function of migrant labour. First, *labour substitution* enabled employers to fill labour shortages and, in addition, allowed native workers to be upwardly mobile and enjoy rising living standards. Settled 'migrants'

Table 6.1 Percentage of Migrant Populations in Selected Countries

Country (year)	Foreign population (000s)	% of total population	Foreign labour force (000s)	% of total labour force
Belgium (83)	890.0	9.0	332	8.7
France (82)	3680.1	6.8	1436	6.4
West Germany (84)	4363.7	7.1	2082	9.5
Netherlands (84)	558.7	3.9	238	4.9
Sweden (84)	393.9	4.7	234	5.4
Switzerland (84)	932.4	14.5	689	22.9
Great Britain (81)	4470.0*	8.5	1858	7.2

* Population in households with foreign-born heads.
Source: Castles *et al.*, 1984, Table 3.9.

probably no longer perform this function and new migrants would now find themselves in competition with native workers for virtually all jobs except perhaps those in the higher professions. None the less, settled migrants and their descendants remain heavily concentrated in the least desirable jobs. The second, *buffering* function of migrant and settled ethnic minorities is plain to see in the unemployment figures for the United Kingdom (Table 6.2).

Table 6.2 Percentage Unemployed among Whites, West Indian and Asians in the United Kingdom, 1981

	Men	Women
White	13	10
West Indian	25	16
Asian	20	20

Source: Castles *et al.*, 1984.

Within the Asian group, men from Pakistan and Bangladesh had an unemployment rate of 29 per cent. Castles *et al.*'s figures for West Germany are 7.5 per cent unemployment for the whole workforce and 11.9 per cent for foreigners. The buffering function is especially obvious in West Germany because the recession was accompanied by return migration, through which West Germany was able to lose about half a million unemployed – and the cost of their unemployment (Castles *et al.*, 1984, pp. 145–6).

The figures for unemployed foreigners in several EC countries were given in a written answer to a European Parliamentary question on 1 August 1985 (Table 6.3). This may be compared with Table 6.1 (showing the proportion of the workforce which is foreign) to demonstrate how much larger a proportion of the unemployed than of the workforce comprises foreigners. If we take an index of 100 for the unemployment of native workers, then foreign unemployment in Belgium is 148, France 186, West Germany 118 and The Netherlands 163.

Table 6.3 Foreign Workers as Percentage of Unemployed in Selected EC Countries

	Men	Women
Belgium	13.1	9.8
Denmark	4.0	3.4
France	12.1	6.9
Luxembourg	44.4	42.5
Netherlands	8.2	6.4
West Germany	11.0	9.3

In Britain, Asian women have tended to work in industries more susceptible to seasonal fluctuation as well as to recession: notably, wool, textiles and clothing. This raises the question of whether members of minorities 'buffer' in the sense of losing their jobs to natives in recession, or simply by being concentrated in those industries where jobs are more likely to be lost. Given the high concentration of immigrants in manufacturing, vehicles and textiles, the latter is more likely to be the case. The outcome in the United Kingdom is that Asians and West Indians – and those of Asian and West Indian descent – have been proportionately more heavily affected by unemployment than the native white population.

I also suggested in 1977 that – in popular terms – migrants served as cheap labour (Moore, 1977a). I presented evidence of low wages amongst migrants in Europe, but the evidence was open to more than one interpretation. Castles *et al.* were to argue in 1984 that by depressing a potentially damaging rate of inflation, migrants helped sustain a boom in which the majority enjoyed high wages. It is safe to reiterate the conclusion that migrants did not undermine indigenous wage levels and, indeed, this was hardly likely, given their heavy employment in well-unionized industries.

Migrants were cheap labour in the sense that through migration Europe acquired mature labour. No costs were incurred in Europe in raising, educating and training young workers. There were no costs for maintaining the income and health of elderly migrants or in supporting families through tax and other allowances, houses, schools and health services. The substantial benefit of this kind of cheapness was to be short-lived and to disappear with the reunion of families and the settlement of migrants.

One function performed by migrants was insufficiently emphasized in the mid-1970s. They were used in the restructuring of work processes and the reorganization of industries. The gap in the analysis has been partly filled, notably by Fevre's (1984) work on textiles and by Duffield's (1985) on the West Midlands iron-founding industry. In both cases, modes of working had, over many years, been established by native employees. These traditions could only be broken by using different workers. New machines and new patterns of work were thus introduced with immigrant workers. Historically, also, we find similar cases: for example, the change from skilled to unskilled labour in the transition from sail to steam in the merchant fleet, where colonially hired stokers replaced British seamen and, as we will see below, this became a focus of considerable hostility in British seafaring communities.

Men and women

Because the use of migrant workers was seen as a solution to an essentially temporary problem, migrants were not encouraged to settle and there were obstructions to dependants joining workers in Europe. During the late 1960s and the 1970s, it became increasingly clear that migrant labour was becoming permanent. Considerable progress was made in the 1970s in improving the political and civil status of migrants in Europe and, as a result, there was an increasing trend for family reunion in Europe (for a discussion, see OCIPE/CCP, 1979). Throughout this period, the United Kingdom reduced the remaining rights to family life of Commonwealth citizens and placed increasing obstacles in the way of reunion (Moore and Wallace, 1975; Gordon, 1985). Because of the concern with family unity and the domestic stability of migrants, there was a tendency to regard women simply as 'dependants', in the sense of wives and mothers with children and with health and language problems, joining their husbands in the European Community. Until recently, less attention has been given to women as workers. Thus, a proper consideration of them raises questions that were not adequately addressed in 1977.

Women workers have two origins. First, in the migration of women who joined their husbands and then entered the labour market. Second, in the substantial migration of women who came in search of work in their own right. In 1980, Kudat and Sabuncuoglu said that 'more than 40 per cent of all migrants and 25 per cent of migrant workers in Europe are women' (1980, p. 11). As Phizacklea (1983, p. 1) put it, 'There are approximately six million women and girls . . . who have either migrated . . . since the 1950s or who have been born . . . to migrant parents.'

In the United Kingdom, white and non-white women are more similarly employed and paid than white and non-white men. This reinforces the view that if there is a 'dual labour market', it is based more on gender than race. In 1981, according to Brown (1984), the median earnings of West Indian men were £20 per week and Asian men £19 per week below white earnings. For women, the differences were: West Indians, £6 *above* white women and Asians, £4.50 below. All women are more heavily concentrated in a narrow range of jobs. In Switzerland, with an economy highly geared to services, migrant women (including seasonal workers) comprise about 46 per cent of all migrant workers. More than one-half of women workers are accounted for by textiles and clothing, hotels and catering, and domestic service. Female occupations in Switzerland are typical of Europe as a whole, where migrant women workers are to be found mainly in textiles, clothing, health services and 'domestic' work – cleaning and cooking, both in industry and commerce and in the hotel and catering trades. Kudat and Sabuncuoglu detect a significant increase in the proportion of women in the workforces of the major European labour importers and they see this as both changing the infra-structural costs of migrant labour and offering opportunities for upward mobility amongst native women (1980, p. 16). Bonney (1987) has suggested that *qualified* women are beginning to have labour-market careers closer to the typical male pattern, while at the other end of the occupational spectrum, 'an increasing number of the male labour force is coming to have the typical labour market situation of women', seeking whatever temporary work is available. Thus, certain changes are under way in European labour markets that are best understood in terms of *gender* and class. For women (and, perhaps, the men who join them at the lower end of the occupational scale), race is not such a major determinant of their economic life chances. At least the arguments of Bonney and Kudat and Sabuncuoglu and the data for Europe and the United Kingdom make this an open question (see also Wilson, 1978, and Churches Committee on Migrant Workers, 1987).

I have written elsewhere that migrant women are at the intersection of three systems of domination: class, colonial and gender (Moore, 1986). The autonomy of gender has been noted in a number of studies but especially clearly, and demonstrating the 'intersection' of systems of domination, in Floya Anthias's discussion of Greek Cypriot women in the United Kingdom (Phizacklea, 1983).

Anthias shows that Greek Cypriot women are overrepresented in manual skilled and semi-skilled work compared with other female Commonwealth workers. This is related to what she calls 'the conditions for the sale' of their labour, namely, a sexual division of labour. The women see themselves as, first and foremost, wives and mothers whose employment is for cash rather than career or self-advancement. Their role in Greek Cypriot society and the Greek Cypriot family facilitates their employment by Greek Cypriot employers. Thus, they find themselves largely in the clothing industry, working for Greek Cypriot men in an

154

industry with low job security and regular lay-offs. Many will work at home and others will work as unregistered workers. Yet employers are linked by kinship and less likely, therefore, to be seen in exploitative relations to the women. The women are reluctant to unionize because this would divide men and women within the Greek Cypriot community.

Ethnicity and gender are, therefore, mobilized in pursuit of profits in a highly competitive trade. Greek Cypriot migrants have organized their section of the clothing industry around the ethnic community and have used traditional gender relations and attitudes to construct the role of women workers within the industry. The expectations that Greek Cypriot men and women have of one another are rooted in Greek Cypriot 'familial ideology' (Barrett and McIntosh, 1982).

In discussing the fashion clothing industry, Morokvasic *et al.* (1986, p. 406) argue that

> The system of sub-contracting provides low paid jobs in outwork or homework for women who have skills in sewing. The only upward mobility in this sector – petty entrepreneurial status – is quasi limited to men. Men from patriarchal cultures can 'naturally' expect their kin and other women to work for them, while women can expect to control and give orders only to other women . . . As has often been the case in the history of migration, exploitation of women has been one of the few ways for immigrant men to accumulate capital.

In these circumstances, migrant women, it seems, stand in the same relation to migrant men as migrant men do to native workers.

'Race', ethnicity, gender and class

I suggested in 1977 that migrant workers performed a buffering function, that they were cheap labour and that they enabled employers more readily to restructure their enterprises. None of these is now necessary given the possibility of compelling the native labour force in conditions of high unemployment. Further-more, with family settlement, the infrastructural costs of ex-migrant labour are no longer so low. This change takes place against the shift from bringing workers to jobs in Europe to taking capital and creating jobs in Third World countries, outside Europe. I have argued also that the position of migrant women needs to be understood as much in gender as racial or ethnic terms.

155

If immigrants served to enable Europe to overcome a crisis in the labour market, they and their descendants now serve additional purposes in a new political crisis. If previously they were located at the intersection of systems of class, colonial and gender domination, they are placed today at a conjunction of class, political and gender exploitation. Migrants are concentrated in inner-city areas. There has been massive disinvestment in private industry and services in city centres and, in the United Kingdom, a decline in public investment (especially housing). Capital withdrawn from the cities has gone either overseas or to greenfield sites beyond the city, with similar results for the city in either case. The circumstances that made migrants so vulnerable in the labour market in the 1960s and 1970s make them politically vulnerable in the 1980s. They are blamed for the problems that befall Western Europe, especially the environmental decline of the inner cities and the rise in crime rates. This has to be seen in sharp contrast with the 1950s and 1960s when the (then) immigrants were seen as *victims* of crime and decline (Gilroy, 1987). Governments have made no systematic attempts to divert this blame, indeed, they have reinforced it through immigration and policing policies. A new dimension to this scapegoating of migrants and their descendants is the right-wing attack on attempts to meet new educational needs through multi-cultural and anti-racist education. Writers, notably in the *Salisbury Review*, present the English language, culture, religion and educational standards as threatened by alien influence.

For these writers, and notably Ray Honeyford, a Bradford ex-headteacher, legal citizenship does not confer 'real' Britishness. This brash and populist racism which has now become central to Conservative thought in Britain echoes the beliefs underlying the speeches of Enoch Powell in the 1960s and 1970s and the features and editorials of the *Daily Telegraph*. These are typified by Alfred Sherman's comment in 1976 that 'A passport or residence permit does not automatically implant national values or patriotism'. Views that cost Powell his seat on the Conservative front benches ten years ago are now Conservative orthodoxy.

Actions against mainly black populations, in the form of restrictive immigration policies, and their stigmatization as a 'problem' during immigration debates has both reinforced the notion that they are the cause of the problems of inner-city crime and justified greater internal surveillance and control (Gordon, 1985). This is typified by the practice of checking the papers of dark-skinned foreigners at Paris Metro stations, by stop-and-search policies in London and by deportation virtually at police discretion in West Germany. Beyond this, blacks have been the objects of casual violence by the police, leading to deaths in custody. Violence of a more organized kind has been directed in Britain against whole black communities in the name of crime fighting, leading to riots in Toxteth, Brixton, Bristol, Handsworth and elsewhere from the late 1970s onwards (see Institute of Race Relations, 1979; Lambeth, 1981; Joshua and Wallace, 1983).

In addition, blacks have suffered violence in the form of attacks by neighbours, youths and organized racist groups (see, for example, Bethnal Green and Stepney Trades Council, 1978). Details of many of these attacks are published monthly in the anti-fascist journal *Searchlight*. The police have been mainly indifferent to this violence and until recently have been reluctant to admit to its racial motivation. The 'criminalization' of the black populations of Europe and the upsurge of violence against them was largely predictable and I described its beginnings in 1977 (Moore, 1977a).

Alongside these developments, the demand for deportation is growing, especially on the far political right. Demands for tougher immigration controls are common across the whole range of right-wing politics. Barker (1981, p. 17) quotes Edward Gardner, MP:

The strength of any nation lies in its unity and, unless a Government is prepared to deal with the problem of numbers, unless they are prepared to make finite and known what is at present infinite and unknown, I believe that the hopes of all of us of creating an homogeneous nation composed of both the immigrant and indigenous parts of our nation will and must inevitably begin to go.

These demands have not been repudiated by political leaders, but echoed and endorsed, as by Mrs Thatcher, in 1979:

If we went on as we are, then, by the end of the century, there would be four million people of the New Commonwealth or Pakistan here. Now that is an awful lot and I think it means that people are really rather afraid that this country might be swamped by people with a different culture. And, you know, the British character has done so much for democracy, for law and done so much throughout the world, that if there is a fear that it might be swamped, people are going to react and be rather hostile to those coming in.

(Barker, 1981, p. 15)

The British Prime Minister has never been known to make even the most mildly liberal statement about wanting to see 'good race relations' in the United Kingdom and, in this attitude, she differs little from her continental counterparts who face, for example, the rise to parliamentary representation of the National Front in France and 24,000 members of 76 extreme right-wing organizations in West Germany (*Searchlight*, No. 50: 13).

What to many white observers and the press are 'riots' are to black communities 'uprisings' and 'resistance', belonging to a historical and international tradition of resistance both to colonialism overseas and racism at home. Joshua and Wallace (1983) divide the modern period of metropolitan resistance into two main periods. The first was 1900 to 1948 and was largely confined to seaports with substantial populations of colonial seafarers. In 1911, the small Chinese community in Cardiff was attacked. The local shipowners had threatened to use Chinese labour to break a national strike of seamen; picketing and intimidation of the Chinese quickly followed. 'Moral' crusaders made their contribution by playing upon hostility to the association of white women with Chinese men and accusing the Chinese of involvement in the white slave trade and other morally objectionable activities. The police did little to prevent the destruction of Chinese property and seem to have confined their activity to dispersing the rioters after the event (Joshua and Wallace, 1983). The Chinese for their part did not mobilize to resist but rather sought to survive by withdrawal.

In 1919 there were riots in London and nearly all major seaports. According to Joshua and Wallace (1983), they were genuine 'race riots' unprovoked by any industrial or other dispute, although the presence of ex-soldiers in many of the mobs may suggest one source of disaffection amongst the whites. Clashes in Liverpool and the South Wales ports resulted in a number of black fatalities. Such was the ferocity of the attacks that the police claimed to be unable to intervene. Black families were, however, taken into protective custody and arrests were made – one attempt to make an arrest led to the killing of Charles Wootten in Liverpool. Blacks suspected of having weapons were arrested and, in spite of being the victims of the riots, were in the majority of those arrested. But, foreshadowing cases in the 1980s, the courts did seem prepared to accept the defence of self-defence. One crucial response of the state was to introduce regulations, ostensibly for the regulation of sea-going labour, which facilitated deportation of colonial subjects and made it easier to subject black settlements to intensive policing.

The media response was to treat the problem as a 'black' problem with themes of 'black violence', 'white reaction' and 'police heroism' (Joshua and Wallace, 1983). Much was made of white postwar unemployment compared with the employment of colonial seamen; men had come home from the war to poverty while coloured men walked the streets with money in their pockets and white girls on their arms (see *Liverpool Courier* and *Western Mail* cited in Joshua and Wallace, 1983, ch. 1).

Black communities have from these earlier days produced their own agencies of resistance, formulated their own political demands and begun, in Britain at least, to influence the politics of the inner city. Caribbean and Asian culture, music, writing, television drama and poetry have also flourished. A black intelligentsia is also helping further to interpret the situation. All these reactions are themselves grounded in the lived experience of a 'racialized' society and a sense of 'racial' history – an important black community facility in Liverpool is called the Charles Wootten Centre, for example (Liverpool Black Caucus, 1986).

It is not the purpose of this chapter to analyse these black responses in any detail, mainly because they are essentially part of a particular British history. Miles and others have, however, raised, in interesting ways, the question of the extent to which 'black' responses have been based upon 'race', class or ethnicity (Miles and Phizacklea, 1980; Miles, 1982). What should be noted is that the presence of black populations and their more recent responses to oppression have provided fertile ground for counter-developments which have strong European and international dimensions. Fascists are now internationally organized and preparing for violence. They are receiving military training in the Lebanon and in Northern Ireland. Joint plans were made to bomb Bologna railway station, the synagogue on Rue Copernic in Paris, the Munich beer festival in 1980, and the Notting Hill Carnival in 1981. Only the last of these was averted, because of the warning given by a long-term infiltrator into the National Front. Bologna bombers meanwhile live in safe houses provided by British fascists (*Searchlight*, No. 122, August 1985; *Searchlight*, No. 128, February, 1986). There has also been a resurgence of 'intellectual' racism ranging from attempts to deny the Holocaust and the financing of a new edition of the anti-semitic forgery, *The Protocols of the Elders of Zion* by the Saudi Arabian government (see Seidel, 1986), to the chauvinism of the *Salisbury Review*.

What this means for the purposes of the present analysis is that although the position of migrants and blacks in the European class

159

structure raises difficult questions of both local analysis (in terms of class, 'race', ethnicity and gender, for example) and international comparison (Moore, 1977a), we can see a fairly unambiguous international mobilization based, *inter alia*, upon racist opposition to their presence in Europe. The opposition to the black population has achieved a degree of international consciousness and organization not achieved by migrant workers themselves, their descendants, or their allies on the basis of 'race', ethnicity, or class. There have, however, been liberal responses to migrant settlement. United Kingdom readers will be familiar with the Race Relations Acts and in England and Wales the wide range of 'Section 11' measures that have been adopted locally. Section 11 of the Local Government Act 1966 enables local authorities to claim money in respect of the problems and needs of ethnic minority communities in their areas. These and other liberal measures address the issue of racial discrimination and disadvantage largely as social pathology, not as a problem of the normal working of British social structure (Moore, 1977a). Liberal measures tend to depoliticize race and the interests of ethnic minorities. A more radical approach is found in what is generally identified as 'anti-racism', which treats the historical and contemporary structures which produce discrimination and disadvantage as the problems. Anti-racists, in other words, seek to address causes rather than effects.

These essentially local United Kingdom questions are important matters of concern to sociologists but the same questions may be, and are, asked on a wider scale, most notably perhaps, through the European Parliament, where, for example, there has been pressure for improved civil rights and for policies such as mother-tongue teaching. Political issues are also addressed at the European level as witnessed by the parliamentary enquiry into the rise of racism and fascism in Western Europe which amassed Europe-wide evidence on the problem (for a short summary report, see Bell, 1986). Both liberals and anti-racists have created organizations and programmes. Liberal initiatives having met with limited success, are now increasingly having to face the challenge of the repoliticization of racial issues in the rise of anti-racism. But both liberal and radical have become the target for opposition – the 'race relations industry' and now 'anti-racists' are the target of the political right.

It is significant that the *Salisbury Review* authors have directed much of their attention to questions of education. This is partly because control of education is central to their authoritarian and anti-egalitarian programme. But it is also in the field of education that the demands of ethnic minorities have been heard and where serious debates have taken place about the steps necessary to create the conditions for a less divided and more just society. This forces both pupils and teachers to ask questions about inequality and about ideology. Such questioning is seen as profoundly subversive by the right. It is also especially fertile ground for the promotion of hostility by white working-class parents towards the black population: policies of equality are being discussed – but not, it seems, for them. Why are equality of opportunity and compensatory measures only being discussed for black children? It has never been on the agenda for white working-class education. Furthermore, it is easy to present these developments as taking place *at the expense of* white children. Although British educational institutions do not entirely serve working-class interests, the working class does have an interest in the educational system. However little the educational system may have done for working-class people, it is easy to present the intrusion of 'alien' interests as threatening, especially in conditions of declining resources. Black parents in inner-city schools may quite properly reply that their demand for educational resources will benefit all children and not theirs alone. *They* might ask why native parents have not raised demands for *their* children's education.

Similarly, in the field of housing, the most deprived will compete to exclude others in similar situations to themselves, perhaps on the basis of skin colour. There is no party capable of mobilizing potential resentment against wealthy owner-occupiers who have received massive housing subsidies while the poor have been deprived. Mobilization such as this might emphasize the common interest of the poorly housed, irrespective of skin colour or culture. Unsurprisingly, perhaps, Phizacklea and Miles found considerable racial resentment amongst white respondents on the housing question, in their Willesden study (1980, pp. 170–1).

In employment, large areas of work where immigrants and women are found are either non-unionized or have been de-unionized. None the less, wherever there are unions, black workers are well unionized. A small number are now becoming full-time officials. But throughout the 1970s, trade unions did not support black workers on racial matters – they did not identify with black interests in any circumstances. White workers and their unions, in certain circumstances, practised policies of exclusion from work or promotion against black workers (Moore, 1977a). Unions supported black workers only when union rights and interests were at issue and campaigned against the far right (notably the National Front) when they threatened unions.

The status gains made by the indigenous working class, partly (as I argued in 1977) as a result of migrants taking the lowest status and worst paid jobs, are now threatened by unemployment. White workers now facing unemployment and downward mobility see black workers below them in competition. Thus, both upward mobility by migrants ('equal opportunities') and downward mobility by indigenous workers (unemployment) are a source of potential conflict and division. Such conflict and division must strengthen the hand of capital and the state and weaken the working class further, by dividing it.

What cannot concern us here – but is of central sociological importance – is how and why it is possible for, for example, skin colour, gender, or national origin to be the basis around which people build theories to interpret their circumstances. In present conditions, people do so. Racial interpretations are, in part, derived from experiences of economic and environmental deprivation, conflict and a sense of powerlessness, and legitimized both by an imperial past and by the acts and attitudes of recent governments (see Moore, 1986). In 1977, conflict seemed to be rooted almost entirely in the labour market, but by no means exclusively so. Today, through the mobilization of actual or potential conflict over education, housing and crime, the 'racialization' of society is increasingly rooted in political conflict over the distribution of material resources and threats to a presumed national way of life from crime and 'alien' cultures. We might reasonably expect similar processes of racialization to be taking place elsewhere in Europe, although each nation has a different imperial and colonial experience. The important point for this analysis is that although 'race', class, ethnicity and gender are all possible overlapping bases for action, they are not only the bases for action by minorities themselves. To a significant degree, it is the far right that has used 'race' as a basis for mobilization throughout Europe. 'Race' in this context is a basis for action on the streets, in areas of social policy, and in education.

In 1977 I raised the question of the *class* position of migrants. A central issue was whether an accumulation of differences of interest between natives and migrants in the working class can become a class difference. Phizacklea and Miles (1980, pp. 6–10) have defined migrant workers as a *class fraction*; Castles and Kosack (1973, ch. 11) referred to them as a stratum within the working class. All argued that migrants are part of the working class but, at the same time, occupy a particular and disadvantaged position in it. Migrants (and now settlers) are a part of the working class, but that class is stratified by race and gender in a way that gives it a distinct form and, according to Miles (1982), creates particular opportunities for capital.

In 1988, it is hard to disagree with Castells' 1975 (p. 54) statement that 'Immigrants find themselves in an extremely unfavourable balance of power which tends to reproduce their separation from the rest of the labour movement'. The level of political victimization is much higher and the process of criminalization of the black population in Britain is much more advanced than in 1975. Blacks remain heavily overrepresented in low-status work, in casual occupations, and amongst the unemployed. Additionally, they are now presented in political discourse in terms similar to the urban 'mob', the 'dangerous classes', at the turn of the century – and there are similarities in their position (not least because many of the 'mob' were recent arrivals). 'The new lumpenproletariat' might, then, best describe black members of the working class in Britain. In European terms, this British class is a privileged class, given the security of residence and political rights they enjoy compared with European migrants and settlers.

There is an alternative interpretation of the 'new lumpen-proletariat', wider than the black population. It grows, according to Halsey (1987), as more people become surplus to the productive requirements of modern industrial society:

> The class structure of industrial societies, including Britain, is developing an under-class of those who cannot be placed in the stable workforce of the formerly employed . . . They suffer a cumulation of social pathologies – education failure, illiteracy, broken families, high crime rates, poor housing, and spatial concentration in the inner city. They are disproportionately recruited from the young and the ethnic minorities, and they tend to adopt a ghetto existence outside the normal social contract of citizenship and with little or no stake in official society.

This alienated minority may be controlled, according to Halsey (1987), by 'the twin weapons of minimum state welfare and efficient police'. Of particular interest for our purpose is Halsey's word *disproportionately* because it raised the question of how and why ethnicity is used to assign a proportion of the non-white population to the underclass. Perhaps the most important trend to be identified underlying Halsey's brief comment is that a larger proportion of the native population is acquiring life chances that, in recent history, were more typically black.

Can we simply assign migrant workers to *one* position in a class structure? As we have seen, 'race' was used to define immigrant workers as suitable for particular modes of employment in the 1960s and 1970s but, by 1985, their ethnicity was being used to define them as problematic and culturally threatening. Ethnicity was rapidly redefined in response to changed circumstances. That the black has been redefined from cheap labour to 'mugger' does not mean that blacks do not still do the worst jobs nor that Turkish workers at German railway stations were not seen as a threat to the German way of life in the 1960s. Only the emphasis has shifted. These changes are real in their consequences, and for both the actors and for sociologists they modify relations within and between classes. Not least, immigrants and settlers find themselves up against the state and the police more often than against their employers.

There will be particular combinations of interest and consciousness which make class, 'race', ethnicity and gender salient and potential bases for action. Examples may be found of action organized around ethnicity and gender *within* the working class. Such action may extend well beyond the workplace, either in extension of work-based conflict when an ethnic community offers a workforce material and moral support, or outside the workplace altogether, when a community organizes for self-defence. Action organized on a 'race' basis is harder to find, given the problematic status of the idea of race. Perhaps the nearest we find are broad-based coalitions either in the workplace or in the community. The Liverpool Black Caucus is a good example of the latter and further serves to emphasize the *political* nature of the definition of 'race', in that a 'black' caucus may include people with white skins. For black workers, the experience of being a member of the working class is not an experience of being a member of a class at large, but as a particular 'fraction' within that class. The fractional nature of their membership may be emphasized if they find themselves in opposition not only to their employers, but to employers apparently in coalition with other workers.

Similar arguments could be developed for women. The Greek Cypriot women described by Anthias (in Phizacklea 1983) are members of the working class. But what they experience is the fulfilment of traditional obligations. That they work for poor wages in bad conditions, like many working-class people, is a

164

result, not simply of their class membership, but of the particular form of subordination of women to men in their ethnic community. That they may be working illegally means that their subordinate status is reinfored by the implied threat of legal sanction. Kudat and Sabuncuoglu (1980) suggest that women in this situation may mobilize for radical action, but their brief account suggests that this was part of wider action not entirely confined to women. None the less, it would be possible for women to develop a sense of their membership of a class fraction and act in that fraction's interests before or without seeing its relationship to broader class structures. Making the linkages is often the function of radical organizations, political, trade-union, or feminist.

What, then, is the position of the migrant worker in the European class structure today? This question must bring us to a consideration of the traditional distinction between class and status. All wage-labour may fall under the classical definition of 'working class' but wage-labour may relate to the means of production in different ways. This depends in part upon the ability of groups and individuals to appropriate property, skills, knowledge, opportunities and rights. We constantly use terms like 'skilled' and 'unskilled' to denote different market positions within the working class. The acquisition of knowledge, managerial skills and minor interests in property by a significant section of the population has fuelled a debate about the 'new middle class' that has spanned the last thirty years of our professional careers as teachers and writers. The question of the 'new lumpenproletariat' may come to dominate the next twenty years. But there is nothing new about imposing a scheme of stratification upon very general concepts of class, or debating whether differences based upon stratification could be transformed into class differences. If one adopts a very simple two- or three-class model and asks 'Do migrants constitute a class?', the answer is probably 'no'. In this sense, the idea of class fraction has some limited value in emphasizing the continuity between migrants' class position and the working class – they are not a *separate* class. Although one may readily agree that the capitalist world is divided into owners and non-owners of the means of production and less readily agree that this might have some 'ultimate' significance for the transformation of that world, this answer does not aid most analyses rooted in our daily experience or our research.

A more useful definition of class, that gives us greater analytical leverage, is that class denotes all persons in the same class

165

situation, namely, the typical probability of procuring goods, gaining a position in life and finding inner satisfaction, which derives from the relative control over goods and skills and their income-producing uses within a given economic order (Weber, 1968). What is, however, crucial in using this definition is that the 'relative control' within a given economic order may, itself, be derived from outside the economic order. In other words, gender and ethnic differences are not derived from an economic order, but the way in which they are incorporated into the economic order may effectively alter an individual's or group's typical probability of procuring goods, status and fulfilment in the economic order. It *may* be arguable that (1) 'races' are in part the product of the incorporation of groups into particular positions within economic orders and that (2) the role of women and the advantages enjoyed by men in the economic order create conditions for the development of, for example, religious and scientific legitimations of the positions of ethnic minorities and women in that order. But it is not our concern to explore this dialectic here – and it is no more than a possibility that such a line of enquiry would be useful.

Within this definition of class, the legal framework within which actors are situated affects their class position. Thus, for example, citizenship – both in formal terms of nationality and in terms of the acquisition or non-acquisition of legal, political and social rights – may, and usually does, influence position in the economic order. The role of the 'political' and of the state is crucial because the state grants and removes rights and creates a legal framework within which the rights may or may not be made effective. The state is also partially responsible for creating climates of opinion in which sections of the population may be more or less included or excluded from civil society and expressions of hostility made more or less legitimate. So, we may argue that Europe's migrant workers are all part of 'class fractions' but that they occupy relatively different positions between and within each nation by virtue of differential citizenship. The effects of the lack of citizenship may also be modified to the extent that the 'home' government maintains surveillance over migrants and their families (Castles *et al.*, 1984, p. 220).

For most of the migrants in most of Europe, we may turn this analysis the other way up: they occupy positions in the European economic order because their differential citizenship enabled them to be employed for particular purposes. Their position in the economic and legal order derives also from the status attributed to them by virtue of their nationality, ethnicity, 'race' and gender. It is unnecessary to labour the point that the positions they occupy then come to reinforce their status. Thus, I go beyond my 1977 argument by looking at the consequences of the projection of this into the political sphere during an economic crisis. I suggest that migrants and their descendants may be seen as performing a key function in obscuring the nature of the crisis. The process of criminalization and political stigmatization in this will have consequences for both their economic and citizenship status.

In 1975 Castells was dismissive of attempts to talk of an international working class; the development of capitalism was uneven and each national proletariat had to work out its own strategy. It is not the function of the sociologist to work out strategies for the proletariat and we recognize the problems of uneven development. None the less, capital is international, there is an international division of labour, and we should be examining the extent to which international class formation and class or trade-union consciousness develops. The interest for sociologists of 'race relations' lies not in the fact that migrants occupy particular positions in European societies, but *how* they come to occupy these positions. The main issues concern the interpretation and incorporation of ethnic and gender differences into the economic and political order. The class positions of different groups of migrants in Europe, whose relationship to the means of pro-duction is modified by status differences, are, perhaps, more similar to one another than they are to those of indigenous working classes. To that extent, this 'fraction' of the European labour force may approximate to a class.

Acknowledgement

I am, as always, indebted to Mike Lyon for comments on this chapter.

7

Social change, division and control in the USSR

DAVID LANE

The October Revolution of 1917 was one of the most decisive events of the twentieth century. It was hailed by 'progressive' and Marxist intellectuals in the West as the beginning of a new era in world history: in the words of the Webbs, it was a 'new civilization' (Webb and Webb, 1938). Its supporters and critics alike regarded the Soviet Union (and later countries following in its path) to be different in important ways from capitalism: the profit motive and the market had been abolished and replaced by planning; the values of collectivism and equality had superseded those of individualism and freedom. Its supporters argued that rationality in human affairs could be achieved through direct human intervention in the form of conscious political guidance and control by the Communist Party and the Soviet state. The age of planning had replaced that of the market. A 'classless' society was on the agenda.

But pessimism about the nature of the Soviet model of socialism and its internal political processes has been expressed from the time of the Kronstadt rebellion when the sailors there revolted against 'communists and commissars'. And opposition has always been voiced by conservatives and liberals who see 'communism' as being antithetical to individual enterprise, progress, liberty and the rights of private property. During the 1980s, moreover, what might charitably be termed the 'hesitancy and doubt' about the Soviet system has turned to disapproval and disillusionment. Two major developments have taken place: first, ideologically, Western critical and leftist writers have adapted features of the right-wing theory of totalitarianism and have linked it to the rise of a new ruling class. Secondly, from within the USSR and other socialist states the inadequacies of the existing political and economic apparatus of planning and political control have come to the forefront of the political agenda. Many of the 'sacred' features of the system have been challenged by the emerging leadership of these societies (including that of the USSR) and a 'recalibration', or 'realignment' of plan and market, of money and political control, and of the individual and the state has taken place.

This chapter is in two parts: the first being more theoretical will evaluate the cleavages in state socialist society as articulated by critical Western writers. The second will outline empirically the social changes taking place and will analyse the underlying social dynamics at work within the USSR. This will involve two theoretical approaches: that of class conflict and that of social structure and social differentiation.

Division as class conflict

Until relatively recently, 'state capitalism' and the theory of the transitional society have dominated Marxist discussion in the West. (For a review see Cliff, 1963; Sweezy and Bettelheim, 1971; Carlo, 1974; Mandel, 1974; Melotti, 1977; Bellis, 1979; Binns and Haynes, 1980.) From a comparative viewpoint, the theory of state capitalism posits a form of single convergence of 'Bolshevist' societies to the model of capitalism described by Marx. A number of different sets of arguments are advanced by such thinkers. First, it is contended that the level of productive forces (that is, of capital investment and productivity) is far too low to justify a qualitative leap even to the preliminary stage of a communist mode of production, which can only proceed from the highest stage of capitalism. Second, the working class is not in fact hegemonic in East European socialist societies: it is divorced from real control of the means of production. The relations of production do not ensure socialism, rather the social formation is a type of capitalism with state ownership and control. A distinguishing feature is that the officials or 'bureaucracy' controlling the means of production fulfil the traditional functions of the capitalist class: they channel surplus product extracted from the direct producers into capital. Concurrently, their social position in the political order turns their administrative privilege into class rights. With the consolidation of the bureaucratic structure a dual class system arises akin to that in capitalist states.

169

In the past fifteen years, a change has occurred in Western Marxist critiques of Soviet-type societies. While earlier, state capitalist writers denied that Soviet planning was socialist, they did concede that state management of the means of production was 'progressive' in the sense that, like early capitalism, it allowed for the unfettered development of the productive forces. 'State capitalism', it was believed, was a more efficient and more appropriate form of capitalism for Russia than that which had arisen in the West. However, the founding of the journals, *Socialisme ou Barbarie* by Castoriadis and Leforte and *Critique* by Hillel Ticktin has led to a theoretical position which has disputed whether planning occurs at all in the East European societies. And the testimonies of East European immigrants in the West conjoined with the dominant American paradigm of 'totalitarianism' applied to Soviet-type societies, has focused on the control of the apparatus of planning as being the crucial foundation to the rise of a new ruling class.

Both these viewpoints regard Soviet-type societies as being destructive: they produce waste and sacrifice the needs of the population to the interests of the dominant bureaucratic ruling groups. As Feher *et al.* (1983, p. 32) have put it: 'there is a contradiction between administratively determined use value and real social utilities'. The essence of this position is that the Soviet system of planning results in exploitation of labour and the extraction of surplus – a process similar to that under capitalism. Claude Lefort describes it as follows:

> The bureaucrats form a class only by reason of the fact that their functions and their statuses differentiate them collectively from the exploited classes, only because these features bind them to a central administration that determines production and freely disposes of power . . . The unity of the bureaucratic class is therefore immediately derived from the collective appropriation of surplus value and immediately dependent on the collective apparatus of exploitation – the state.
>
> (Lefort, 1986, p. 72)

For Feher *et al.*, 'Soviet-type societies' are not capitalist in the traditional sense but neither are they socialist; the antinomy between market and plan, between the production of use value and exchange value is rejected. The nationalization of the means of production is not socialist because it does not, in the state socialist societies, lead to the 'effective transformation of economic relations, establishing a collective–social property in the sense of the real power of immediate producers to decide and dispose collectively over the conditions and products of their labour' (Feher *et al.*, 1983, pp. 18, 19).

This new social formation has the character of a modern and new form of oppression and political exploitation. The bureaucracy is dominant: 'not only the technical organization of the process of production, but also all the socio-economic decisions concerning what to produce and how to employ the gross product socially are established and made by a distinct and separate social group [the bureaucracy] whose corpus is continuously replenished through mechanisms of a selective co-optation and which is essentially self-appointed.' There are no centres of institutional autonomy; Eastern European countries are 'mono-organizational societies'. The party 'penetrates all these structures of the administration control' and the party elite 'exercises command' over the bureaucratic hierarchy. This, in turn, exercises power by effecting 'the perfect atomization of the individual' who is 'coercively organized'. This school of thought echoes Raymond Aron when it conceives of the 'classless' society – in the sense of a pulverized and fragmented social structure (Feher *et al.*, 1983, pp. 45, 107, 247–8, 250).

The quintessence of this new ruling class lies not so much in its distributional privilege but in its institutionalized power. The bureaucratic apparatus as a whole 'actually exercises all the functions of disposition and control over the nationalized means of production . . . [through] this power to dispose over the resources and the surplus produced, this group actually realizes its common interests.' The relationship of this group to the population of the country is one of 'mutual opposition of interests centering around the disposition and appropriation of surplus product' (Feher *et al.*, 1983, pp. 57, 60, 118). Planning lacks rationality, the political leadership responds to exogenous forces and consequently planning is an inferior 'cohering mechanism' to the capitalist market.[1] Rather than the division of labour, reflected in a graded hierarchical social and political structure, these writers conceive of antagonism which culminates 'at specific historical moments' into 'overt antagonism' between the members of the apparatus as a corporate ruling group and the whole working population. Unlike capitalist society in which politics and social stratification are (in the last instance) outgrowths of economic-based class relationships, Soviet-type societies ensure the 'primacy of the political state over the whole of societal life; society is an annexe to the omnipotent political state rather than a relatively independent entity'. Individual and group demands are not articulated and 'command . . . irredeemably comprises the elements of arbitrariness and the deliberate disregard of needs' (Feher *et al.*, 1983, pp. 130, 253, 254).

While Feher *et al.* in places concede that the powers of the political party elite are limited, it is clear that social outcomes are largely shaped by politics; the reproduction of the system is at the behest of the political bureaucratic ruling class. Societal forces play at best a marginal role. In my view, this approach is best conceived of as a contemporary version of the state capitalist thesis, save that it locates the source of class power in political control of the means of production and violence. Hence the penetration of society by the state and the control of the state by the political power of the party elite make changes of political leadership of much greater significance in state socialist society than in Western capitalist ones.

Evaluation of the bureaucratic class theory

These contemporary critical approaches highlight three significant aspects of state socialist societies, but in three other respects they may be faulted. It is correct to point out that the 'deformations' or inequalities of state socialist societies are not just things that are 'left-overs' from pre-socialist formations. They are replicated by structures within state socialist societies. Second, such societies lack advanced forms of participation by the 'direct producers'. Writers such as Lefort remind us that the state has a coercive role as well as an organizing capacity, that the state generates social interests which drive the system and which may be in conflict with the ideological goals of socialism, with other interests, or even with the general interest (1986). Finally, I would agree that such societies are characterized by a ruling elite and by forms of inequality and privilege incompatible with the ideals of a socialist system. Such malformations I would explain in terms of several factors: (1) Cultural and economic backwardness was particularly important in the formative years of the USSR when the political structure was shaped without the participation of a mature working class. (2) Traditional social institutions which replicate inequality: the family, for instance, is a font of cultural capital derived from education and place in the division of labour, and the social destination of children is now strongly influenced by that of their parents. (3) Bureaucratic politics which give inadequate popular control.

However, I would disagree that the form of exploitation and 'class rule' is analogous to that of the feudal or capitalist mode of production. The system of planning in the USSR has abolished the valorization of commodities through market exchange. Revenues comparable to profits given by ownership rights over property or labour power do not exist. Hence, officials, executives and intellectuals in these societies who enjoy privileges do not create a ruling class in a *Marxist* sense. A Marxist 'ruling class' has to be defined not only by relations of domination over the direct producers but also by forms of exploitation derived from the social relations of production (Wright, 1980, pp. 325–6). For Marxists, economic exploitation is not just one form of asymmetrical relationship but a qualitative one having manifold effects – over status, power and wealth.

Second, these writers attribute the non-fulfilment of needs to a 'dictatorship' over the primary producers. Clearly, the elites of these societies enjoy unearned privileges. But any political system, I would argue, located in Eastern Europe after the Second World War would have been unable to fulfil all the population's 'needs'. Even if one concedes that an overinvestment occurred in heavy industry one cannot overlook the severe shortage of resources in state socialist societies which such investment in the long run sought to reduce. The causes of shortage cannot be attributed to 'planning'. Market-type systems also involve unearned elite privileges and the non-fulfilment of needs of the population in capitalist societies. Market systems effectively ration by price and ability to pay those needs which may be fulfilled and those that go unfulfilled. Moreover, the notion that state socialist societies produce 'waste' through the incompetences of planning is far too simplistic. While the quality of consumer goods may be inferior to those of advanced market societies, state socialism does not have an equivalent level of 'waste' with respect to unemployment of labour or the underutilization of capital which are endemic to advanced capitalist societies.

Third, the costs and benefits of state planning are not properly evaluated by these writers. In the early post-revolutionary period, macro economic and social change benefited the masses through land reform, provision of rudimentary education, health and welfare services; and rapid industrialization gave full employment and social mobility. While there is no industrial society with an equal distribution of resources, commodities and services, developed socialist societies have overall a qualitatively more equal form of distribution than capitalist ones. Of course, this is not a black and white contrast. Some Western welfare states have secured a fairly equitable distribution of earned income through taxation, and also have made possible comparable or even better advancement for women. The leading capitalist states, moreover, such as the USA and Japan are characterized by severe distributional inequalities. This is a consequence of the division of wealth which gives owners of capital massive incomes. The wealth and income of a capitalist class cannot be ignored or regarded as unimportant. And it is perhaps appropriate to compare the leading socialist state, the USSR, with what Margaret Thatcher has termed 'the flagship of freedom', the USA. In the USA, as Lenski has reminded us, '94% of all people with adjusted incomes [for tax purposes] of one million dollars or more received the largest share of their income from capital gains [despite the fact that half of capital gains are not even recorded as income] or from dividends' (Lenski, 1978, p. 370).

It is true that the aspirations engendered by an overoptimistic leadership have not been fulfilled and this has led to popular disgruntlement. The frustration of popular expectations is indicated by a Soviet survey of people's attitudes to various aspects of life (Levykin, 1984, p. 94). When asked in the early 1980s 'whether the situation had improved during the past 5 years', 68 per cent responded that material conditions were better (data for USSR as a whole), 75.8 per cent in rural locations thought so, as did 65.3 per cent of respondents aged 18–29. As for food, the proportions of positive responses fell to: 54.8 per cent (USSR), 67.1 per cent (villages), but only 48.5 per cent of the 18–29-year-olds and 55.6 per cent of people living in large towns. When asked about the improvement of possibilities for enjoying leisure time, the figures were much lower: only 37.5 per cent (USSR), 36.1 per cent (large towns), 42.6 per cent (villages), 22.6 per cent (18–29 age group). Over a long period expectations generated in the 1960s had not been fulfilled: national income was 36 per cent lower than planned, gross agricultural production was 56 per cent short of the long-term plan.[2] Nevertheless, by the mid-1980s conditions had improved and it can hardly be doubted that standards have been rising. In industry as a whole the working week has shortened from 47.8 hours in 1955 to 40.5 in 1985, and the average number of days holiday had risen from 18.5 in 1958 to 22 in 1983 (Narkhoz, 1986, p. 399). The index of consumption has risen from 100 in 1970 to 176 in 1981 (and remained the same in 1982); it rose to 189 in 1984 and 196 in 1985 (Narkhoz, 1986, p. 441). Even according to estimates made by the Central Intelligence Agency of the USA, the USSR has had an annual rise in gross national product of from 2 per cent to 2.5 per cent in the early 1980s (Oberdorfer, 1987). Of Western European states, according to OECD figures, this record is only matched by Ireland in the 1980–5 period; the Federal Republic of Germany had an average rate of 1.3% between 1980 and 1985 and the UK 1.2% (*Manchester Guardian Weekly*, 1987). However, the Soviet Union has experienced a long-term decline in its rate of economic growth. Official figures show a reduction in growth rates; the average increase in produced national income being 8.9 per cent in 1966–70, 6.3 per cent 1971–5, 4.7 per cent 1976–80 and 4.0 per cent 1981–3 (White, 1986, p. 466).

It is also true that the direct producer does not receive in income the total return from his or her labour. Surplus is extracted by the state (as under feudalism, or capitalism); Marx, however, acknowledged that in all types of society 'surplus-labour in general must remain' (Marx, 1959, Vol. III, p. 799). It is necessary for the expansion of the process of production, for the renewal of capital as well as for the maintenance of non-productive labour, such as children and other dependants. The distinctive feature of a ruling class is that it does not exchange income for labour but is a parasitic stratum. State socialist societies have channelled surplus into capital formation and renewal, indeed this has been a characteristic of such societies. One can agree with Roemer that 'the historical task of the socialist revolution is to eliminate that form of exploitation due to differentiated ownership of alienable assets' (Roemer, 1982, p. 238). Unjustifiable privilege, however, is a characteristic of Soviet society. It is founded on the excessive rewards, both material and cultural, which may be exacted by people in executive and administrative posts. We shall return to these points later.

The 'crisis' of Soviet planning

Ironically, the 'critical' class conflict approaches discussed above have been given sustenance in the 1980s by reformers of the system of planning in the socialist states themselves. Reforms have taken place in Hungary and China which move away from the system of state planning to the market. In the USSR a major divide is manifested in the rise of Gorbachev. The leadership of Gorbachev, however, does not merely criticize the system of

planning in the USSR but extends the analysis to the 'contradictions in the development' of Soviet society (January 1987
Plenum). Gorbachev, in his speech to the Twenty-Seventh
Congress in 1986, criticized the state system, the bureaucratic
nature of control, 'the lack of correspondence between productive
forces and production relations', between socialist property and
the economic forms of its implementation, the relations 'between
goods and money' and in the 'combination of centralization and
independence of economic organization'.

Gorbachev locates changes necessary in the form of planning in
a social and political context.

> The forms of production relations, the system of running and
> managing the economy . . . took shape . . . in the conditions of
> an extensive development. Gradually they become obsolete,
> they began to lose their role as incentives and here and there
> they turned into impediments. Currently we are striving to
> change the thrust of the economic mechanism, to overcome its
> cost-intensive nature, to target it towards enhancing quality and
> efficiency, accelerating the progress of science and tech-
> nology and the strengthening of the role played by the human
> factor.
>
> (Gorbachev, 1986)

It involves a movement away from administrative methods of
control of the economy to greater reliance on economic ones. As
Zaslavskaya (1985) has put it: What is now necessary is making 'a
rational calculation between administrative and economic
methods of management under new conditions'. There is no
mention in the Revised Party Programme adopted in 1986 of
increased public consumption, of the withering away of the state
or of the decline of money. Notions of class struggle in capitalist
countries and optimism about the 'building of communism' in the
USSR are absent from Gorbachev's speeches.

How then can one explain this change of emphasis? Those
advocating the totalitarian approach, considered earlier, would
regard 'politics' as being determinant. This does not explain
differences between factions of the political elite involving
changes in policy and political process. A sociological approach,
rather than seeing the social structure as an *outcome* of the activity
of a ruling class or power elite, would consider changes in the
social structure and the impact they have on political leadership.
The latter is conceived to be an outgrowth of, and limited by, the

social structure, which is far from being 'an annexe to the omnicompetent political state'.

The Soviet political leadership is confronted by a different type of society to that inherited by Khrushchev and Stalin. In policy-making a government has to take into account the maturation of class, ethnic, or other social groups, the appropriateness of ideology, changes in the nature of values and beliefs, developments in science and technology, and the ability of the existing structures to cope and to innovate. Only one of these aspects can be considered here: the changing occupational structure.

The changing occupational structure

During the past forty years the USSR has experienced a large and rapid movement of population from the countryside to the towns concurrent with the formation of a large manual working class, the rapid expansion of professional and executive strata (the 'intelligentsia') and the decline of the traditional peasantry in the collective farm. The major changes of the population by sector of the economy are shown on Table 7.1. By the mid-1980s, if transport is included in the service sector, the latter was the largest in the Soviet economy having 42 per cent of total employment, compared to only 23 per cent in 1940. Though this is smaller than in advanced Western states, the industrial and occupational structure has now more similarities to than differences from them; and this is particularly so if one uses for comparison the European areas of the USSR.

Until relatively recently, collective farmers were a significant social group in the social structure.[3] Over time the numbers of collective farmers have fallen steadily. In 1986 they accounted for only 9.47 per cent of the workforce compared to 26 per cent in 1960 and 46 per cent in 1940 (see Table 7.2). Collective farmers occupy the bottom rungs of the stratification order in the USSR, though the status of this group has improved qualitatively in recent years.

Table 7.1 Employment by Economic Sector, 1940–1986

	1940 %	1960 %	1986 %
Agriculture	54	39	19
Industry and building	23	32	38
Services (including transport)	23	29	43

Source: Narkhoz Za 70 let, 1987, p. 410.

Table 7.2 Average Numbers of Manual Workers and Non-Manual Employees in the National Economy and Collective Farmers Engaged in the Social Economy of Collective Farms (millions)

	1940	1960	1970	1980	1986
Non-manuals	10.0	15.8	25.3	33.7	36.4
Manuals	23.9	46.2	64.9	78.8	82.1
Collective farmers	29.0	21.8	16.6	13.1	12.4
Total	62.9	83.8	106.8	125.6	130.3

Source: Narkhoz Za 70 let, 1986, p. 390.

Collective farmers are now issued, like urban workers, with internal passports giving them the right to travel, they are able to join the Agricultural Workers' Trade Union and have rights to social security provisions, and they have considerable participation in the Communist Party. In 1986, 11.8 per cent of the party's total membership was constituted of collective farmers, 45 per cent were manual workers and 43.2 per cent were non-manuals ('KPSS v tsifrakh', 1986, p. 22).[4]

The traditional way of life of the peasant with its 'attachment to the soil' has been vitiated by the organization of the collective farm which controls the labour input of the farmer, fixes rates of remuneration, and determines the content of agricultural production. The collective farmer, however, is still separated – socially and economically if not politically – from the urban manual worker and non-manual employee. This may be illustrated by considering educational levels and the structures of family income and outgoings. In the census of 1979, of every 1000 manual urban workers, 351 had had a middle education, the corresponding figure for collective farmers being 220. The differences were somewhat greater for women: 350 and 201 respectively. When one considers higher (and incomplete higher) and middle specialist educational levels, differences were much more marked: 102 per 1000 for urban manuals (men and women) and 58 for collective farmers, and data for women were 41 and 19 respectively (Itogi, 1972, p. 46; *Vestnik statistiki*, 1981, p. 63). Ratios of real income between collective farmers and manual and non-manual workers have risen from 70 : 100 in 1960 to 80 : 100 in 1970 and 90 : 100 in 1984 (Narkhoz, 1985, p. 426). Measurement of the trend in real income (per employed person) shows that it has risen 4.1 times between 1940 and 1981 for manual and non-manual workers and 7.2 times for collective farmers (*Vestnik statistiki*, 1982a, p. 63). This is a significant equalizing tendency in Soviet society.

Table 7.3 Family Income and Expenditure of Industrial Workers and Collective Farmers 1960, 1970, 1984

	Workers			Collective farmers		
	1960	1970	1984	1960	1970	1984
Income						
Wages of family	74.8	74.4	72.4	8.5	8.4	9.2
Pensions, grants etc.	20.4	22.2	25.0	10.3	17.9	19.2
Collective farm earnings	–	–	–	35.3	40.0	45.2
Private farming	1.5	1.3	0.7	42.9	31.9	25.1
Other services	3.3	2.2	1.9	3.0	1.8	1.3
	100	100	100	100	100	100
Expenditure						
Food	37.9	35.7	29.4	53.2	40.4	33.6
Purchases of goods	16.8	15.5	15.1	16.0	15.7	15.6
Social and cultural services (including education and other government-provided services)	21.4	23.5	24.2	11.3	15.0	14.9
Savings	2.0	4.1	7.8	1.5	6.4	10.5
Taxes	7.5	7.9	8.8	2.2	1.3	1.6
Other outgoings	7.3	6.8	6.2	7.4	11.7	13.5
	100	100	100	100	100	100

Source: Narkhoz, 1985, p. 434.

The Soviet 'intelligentsia'

While the collective farm peasantry is in numerical decline and is destined to 'merge'[5] with the manual working class, at the other end of the scale the professional, technical and executive personnel – the 'Soviet intelligentsia' – represent the dynamic elements in Soviet society. The term 'intelligentsia' is an ambiguous one, its meaning ranging from independent political critics rooted in cultural traditions, to people who work 'with their brains'. In the contemporary USSR the Soviet intelligentsia is considered to be a social group distinguished by higher and specialized secondary education, performing superior technical, executive, or administrative work roles.[6] The Soviet intelligentsia in recent years has grown enormously in size. Taking as an index people with higher education, in 1939 there were only 1.2 million people in the USSR with complete higher education (that is, 8 per 1000 of the population aged over 10). By 1984, the number had risen to 18.5 million (82 per 1000) (Narkhoz, 1985, p. 29), and in addition there was another 3.6 million with incomplete higher and 28.2

million with a secondary specialist background. Even between 1980 and 1984 the number of specialists employed in the economy rose by 4.5 million – reaching a total of 33 million (Filippov, 1985, p. 4). The numbers of the elite of the intelligentsia – those with higher degrees – rose from just over a third of a million in 1960 to 1.4 million in 1981 (*Vestnik statistiki*, 1982b, p. 68).

Table 7.4   The Soviet Intelligentsia

	1939 mills	1959 mills	1984 mills	1987 mills
Higher education: full	1.2	8.3	18.5	20.8
incomplete	–	1.7	3.6	3.5
Middle specialist education	–	7.9	28.2	30.9
	1941	1960	1984	1986
Specialists employed in economy	2.4	8.78	33	34.6

Sources: Narkhoz v 1984g, 1985, pp. 29, 420; *Naselenie SSSR*, 1983, p. 115, *Narkhoz Za 70 let*, 1987, p. 523.

All Party Members	Education of Party Cadres					
	1971		1981		1986	
	N (mills)	%	N (mills)	%	N (mills)	%
Higher education	2.81	19.6	4.88	28	6.04	31.8
Incomplete higher education	0.337	2.4	0.391	2.2	0.398	2.1

Leading Cadres
A   Members and candidates of City, District (*raykom*) and Area (*okrug*) Committees and Auditing Commissions

	Elected prior to 26th Congress (1980–1)		Elected prior to 27th Congress (1985–6)	
	N	%	N	%
Higher education	218,069	54.8	230,926	56.7
Incomplete higher	8,535	2.1	6,408	1.6
Higher academic degrees (*uchenoe zvanie*)	5,575	1.4	5,828	1.4

B   Members and Candidates of Central Committee and Auditing Commissions of Central Committees of Union Republican Parties and Provinces (*obkom*) and Territories (*krai*) Committees.

Higher education	21,974	69.9	22,118	69.4
Incomplete higher	311	1.0	220	0.7
Higher degrees	2,193	7.0	2,295	7.2

Source: 'KPSS v tsifrakh', *Partiynaya zhizn'*, no. 4, 1986, pp. 23, 29.

The rise of this social stratum of urban non-manual personnel has great significance for the political culture of the USSR. This group has a higher level of expectations, a more sophisticated view of the world, and greater political awareness. Its role in politics is a matter of controversy. Three different approaches may be delineated in the literature: first, as an integral and loyal support of the Communist Party and the communist order of things; second, as an opposition to the communist system and a potential, if not actual, new ruling class; third, as a heterogeneous group in support of the system but with critical and specific interests.

The first line of reasoning is put by more conservative thinkers in the USSR and was the line adopted under Khrushchev. The *Soviet* intelligentsia loses the traditional role of critical opposition and becomes an integral part of society. It serves the nation and the party. Differences in style of life and material rewards are legitimate, reflecting the greater contribution of the intelligentsia to society. The essence of a socialist society, from this viewpoint, is harmony, collaboration and co-operation.

This conception is questioned by many critical writers, both in the USSR and the West. The second approach mentioned above regards the intelligentsia as a dominant social group in all modern advanced societies. In capitalist countries it is said to have displaced the old moneyed bourgeoisie and has dislodged the formally elected legislators to parliaments. The crux of the argument is that, in modern technologically advanced societies, specialized knowledge is necessary for planning and manage-ment, for innovation and achievement, and for political control and security (both internal and external). (Advocates of this point of view are Bell, 1974; Gouldner, 1979; Feher *et al.*, 1983.) In socialist societies of the Soviet type these arguments are said to have even greater force because the property-owning 'moneyed bourgeoisie' has been destroyed. (This line has been put cogently by Konrad and Szelenyi, 1979.) The 'socialist intelligentsia', then, is in a position to 'direct' society because social planning is guided by technical experts. Moreover, and as we noted above, in the disposal of surplus product a form of exploitation of the direct producers (workers and peasants) takes place. The intelligentsia, it is argued, assumes the position of ruling class rather than supportive stratum because it has a distinctive and superior level of education, and has the authority to appropriate surplus and privileges in the form of income, life-style and opportunity for self and offspring. The ideology of efficiency and effectiveness, which replaces a Marxist world view, legitimates these rights.

This approach, while being a necessary corrective to the more naive views mentioned earlier may be faulted on many counts. The various groupings of the intelligentsia (elites from the arts, sciences, administration, economy, police, military and party) lack cohesion and class identity. Ways of thinking and acting, life-styles and political power vary greatly between these groups. A white-collar position with authority and privilege is insufficient to constitute a class. Moreover, enhanced efficiency and effectiveness of the economy may lead to greater productive capacity all round allowing, for instance, the peasantry to improve greatly its relative position. While there are undoubtedly privileges (earned and unearned), the trend has been towards an equalization of 'earned' money incomes. Soviet published data are inadequately detailed to pinpoint elite incomes, though there can be no doubt that considerable advantages accrue to people in authority positions – not least from access to illegitimate forms of resources (special shops and the black market). (See review of literature in Lane, 1985, pp. 180–2.) Manual workers, moreover, have bettered their position *vis-à-vis* the technical intelligentsia and other non-manual workers, and the contemporary political leadership is seeking to reverse these trends. In Table 7.7 the manual workers' wage is calculated as 100, managerial/technical was 2.1 times greater in 1940, but only 1.1 times in 1986; the office workers' differential fell even more, from 1.09 to only 0.79 times between these two dates.

Table 7.7 Wage Ratios of Managerial/Technical, Office Workers and Manual Workers in Industry 1932–1984

	1932	1940	1960	1970	1985	1986
Workers	100	100	100	100	100	100
Managerial/Technical (ITRs)	263	210	148	136	110.1	110.4
Office workers	150	109	82	85	77.7	79.5

Sources: Narkhoz, 1985, p. 417; Za 70 let, 1987, p. 431.

The third categorization noted above – that of a heterogeneous set of groupings having different attitudes but making demands on and within the political apparatus – is the most satisfactory way to think of the intelligentsia. Groups have developed within this category with activist orientations to politics. With the processes of modernization come the spread of notions of individual and group rights. If one assumes that the political leadership is dependent on the loyal support and creativity of the intelligentsia, it seems likely that as they grow in size and maturity their opinions, particularly with respect to their professional competence, will increasingly be taken into account. However, this does not necessarily lead to 'democratization'. The political leadership is confronted by different groups of intellectuals from the arts, sciences and economy; the army, police and party also have their intellectual cadres. The 'intelligentsia', therefore, should not be considered as a homogeneous group, but rather as different constituencies with various ways of thinking and acting and presenting 'inputs' to, and even vetoes on, the political leadership. Coinciding with the rise of the Gorbachev generation, the Soviet political culture has moved from being a 'subject' one to a 'subject-participant' one. (That is, people change from being mere 'recipients' of government outputs to having in addition their own conception of their interests, see Almond, and Verba, 1963.) Gorbachev's recognition of 'deficiencies' and 'short-comings' in policy has been triggered particularly by the lack of fulfilment of the aspirations of groups of intellectuals. And the policy of *glasnost* (or public discussion) is recognition of a surge of individual and group demands. In addition, the group interests of executives and administrators may be antagonistic to govern-ment. This comes about because the maintenance of their own positions in authority may be undermined by the development of the productive forces; administrators in the government bureaucracy may hinder the growth of market forces. This is an example of what Gorbachev has called a contradiction between the forces and relations of production under socialism.

The working class

The relationship of the 'intelligentsia' to the manual working class is also much more complicated than suggested by 'ruling class' theorists. While it is an overstatement to depict the working class, as does the Soviet Constitution, as the 'leading force' in Soviet society, the working class has an influence much greater than in Western capitalist society. It acts as an effective 'veto group' both on the political elite and those who seek to increase the extraction of surplus by increasing its productivity. At least symbolically, it participates in the institutions of Soviet power. Its share of membership of the Communist Party rose from 40.1 per cent in 1971 to 45 per cent in 1986 ('KPSS v tsifrakh', 1986, p. 22), that is, a rise from 5.759 million to 6.443 million. (Of new party members the share of manual workers rose from 57 per cent (1971–5) to 59.4 per cent (1981–5), KPSS v tsifrakh', 1986, p. 21.) Approximately 10 per cent of all manual workers (in appropriate age categories) are party members. This is the political ballast of the ruling groups.

The working class has high job security; the worker is cushioned by overful employment and a labour shortage. There is lax labour discipline and low labour productivity. Nevertheless, there has been a slow but constant rise in wages coupled to low price inflation: the index of real income for manual and non-manual workers rose from 100 in 1970 to 169 in 1984 (Narkhoz, 1985, p. 426) and the number of hours worked per week fell from 48 in 1955 to 40.5 in 1984. A contented working class has been at the basis of the political stability of the Soviet system. Until the advent of Andropov it was cultivated by all Soviet leaders. However, the cost of such stability has been in terms of absenteeism, poor labour discipline, and poor quality production: in short, low labour productivity. (For details, see Lane, 1987.)

Here then is the dilemma for the Soviet political leadership. In the train of modernization, the population has come to expect a rising standard of living and a better quality of life. Partly due to the influence of the West, but also because it has been realized that people will have no incentive to work harder unless they have goods to buy, the idea of a consumer society has gained ground. 'Moral' incentives and a commitment to work as a collective duty are not regarded by the present leadership as being effective. As noted above, the falling levels of economic growth and the non-fulfilment of plans have led to widespread consumer dissatisfaction despite the fact that living standards have improved. Moreover, unlike Khrushchev who presided over a fairly quiescent population (a legacy from Stalin's ruthless suppression of dissent), the leadership of Gorbachev is confronted with a more mature and articulate people. He has been faced with external threats to security in the shape of a more assertive American and British foreign policy which can only be met by improved technology.

Changing principles of control

The policy adopted after the demise of Khrushchev was one of 'social contract'. It was predicated on consensus, harmony and social welfare and associated with leaders like Brezhnev, Suslov and Chernenko. Harmony was ensured by the unitary class system (that is, in the sense of all adults having to sell their labour power) and social welfare was conceived of in terms of gradual improvement for all within the existing system of central planning and party control. In practical terms this policy meant: a relatively slow rate of economic growth, increasing equality of *earned* incomes, low prices with high subsidies of essentials (bread, accommodation) with consequent shortages of goods in the shops – in short, a low-wage full-employment economy with job security. The ideological underpinning to this policy was the notion of 'developed socialism'. The transition to communism would be a long and protracted affair; it legitimated a slower rate of growth than that promised by Khrushchev and conceded that contradictions (for example, between town and country, between aspirations for education and skilled jobs and their provision) would continue during the period of socialism. The major organizing principle of the Brezhnev period was solidarity, the objective was to maintain social integration – even at the cost of efficiency and effectiveness. 'Moral corruption' (nepotism, bribe-taking, unearned income), lack of incentives, falling labour and capital productivity, and general complacency were the other side of the coin.

The 'modernizing' policy of Gorbachev has emphasized growth, investment, new technology, individual initiative and incentive, and discipline. The chief ideological concept is that of acceleration (*uskorenie*) of the socioeconomic development of the country, 'of the perfection of all sides of life of society'. This involves 'the reform of the material–technical bases of production, the perfection of the system of social relationships, most of all those of an economic character, the development of people, the qualitative improvement of material conditions of life and labour, and its spiritual character' (Plenum on Ideology, cited in editorial, *Sotsiologicheskie issledovaniya*, no. 2, 1985.)

Rather than a 'social contract', Andropov during his short period of rule emphasized integrity and commitment as organizing principles. He opposed the material and moral corruption of the Brezhnev era. He sought to provide a framework of discipline and law to enforce a revived 'socialist morality'. Gorbachev in turn has put much emphasis on the organizing principle of efficiency. He has stressed the role of the market and money to 'attain a superior level of organization and efficiency for the Soviet economy' (Gorbachev, *Pravda*, 16 October 1985). Increases in labour productivity are a crucial component of Gorbachev's policy: as he summed it up in his meeting with the Stakhanovites in September 1985: 'Pace, quality, thrift and organization are the main slogans of the day' (*Pravda*, 21 September 1985). In his report to the Twenty-Seventh Congress, Gorbachev emphasized the need for 'A new quality of growth: the all round intensification of production on the basis of scientific and technological progress, a structural reshaping of the economy on efficient forms of managing, organizing and stimulating labour'. This is a wager on the strong: the harder one works, the more one receives. The role of money is heightened. The improved operation of the economy is 'decisive' in the present leadership's quest for development. (See Gorbachev on the Revised Party Programme, *Pravda*, 16 October 1985.)

In this context, economic reformers in Hungary and China have introduced the 'market mechanism'. Briefly, this involves central planners fixing the macro level of bank credit and of allocating raw materials to ministries. Enterprises, however, are subject to market forces. Prices and level of output are fixed by supply and demand. This has consequences also for levels of employment and wages. In addition to changes in the state-controlled sector, there is a considerable increase in economic activity unconstrained by the state plan: there is a development of 'free trade' in agricultural production, artisan activities and services.

This system is to be only partially adopted in the USSR. 'Individual enterprise' in services and in crafts is legalized, though employment of hired labour is prohibited.[7] The reforms of industry strengthen central planning on the one hand and fortify the industrial enterprise on the other. The control of ministries under Gosplan is to be stiffened and concurrently enterprises will be given increased powers. The idea is to allocate to enterprises realistic targets for output, increases in labour productivity and product quality. The enterprise will have more autonomy in the organization of production and in the payment of wages, and there will be incentives to 'free labour', that is, to create redundancies, thereby lowering labour costs. While prices and output will be fixed in the factory's plan (given from above), surpluses may be traded freely and their prices determined by supply and demand. Enterprises will thus have financial incentives to overfulfil the plan and to economize on labour and material costs. Nevertheless, full employment at a macro level is to be ensured. 'Redundancies' will be mopped up through labour mobility. (The Soviet equivalent of 'Get on yer bike!'.)

The present leaders do not intend to carry out major structural change. They do not seek the weakening of the present hegemony of the Communist Party, the subversion of central planning by the market, or the privatization of nationalized property – though to be sure policy is unclear and ambiguous. This has disappointed many Western commentators. What are more important are *relational* changes – between polity, economy and society – and motivational principles. The notion of *glasnost* will enhance exchange of information and allow far greater public criticism. *Self*-expression promotes the public interest as does self-interest in the economy. The organizing principle of central detailed direction will be superseded by exchanges dominated by individual and unit self-interest. Money will become a more important medium in the economy and 'influence' rather than 'power' will take precedence in the dealings of the government. The party will become an agency of rule application rather than one of administration, that is, it will 'check up' on activities rather than organize them. In future the power of the party will decline, and self-interest will become a driving force.

For the worker, the concept of *self*-management (*samoupravlenie*) is linked to the brigade system. This divides the workforce up into groups contributing to a final product. All members of the brigade have responsibility for a given output and they work out production schedules. The brigade is paid by results and it distributes bonuses to its members. It is believed that the social pressure of efficient workers seeking more pay will raise the productivity of slower, careless and undisciplined workers. The brigade will legitimate the declaration of redundancies which will in turn increase members' wages and raise productivity. Self-management is a spur to greater labour productivity.

The motivating principle is individual and unit *self*-interest. Policies are designed to link workers' rewards to the quality and quantity of work they perform. Social justice is about punishing idlers and those who do not work. This brings into focus the motivating principles of discipline and control which seek to curb such 'negative phenomena' as unearned income, bribery, drunkenness, alcoholism and parasitism. These again are motivating principles of ascetic puritanical capitalism and they go some way to explaining the affinity between Margaret Thatcher and Gorbachev – a man with whom she believes one can 'do business'. I do not suggest that both equally proclaim the values of competitive capitalism, merely that both share a similar belief in an individualistic calculus as a motivating principle.

Support and opposition

What levels of support for, and opposition to, these policies are likely? At first sight (and this view will be modified later) it appears that the leadership's policy is based on alliances between the military and security forces, provincial party secretaries, groups among the intelligentsia, and the younger and skilled sections of the labour force. These interests support – though not unequivocally – the leadership for quite different reasons: the military in its concern to catch up with American technology, groups of the intelligentsia attracted by openness or *glasnost*, economists and planners who give priority to efficiency as a professional value, regional party officials who would stand to gain by decentralization, ambitious industrial managers and well-qualified workers who believe that they would benefit from a system more in accord with payment for achievement. Professional non-manual workers in occupations in the 'public sector' (teaching, medicine) may consider that payment according to 'deserts' applies particularly to them in view of Gorbachev's concern for 'social justice' and his commitment to pay rises for teachers, cultural workers and doctors. On the other side are those who stand to lose by Gorbachev's policy. These are: the government administrative elites in the industrial ministries, factory managers and administrators, older less qualified workers and the more traditional party functionaries. Life would be much more difficult for these people – their established administrative practices would be swept away. Initiative and innovation would be at a premium. In a survey conducted in Moscow in 1987, 23 per cent of the respondents recognized that 'restructuring' infringed certain people's interests (V. Ivanov interviewed in *Izvestiya*, 5 May 1987).

The greatest problem faced by the political leadership lies in the resistance of the centralized industrial ministries. Ministries should be the servants of, and responsible to, the Supreme Soviet (Parliament). In practice, however, they have developed into self-regulating bodies having a tendency to inertia and they resist outside control. John Stuart Mill (1986, p. 183), writing in 1859 on the Russian Empire said 'The Tsar himself is powerless against the bureaucratic bodies: he can send any one of them to Siberia, but he cannot govern without them, or against their will. On every decree of his they have a tacit veto, by merely refraining from carrying it into effect'. (Quotation attributed to Gorbachev on his meeting with Soviet writers in June 1986, listed by Trehub, 1986, p. 1.)

Managers would be faced with market uncertainty and more stringent output requirements. At present they largely 'write their own plans' which stipulate prices, output and wages. There is no competition, inefficiency is not shown up by market forces and no enterprise is made bankrupt. Managers seek 'realistic' plans which are not too difficult to overfulfil, and to do this they want labour reserves. This in turn ensures full employment. Workers desire job security, a not too strenuous working day and rising wages. Management and labour have a common interest in procuring a plan maximizing the level of inputs (including wages) and minimizing output. Moves towards raising labour productivity leading to redundancy would be resented and resisted.

More traditional communists oppose elements of 'modernization' on ideological grounds. The 'market' is an institution alien to planning which introduces anarchy, inequality, and diminishes political control and vitiates social priorities. The editor of *Kommunist*, R. Kosolapov (who was subsequently replaced), opposed the move to consumerism which he regarded as undermining the socialist ethic of the USSR. And the then Moscow party secretary, Boris Eltsin, insisted in his Congress speech: 'We are not going to submerge in the quagmire of consumerism'. Implications that involuntary unemployment could be consequent on labour productivity increases have been denounced as alien to socialism. Ligachev at the Congress pointed out, 'Socialism cannot allow and will not allow large groups of working people – and the count may be millions – to find themselves redundant in society as a result of scientific and technical progress, not prepared for work in new conditions'.

This kind of group interest or analysis, however, is only part of the explanation. Gorbachev's policies are not unequivocally supported by any one social group. Supporters and opponents of Gorbachev-type policies are to be found across the board of all groups and institutions. A major social divide is likely to be based on a syndrome of age, qualifications and education. The younger, better trained and more highly qualified cadres may be assumed to favour the Gorbachev line. The 33 million qualified specialists, the 16 million skilled workers who graduated from trades schools between 1960 and 1984, the ambitious factory director or party secretary (or budding secretary), the 6.8 million party members with full higher education – these are the people likely to support a policy of restructuring (*perestroika*) or acceleration (*uskorenie*) 'on the basis of scientific and technical progress . . . and efficient forms of managing, organizing and stimulating labour' (Gorbachev). They will gain at the cost of those tied to old ways, feather-bedded by administrative rules and succoured by unearned and undeserved privileges. This will occur at the expense of those untrained and unable to adapt: in the 1979 census, for example, it was reported that 60 per cent of manual workers had less than full secondary education.

Conclusions

The 'grand sweeps' of social and political concepts – totalitarian-ism, ruling class, socialism and capitalism – do not enable us to grasp the reality of social and political change in contemporary socialist societies. Their utility is ideological in the sense of masking contradictions or sustaining political claims of illegitimacy. The state capitalist approach is faulted, in my view, because of its inadequacy in locating a mechanism for the extraction of surplus; totalitarianism is incompatible with socially structured political demands. There are, of course, forms of exploitation and bureaucratic domination, but not having the determinant effects claimed by writers adopting a ruling-class paradigm. Power in the USSR is not the mutual opposition of classes over the disposition of economic surplus. Social structural analysis in terms of interests based on education and occupation is a more appropriate approach than that of ruling-class or bureaucratic domination. Policy in the Soviet Union and the dynamics of social change should be regarded as multi-dimensional and containing many contradictions. Gorbachev's stated priorities contain a drive for modernization based on self-interest, greater use of market relationships combined with traditional administrative means – the use of police to enforce discipline and to prevent 'parasitism'. He champions '*glasnost*' and advocates freedom of discussion – though within a framework of Soviet values and institutions. The interests supporting Gorbachev's reformist sweep need to compromise with the security elements and the more traditional communist functionaries. The conflicting forces of market and plan, of exchange and administrative direction, involve incompatibilities and contradictions between collective and individual interests, between need and desert.

There are a number of unknowns in predicting how these contradictions will be resolved – particularly demands stemming from international considerations. The dynamics of internal developments will lead to a wager on the strong, to greater modernization, to a weakening of job security, to more emphasis on consumerism and on money as a unit of exchange. There are likely to be higher earned money incomes for some at the cost of greater differentials. These will be less dependent on formal trade or qualification but more on the ability of a production enterprise (or units within it) to pay. Such exchanges will upset adminis-tratively sanctioned income priorities. At the same time, however, the political leadership is legitimated in terms of socialist values.

Other developments will lead to improvements for previously under-rewarded groups: pay rises for teachers and old-age pensioners. An increase in incomes of collective and state farmers will diminish even further the difference between them and urban workers. The proposed strengthening of the family and the provision of part-time and homeworking for women are likely to reduce stress but concurrently will increase inequality relative to men. The greatest tension in Soviet society will be between communist values emphasizing an ethic of social service, of goods in kind, of distribution according to need (including employment) and a more instrumental and privatized policy based on self-interest, money and market forces. This contradiction, in my view, will be resolved to the advantage of the latter. The more the USSR's policy of *rapprochement* with the leading Western capitalist states is successful, the sooner will the socialist states be drawn into the international division of labour bringing with it a greater role to market forces. However, one should not expect logically consistent outcomes but, as in all modern states, a mixture of contradictory positions reflecting political priorities and the maximization of individual interests. If one were forced to speculate, to extrapolate from recent trends, one is brought back to ideas of a certain convergence in the processes of industrial societies. The Soviet Union is moving away from the centralized plan to greater modernization, from collective solidarity to individualism, from a primacy on politics to economics. Moral ideas of a classless society, of a hegemonic Communist Party leading the working class to a world order of communism are being superseded by political pragmatism, and by an individualized consumerist morality. Freedom rather than equality will become a dominant value. People will get what they deserve according to their individual performance, not what they need. The idea of a classless society governed by conscious human decision through a plan will be replaced by increasing inequality, market exchanges and a greater role of the profit motive.[8]

Notes

1 The idea that the political leadership organizes 'around the forces of spontaneity' is developed by Furedi 1986.

2 Figures based on projections of goals of the Party Programme (1961) with their realization in 1980.

3 In Soviet Marxist terminology, collective farmers are not hired labour, and paid wages (like workers) for their efforts; they work in a collective, the means of

production belonging to the state but the produce being owned by the collective farm.

4 In 1985 the weights of these social groups in the population as a whole were: collective farmers, 12.4 per cent; manual workers, 61.6 per cent; non-manuals, 26.0 per cent (*Narkhoz v 1984g*, 1985, p. 7).

5 Due mainly to the improvement in conditions mentioned above and to the growth of agriculture in the 'state' rather than collective sector – though the number of collective farms has been stable in recent years.

6 Lower-level white-collar workers (*sluzhaschie*) are excluded here. For further discussion of Soviet interpretations see Churchward, 1973.

7 See, for example, the statutes on private trade published on 19 November, 1986. (Translated in *Current Digest of the Soviet Press*, vol. 38, no. 46, 1986, pp. 6–8.)

8 My thanks to the Peace Studies Program at Cornell University which supported some of the research in this paper.

8

Crisis and conflict in East European state socialism

HOWARD DAVIS

The spasmodic occurrence of social and political movements in postwar Eastern Europe, including the Hungarian uprising of 1956, the Prague Spring of 1968 and the emergence of Solidarity in Poland, can be compared with activity along fault lines in a normally stable geological structure. The lie of the land does not change in a fundamental way but at intervals, and often unpredictably, pressures are released which send shock waves throughout the entire area. The problem is to explain the relationship between the slow build-up of strain in the underlying structures and the relatively sudden, 'superficial' movements. The boundaries between the disciplines of economics, political science and sociology have often discouraged this kind of understanding or explanations based on the relationships between economic development, social structure and political culture in state socialist countries. Sociologists have been inclined to interpret state socialism as a type of society generating significant social inequalities and divisions which are normally held in check by a centralized and coercive one-party political system which ensures greater continuity and stability than in Western capitalism. Few have undertaken any systematic study of social movements. Political scientists have understandably concentrated their efforts on the inner workings of the party system, its pattern of recruitment, discipline, ideology and power struggles. However, they have tended to ignore questions of public opinion, popular movements, dissent, protest politics and legitimation which figure so prominently in their studies of Western political cultures.[1]

This chapter attempts to make connections between the dynamic aspects of state socialist politics and ideology and the variety of social structures in Eastern European societies. The assumption is that the categories of theory which are used to define and analyse the institutions of the economic system and social structure – economic agents, classes, strata – should play an important part in the interpretation of political processes and change because they are intrinsically related. This perspective is indebted to current developments in Western and Eastern Europe which are replacing the traditional themes of 'convergence', 'totalitarian systems' and 'state capitalism', for example, with alternatives which treat Eastern European societies and the Soviet Union as *sui generis* not a distorted or retarded version of Western societies.[2] They are assumed to have a capacity for self-transformation through internal means.

The central issue of whether there exists in state socialism a particular kind of relationship between social divisions in the sphere of production and political change at the macro level involves three distinct types of question. First, the essential character of the social relations of production needs to be defined. This has proved to be a contentious issue with different writers reiterating the themes of class theory or systems theory and disputing the definition of boundaries in the social structure, the degree of conflict between groups, forms of control and so on. The view adopted here is that state socialist societies are defined by a mode of capital accumulation in which property is publicly owned and the state planning system ultimately determines the process by which the economic surplus is produced, appropriated and distributed. The fact that this is a 'public', state-directed process gives a distinctive character to state, politics and society: they merge into a barely differentiated system. This, secondly, raises a question about the mechanisms of power and decision: the linkages between the institutions of the party, the planning system, enterprises and trade unions at the national, regional and local levels. What are the points of pressure, who can exert influence, how are decisions made? The third question or problem area relates to the interpretation of current events, especially calls for economic reform (not new, of course, but with a greater impetus and broader social dimension since Gorbachev's leadership of the Soviet Union) and parallel social and cultural changes. While each of these questions might be answered by a historical, longitudinal analysis of the development process in state socialist societies, the strategy adopted here is to focus on a structural account of tendencies towards crises and manifestations of these in the state socialist system. The term 'crisis' is used advisedly. It refers to the characteristics of the system which, without adjustment, would lead to its chronic instability, general decay, or collapse. At the political level it refers to ideas, movements, groups and associations which threaten or symbolize a threat to the prevailing order: for example, erosion of popular commitment to leading institutions, the existence of groups such as trade unions seeking 'legitimate' demands which cannot be met, and the entry of autonomous institutions such as churches into public debate. These are some of the symptoms of crisis, the causes of which lie deeper.

The chapter begins with an examination of the nature of these tendencies within state socialism: their origins, development and present direction. The second section investigates the central theme of social divisions within state socialism and their relationship to political crises, using examples from each of the major social groupings (the peasantry, working class, intelligentsia, and the elite). The third and final section is a discussion of some contemporary manifestations of social and political change and the responses to them in several East European countries.

The nature of crises within state socialism

Just as economic production and transformation in state socialism differs substantially from that of capitalism so, too, do their *economic crises* have their own unique features. While the capitalist countries experience characteristic cycles of boom and slump, or fluctuations in profitability modified by state fiscal and other measures, the state socialist countries have another distinctive pattern of recurrent crises or interruptions in the process of capital accumulation. These do not reflect market activity – since markets are not the main engines of economic development – but rather the political response to a range of problems including sluggish growth, price rises and consumer goods shortages. They reflect the planning system's limitations in organizing investment and allocating the economic surplus. Since rates of profit have not been particularly relevant performance indicators for the state socialist countries, economic crisis is manifest above all in slow rates of growth, or no growth at all. Problems of growth are not a new phenomenon but they have become general throughout Eastern Europe since the mid-1970s.

This contrasts sharply with the phase of forced industrialization in the Soviet Union when growth rates were high as the goals of industrial strength and military security were given priority over social and consumer goals. They were also high in the countries of Eastern Europe starting from a low industrial base after the Second World War. With the end of this phase and the subsequently slower transformation of the industrial structure, growth rates were less rapid and subject to more interruptions, such as occurred in Czechoslovakia in 1963 and Poland in the years up to 1970.

The economic sources of crisis have a close counterpart in social relations. The relations of production under state socialism contain a key division between the functions of capital, synonymous with the state planning function as there is no significant private ownership of capital, and the functions of labour (Davis and Scase, 1985). With regard to the first, the role of state planning is fundamental, both economically and politically: it determines the processes whereby the economic surplus is produced and appropriated. It dominates all productive activity. The functions of labour are therefore systematically subordinated to plan requirements and the general level of wages is determined by the central planning process. Accordingly, there is no direct parallel in state socialism with the endemic conflict between employers and employees over wages and working conditions in capitalism. Provided the party and planning system retains its authority (either through its ideological apparatus or simply through the appeal of a continuously increasing standard of living, or both) the division between the functions of labour and the state planning function does not engender group conflict. When the working class has been mobilized into opposition at times of crisis it has typically been an expression of discontent at the failure of the state to achieve certain planned objectives, not so much a challenge to those objectives themselves.

In contrast with the structures of capitalist societies, where the boundaries of conflict have tended to be drawn most sharply between the working class and the bourgeoisie, under state socialism it is the groups which make up the administrative class which may find themselves in direct conflict with the state planning apparatus over the goals of the plan. In fact, the state planning bureaucracy is where the symptoms of crisis are likely to be felt at an early stage. The groups and individuals most directly involved in the economic planning process have often been the first to challenge the party's decision-making monopoly. At other times a wider range of groups may be drawn into a society-wide movement, as occurred in Hungary in 1956, Czechoslovakia in 1968, and Poland in 1980.

In state socialism the economic struggles of workers or the contest of other groups over the goals of the planning system translate rapidly into political struggles because of the highly politicized nature of the system of economic management. The party-state is literally represented at every level of economic decision-making so that a challenge to economic decisions is more than likely to be seen as a challenge to the party itself. There is, however, an alternative and more widely diffused form of economic activity and social organization which avoids direct political confrontation, namely what has come to be known as the 'second economy'. It consists of income-generating activities and systems of exchange carried out by households or individuals outside the organizations of the socialist sector, although in close relationship with them. Some activities are peripheral or illegal, or both. Others, such as private agricultural production, are legitimate and gain approval for the contribution which they make within the system of state socialist production. Much discussion of the 'independent' activities lays stress either on their illegality (Grossman, 1977) or the problems of containing the second sector within a socialist political framework. In these respects, it could be said to illustrate the economic and social crisis tendencies of state socialism. On the other hand, there is increasing evidence to show that the second economy is quite thoroughly implicated in the relations of production of state socialism and that it is generally limited and controlled by the state planning system. It represents a form of 'independence' only in so far as workers are able to dispose of their own labour power. Only very rarely does it allow workers to employ others full-time and have access to capital, resources and markets on a large scale.

The second economy is therefore one type of response to the crisis tendencies of the state socialist countries because it contributes to solving problems caused by the rigidities of the command system of planning. But it is a 'solution' of limited significance because of its lack of official support and recognition. While it continues to be localized and fragmentary and to have doubtful status within state socialism, the boundaries of contact between the 'second' and the 'first' economies are unlikely to become a major focus of political movement and change.

There have been several distinct phases in the political development of Eastern Europe in the postwar period. Under the tutelage of Stalin and the Soviet Union the 'people's democracies' in Eastern Europe experienced the generally successful attempt (except in Yugoslavia) to transplant the Soviet type of political system by the consolidation of one-party rule, the development of state bureaucratic hierarchies in all areas of administration and management, and the systematic exclusion of political opposition, by force where necessary. The first systemic *political crisis* came with Stalin's death in 1953. The difficulties of managing the monolithic, bureaucratic apparatus of control had become apparent, not to mention the political costs of personal dictatorship and terror. There was, then, a period of cautious de-Stalinization originating from the party leadership and always within the framework of state socialist one-party rule. Political analysts have tended to portray this period in terms of power struggles at the top level in the Soviet Union (between Beria, Malenkov and Khrushchev) and have described the nature of the crisis as being the problem of consolidating the dictatorial system while allowing a degree of 'liberalization' in economic management. In practice there was some reorientation or relaxation of economic policy in the context of slower rates of economic growth. This has been the dominant theme in subsequent periods.

While it is true that these changes were not the direct result of pressures from below, they gave long-term significance to movements such as the workers' revolt in the German Democratic Republic in 1953, the 1956 riots in Poland and the Hungarian uprising in 1956. These events were a characteristic expression of the crisis of state socialism in its most intensive, Stalinist phase. Popular pressure invariably met with brutal repression but it contributed to the process of economic reform. In Hungary and Poland, where members of the intelligentsia and party officials as well as workers were involved in the various events and movements, there were even short-lived experiments in institutional reform, such as workers' councils.[3] Economic policies were adjusted to relax the pace of collectivization of agriculture and industrial development and to give slightly greater priority to consumption.

These measures of economic adjustment, in the period from 1953 to 1956, known as the 'New Course' were the beginning of regular, almost continuous, attempts at economic reform in Eastern Europe (and to a lesser extent in the Soviet Union). In many respects, the 'normality' imposed after the turbulence of 1956 was that of the Stalinist period and a high rate of investment and industrial development was again the major goal of economic policy.[4] However, there was an increasing acceptance that gradual reform was needed to correct the faults of overcentralization and the rigidities of the planning system. In 1963 'Guidelines for the New Economic System' were approved in the GDR and similar proposals for 'improvement' and 'reorganization' were adopted in other countries in Eastern Europe. The most significant and successful development of this kind was the adoption of the New Economic Mechanism by Hungary in 1968.

These measures were undertaken with varying economic success throughout Eastern Europe but they hardly constituted a solution to structural problems, as the experience of Hungary shows. One condition of success of a reform policy in a state socialist country is that it is initiated from the top, from the party leadership, but this is not a sufficient condition. The continuing dictatorship of the party over a largely passive and indifferent mass of producers is constantly found to be in contradiction with the aims of reform in the economic sphere. Whatever the economic merits, there tends to be a lack of political endorsement for decentralization in enterprise decision-making, the use of incentives and mechanisms for workers' and managers' self-advancement.

The critical importance of the connection between economic and political change is shown in the reform movement in Czechoslovakia in 1968. The circumstances which gave rise to the movement were similar to those in other countries (decline in the rate of economic growth, opposition between Stalinist hard-liners and reformers) but the programme of democratization instituted by Dubček after March 1968 was on a far greater scale than any previous 'reforms'. The political crisis became acute when the programme began to slip from the control of the state and party apparatus. The relaxation of many bureaucratic restrictions in political and economic life led to the creation of independent organizations and to public debate far beyond the officially sanctioned boundaries. The dilemma for the state bureaucracy was that reform was necessary for revitalizing the economy and to obtain popular support for party policies, but, at the same time, reforms would have to be strictly contained if the bureaucracy were not to lose its dominant position. The rapid spread of the changes, loss of state control and the scale of the popular movement for liberalization provoked the August invasion by the Soviet Union and subsequent 'normalization'.[5]

Only a decade later, events on a similar scale occurred in Poland, where economic circumstances were even more critical. It was apparent by the mid-1970s that economic reforms and the accumulation strategy based on large-scale borrowing from the West was failing. In 1976 increases in food prices led to an outburst of spontaneous protest. By 1979 the economic situation had deteriorated to such an extent that there was significant negative growth and popular support for the party declined from an already low level. An increasingly vocal and organized opposition eventually formed into the independent trade-union movement, Solidarity. The object of the strike movement of the summer of 1980 was initially about food prices and wage levels but these economic demands were rapidly extended into political demands for greater access to the media and the right to form free trade unions. The result was the first extensive and officially recognized opposition movement in a state socialist country. The emergence of Solidarity was, potentially, as radically disruptive as the Hungarian uprising of 1956 or the Czechoslovak reform movement of 1968, yet the outcome was significantly different. Solidarity avoided a direct political challenge to the rule of the Communist Party despite its demand for free elections to the Polish parliament and its strength in the political arena was never tested to the limit. The combined effect of a powerful trade-union movement which was 'self-limiting' in the sense that it held back from adopting the role of an opposing political party, and an incapacitated party, created a vacuum between the popular movement and the state, a situation of stalemate. The military coup of December 1981 filled the vacuum and in the familiar conditions of the aftermath of crisis in a state socialist country, there was a return to the status quo of one-party dictatorial rule, but with an acceptance of significantly more economic flexibility and ideological non-conformity within the political and military strait-jacket.

There are exogenous as well as endogenous factors in the crises of state socialism. In the early years of the Soviet Union, the project of 'building socialism in one country' was compelled to make adjustments for the hostile external environment in terms of foreign policy, military security and patterns of trade. The Second World War and the German invasion were the deepest crises the country faced. Today, although military invasion is not in prospect, other exogenous factors create circumstances which contribute to crisis tendencies. The state socialist countries form part of the world system of trade and consumption and are increasingly exposed to fluctuations in world commodity prices, flows of capital, consumer demand and political barriers to trade.

The pressures have been felt more strongly since the 1973 oil price shock and most acutely in those countries in the Soviet sphere, especially Poland and Hungary, which have become heavily indebted to Western financial institutions. However, the endogenous factors contributing to crisis are more fundamental. One of the main reasons why Eastern European countries have become more closely involved with the capitalist economic system is because they have seen this as a way to overcome endemic problems in their own system.

The economic conditions of the 1980s in the Soviet Union and the rest of Eastern Europe continue to display the symptoms of low growth, large imbalances (in trade and foreign debt), the absorption of the reserves of agricultural labour, and technological lag. With the possible exception of Hungary, these endemic problems have so far been met with few significant institutional reforms. An assessment of the future direction of economic and political reform in state socialism, including the outcome of *perestroika* in the Soviet Union, needs to recognize that at each stage of development there have been contradictory tendencies within the central planning system and the political system. The party's role has increasingly been one of directing and ensuring the success of the economy, but there are ideological and political risks entailed in such a close identification with economic performance. The first type of crisis came with the end of the phase of rapid industrialization and accumulation based on the extraction of the maximum possible surplus from the peasantry and working class. The riots and revolts of the 1950s can be understood largely in these terms. The second was a crisis of administration created by the inefficiencies of the central planning system in a more mature industrial phase. The variety of economic reforms since 1968 have been attempts to find solutions to these problems. The third and most recent form of crisis comes from exposure to the competitive pressures of the global economy, indebtedness to the capitalist countries and the relative neglect of non-industrial aspects of the economy (such as infrastructure, housing, personal consumption and cultural development). The causes overlap and interact but each crisis phase can be traced to basic contradictions between the forces and relations of production in the developing state socialist mode of production. The political and economic remedies which have been applied at successive stages have merely set the scene for the next phase of crisis. Thus, the system of state socialism is less monolithic than it appears and is often portrayed to be. It is prone to recurring economic crises and political conflicts. The following section explores the boundaries of conflict and their relationship to the broader social divisions within state socialism.

Social divisions, consent and conflict

The basic division in the production relations of state socialist societies between the categories of the population which perform the functions of state planning and those which fulfil the labour function is invariably expressed in a hierarchical system of income and institutional inequality (Davis and Scase, 1985). Some sociologists from both Eastern and Western Europe have found it appropriate to refer to this as a 'class' system (Cliff, 1974; Rakovski, 1978) but there are disagreements within both Marxist and non-Marxist analyses about the significance of the main lines of cleavage. The debate is too large and space here too limited to deal with all its ramifications.[6] It is sufficient to recognize that the boundary between the 'administrative class' and the 'working class' figures in all accounts as a significant site of social and political conflict. It may be argued, for example, that the relations of production in state socialism, like capitalism, involve economic exploitation and that both systems therefore entail class antagonism (for example, Harman, 1983). On the other hand, according to many Western and Eastern theorists, differentiation in positions within relations of production does not imply exploitation because capital and property ownership are formally socialized. The functional differences between social classes which remain are a basis for inequalities in power and prestige, and acute conflicts may emerge over the direction of the planning process, but issues relating to the appropriation of the surplus are decided in the political (that is, party) sphere. This form of class relations is sometimes described as 'non-antagonistic' in order to show the contrast with capitalism (Lane, 1982, pp. 28–33; Davis and Scase, 1985, pp. 96–8). The terminology is less than entirely helpful because it overstates the potential for class conflict in capitalism and understates the potential for conflict in state socialism. But the value of the distinction is that it draws attention to the origins of conflict within each system and to the forms which it may take.

The present divisions within the state socialist countries cannot be defined abstractly, without reference to their stage of economic development, their political history and culture. The main social groupings considered here are agricultural and industrial workers, the intelligentsia, and the party elite. This is not an exhaustive list but it includes the boundaries which have the greatest political and ideological significance within state socialism.

The industrialization of the Soviet Union and Eastern Europe has gone a long way towards eliminating the 'peasantry' as a class with strong attachment to the land and forms of ownership and production based on the household. The rural workforce diminished rapidly with migration to urban employment, and, with state or collective farming, wages and working conditions resemble more closely those of industrial workers. According to official ideology, the peasantry has been experiencing 'emancipation' from its traditional past under the leadership of the party and the working class. Other accounts describe the changes in rural industry and occupations in terms of the 'modernization' of production. In some countries, including the Soviet Union and Poland, the agricultural sector is still large (19.5 per cent and 30.1 per cent of their respective populations economically active in 1984) and relatively resistant to capital-intensive and collectivized techniques. However, even in these countries there is a definite convergence towards the industrial working class in terms of income levels and access to state services although, as Lane describes, profound social and cultural differences continue to exist between town and country (Lane, 1982, pp. 42–6). In some countries, notably the German Democratic Republic, the convergence is more complete but elsewhere it must be assumed that the incomplete transition to a socialized system of production gives the rural workforce a distinct identity. There is evidence that the values and political orientations of this group are less identified with those of state socialism than other social strata (Hill, 1975). In practice, the 'independence' of the rural population is most likely to find expression in forms of private production rather than through political expression.

Industrial manual workers, unlike agricultural workers, rarely have any 'independent' access to means of production and have the status of wage-workers in state industries, occupying a subordinate position in the processes of production and accumulation. The pattern of accelerated industrialization in state socialist countries has led to the rapid expansion of the working class (a process now reaching its limits in the most industrially developed country, the GDR), the growth of women's employment, and the integration of workers into large, hierarchically structured organizations to the virtual exclusion of small-scale artisan and craft activities. In many respects, as Lane observes (1982, p. 52), the system of occupational stratification, skill ranking and even pay, has broad similarities with that of Western capitalist societies. The functions of labour are characterized by the application of machinery to the productive process, the detailed division of labour and forms of work discipline and 'exploitation' which often parallel those in the monopoly stage of capitalism. Although the motive for production is not the pursuit of private profit, the criteria of efficiency and productivity are still applied in the competition for resources, funds, and other advantages in the centralized planning system. Since the general level of wages is determined by the state planning process and the party's control functions extend into all sectors of state activity, the potential for the coercion of industrial workers and exploitation of their labour has been very great. The political position of the stratum has been correspondingly weak. However, similarities of condition between the working class in capitalism and the working class in state socialism cannot be extrapolated into a fully fledged class analysis of social and political relations. The patterns of class awareness, collective organization and political conflict which have characterized the development of most Western capitalist societies are not found in state socialism (Davis and Scase, 1985). Conflicts which arise are likely to involve more limited claims, be less institutionalized and have administrative rather than political consequences. Typical work disputes in the Soviet Union, for example, involve employees protesting about some form of illegal practice by the management of an organization. In such cases of 'whistle-blowing', employees will appeal to the party and publicize the complaint in the press (Lampert, 1985). The hierarchical structures of state bureaucracy tend to inhibit the expression of collective views and demands which range across organizations and institutions but cannot exclude them entirely. Indeed, industrial enterprises sustain forms of internal solidarity and they can become foci in their own right against centralized control.

Work units have many vested interests and display a certain degree of solidarity in their dealings with the external environment. . . innumerable informal activities take place: the tasks and requirements which the authorities try to impose and enforce are relentlessly modified and restructured or even counteracted by the endeavours of those who act at the lowest or intermediary levels of administrative structures.

(Hamilton and Hirszowicz, 1987, p. 237)

While manual workers have been systematically integrated into the structures and institutions of the productive system, they have also been integrated into the social system in a comprehensive way through educational and cultural mechanisms and an ideology which gives positive value to the contribution of manual labour and the political role of workers. At the same time, the transformation of semi-industrial societies into developed state socialist industrial societies in only two or three generations has provided an opportunity for long-range social mobility for a significant proportion of the lower strata, as well as the prospect of movement into higher-level technical occupations. Manual workers under state socialism are less divided by the economic structures which cause fragmentation in the Western working class: large-scale unemployment, a dualistic labour market and ethnic divisions. The social and political framework of manual workers' existence also tends towards homogeneity and therefore 'incorporation' (Lane and O'Dell, 1978, pp. 50–2).

The processes of industrial development in both capitalist and state socialist societies have led to changes in the structure of skills and occupations. The GDR is probably the only country in Eastern Europe which has reached the stage of maturity at which the rise of technical specialisms on the one hand and the tendency for de-skilling to occur in areas of automated production on the other, are reinforcing social differentiation and causing problems of restructuring not unlike those in some contemporary Western capitalist countries (for example, Dennis, 1986). This stands in sharp contrast to the official view that social inequality and income differentials should diminish over time. Changes in the division of labour could therefore be a precursor of greater competition between social groups for income and privileges.

Routine non-manual workers in state socialist countries form a relatively smaller proportion of the working population than in capitalist countries. This is for a variety of reasons, including the lower levels of technical and economic development, low status and rewards of this group compared with skilled manual workers and, not least, the general ideological aversion to what is seen as 'unproductive' labour. While rates of upward mobility into the intelligentsia are relatively high, the alternatives which are available to the corresponding categories in capitalist societies (self-employment, small retail businesses and other activities of the *petite bourgeoisie*') rarely exist. The factors which make this a politically significant, if volatile, stratum in Western societies do not apply. From her study of Soviet data on lower white-collar workers, Christel Lane aptly concludes that 'this social category has become no more than a kind of shunting yard for those waiting to move to other destinations' (C. Lane, 1987, p. 193). The tendencies towards dispersal work directly against group awareness and identity so that there is no state socialist equivalent to the politics of the lower middle strata in Western capitalism.

It is generally recognized, however, that the higher qualified non-manual groups which carry out administrative functions within the state bureaucracies constitute a significant, even key, category. 'Intelligentsia' is the term most commonly used to describe these groups which include scientific, intellectual and cultural workers with higher educational qualifications: administrators and managers, scientists and engineers, teachers, doctors, lawyers, media and cultural specialists. Despite its occupational diversity some authors have seen the intelligentsia as a new, rising class in the process of formation (Djilas, 1966; Konrad and Szelenyi, 1979). It exists in a relationship of tension with the party elite, depending for all its power and influence on participation in the state bureaucratic structure and yet having a role to play in the setting of priorities for the distribution of the economic surplus. Thus, while the intelligentsia is charged to develop the scientific, productive and creative forces necessary for the construction of socialism according to the priorities of the state plan, the intelligentsia's understanding of these priorities may diverge from those of the party elite. The growth of professional influence and 'expertise' in the process of decision making previously dominated by the elite is almost certainly of greater significance for changes in the power structure than the widely publicized dissent of groups of leading intellectuals. But over against this, it must be recognized that the essential characteristics of this class or stratum derive from its position in a unitary, centrally controlled bureaucratic structure. To a far higher degree than in Western capitalist countries, the salaries, life chances and working conditions of the intelligentsia are determined by the state. This leads to their dependency rather than autonomy, conformity rather than dissent. In practice, the relative power of the administrative class or intelligentsia and the working class is variable and not always weighted towards the former. According to Hamilton and Hirszowicz (1987, p. 260) 'whenever the authorities are faced by a hard choice of whether to improve the economic position of the lower ranks of the intelligentsia or of the workers, they are aware that the discontent of the workers is by far the more damaging for the economy and more dangerous in political terms'. Education, expertise and proximity to the power elite do not guarantee political influence.

The concept of 'elite' is used here to refer to the relatively small, self-conscious group which occupies the summit positions in the hierarchical organizations of the state. To a large extent, the state socialist elite is a group defined by its political power and authority although it also has a distinctive life-style, status and privileges which come from the occupation of high office (Matthews, 1978). However, the use of the concept involves a number of problems of definition. In a hierarchical system it is not easy to identify a boundary between the highest groups and those next in line. The state socialist elite is not in a position to become a self-sustaining and closed social group because it has no legal claim to ownership of wealth or property and cannot use inheritance as a mechanism of closure. On the other hand, there are sets of positions which have national rather than local importance, exert direct influence on the political leadership, and control the activities of entire organizations. These justify the appellation 'elite', as does the method of filling these positions by appointment from a *nomenklatura* list.[7] In state socialism the cohesion of the elite is relatively high because there is less institutional separation between the state, polity and economy than in Western capitalism. This does not preclude important divisions and differences within the elite which arise from the complex processes of policy formation and divisions of responsibility between the party apparatus, the state administration, the army, the police and the centralized economic management. Hough and Fainsod (1979) argue that this amounts to a system of 'institutional pluralism' because the actors in the political structure tend to be compartmentalized and, within their own sphere, can formulate objectives and build support for them. The system of power is not monolithic or 'totalitarian' in the sense that every policy and decision is handed down from the party leadership and implemented by detailed directives to the lowest level. In some areas of policy, like transport, the amount of institutional autonomy may be relatively high while in others such as defence or foreign policy it is low. Perhaps the issue most actively contested by sections of the elite is economic management because all are directly involved.

The history of economic reforms within state socialism can also be interpreted as the political history of relations between the party and the administrative apparatus. The interest of the party in promoting controlled change in the economic sphere without political change has not always matched the interest of economic ministries in maintaining the status quo of bureaucratic administration. And the relationship between the party and economic managers has not been without variation. The years of rapid economic growth and development saw an increasing degree of identification between the two, but with accelerating problems of economic management and control there is evidence that the party has taken steps to avoid this, or at least recognizes that the political stakes are very high.

The social divisions and conflicts described so far derive from the fundamental economic and social processes of state socialism. Each of the lines of cleavage – between the rural workforce and other strata, the manual working class and non-manual groups, and between the party elite and the intelligentsia – has been significant in the history of state socialism. For example, alliances and conflicts between peasants and workers were most crucial in the early years of the Soviet Union but even today the success of economic development depends as much on the incorporation of reluctant rural communities into the system of state socialist politics and ideology as on the socialization of agricultural production. The boundary between manual and non-manual workers is typically reflected in inequalities of income, status and political power, and especially in the methods which each group is able to use to protect and enhance its position. Thus manual workers are more likely to find sources of collective strength in and through their work organizations, which can mean conflict with the state bureaucracy; the intelligentsia is more likely to be identified with the bureaucracy in the occupational sphere but the existence of a variety of artistic, religious, environmental and other movements shows that the educated strata can construct 'autonomous' spaces for activities which are not defined or controlled by the party–state. The boundary between the elite and the rest of state socialist society has changed in character according the phases of development from the early revolutionary period, through Stalinism, to attempts at economic reform. The current question for the state socialist elites is how far the present requirements for economic reform can be reconciled with dictatorial rule through the party and whether the pressures for political change will bring about a realignment of this boundary.

The above 'class' divisions in state socialism bear some resemblance to class divisions in Western capitalist societies (so, for example, it is possible to draw certain parallels between the 'service' class and the intelligentsia or between the condition of manual workers in both types of society) but they have a distinctive character which comes from state ownership of the means of production, the party–state apparatus and socialist ideology. This does not rule out the existence of other divisions within state socialism such as regional, national and gender divisions. According to circumstances these may be very pronounced and may have far-reaching consequences. For example, the ethnic question in the republics of the Soviet Union has been increasing in importance because of the changing balance of population in favour of non-Russian nationalities and the unresolved claims of certain national groups to territory or political rights (Karklins, 1986). Problems of nationality or religion, however, are not unique to state socialism and they are neither more nor less likely to occur within state socialism than elsewhere. In terms of the present analysis they may be both a contributory cause and an expression of crisis tendencies which are system-specific. The mass demonstrations in Armenia in early 1988 can be interpreted in this way: they would probably not have occurred without the background of *glasnost*, the relaxation of controls on public debate, but neither would they have occurred if there had been a political system capable of giving broader expression to national aspirations.

Opposition in Eastern Europe

Contemporary oppositional movements in the Soviet Union and the countries of Eastern Europe are an expression of the structural divisions and crisis tendencies discussed in the previous sections, but each contains a unique combination of social forces and circumstances. The purpose of this section is to consider how far they can be explained by reference to the stage reached in development of the state socialist productive system, power relations between social classes or strata, or changing patterns of political culture. Only brief details of each example can be given but the cases well illustrate the dynamics of oppositional and unofficial movements and their contribution to social change.

The emergence of Solidarity in Poland in 1980 was a landmark in the process of change in Eastern Europe because it combined the not unfamiliar demands of industrial workers for better wages and stable prices with a far-reaching and still unsatisfied challenge to the party's monopoly of power.[8] The movement was a response to the economic crisis of the 1970s which was manifested in stagnation, poor control of investment and unprecedented levels of international borrowing. The failure of the reform strategy became apparent by 1975 and in 1976 there was an outburst of spontaneous protest as food prices were increased. In contrast to 1970, when armed police fired on strikers in similar circumstances, the relatively weak party gave in to the protesters and cancelled the price decree. This strengthened the position of the workers but also gave new vitality to a variety of unofficial groups of both workers and intellectuals (Reports by the Experience and Future Discussion Group, 1981). The economic crisis worsened towards the end of the decade, living standards fell, and workers in key industries faced harsh measures to increase productivity as well as wage cuts and reduced bonus payments. An opportunity for widespread protest was provided by the ending of meat subsidies in July 1980 and it led to the mobilization of workers through local factory committees and strikes in the Baltic shipyards, the Silesian coalfields and other major industries. However, the ferment cannot simply be explained in economic terms, for wage claims quickly extended to issues of collective and personal con- sumption, political authority, and democracy in industrial relations. The independent trade union Solidarity was formed in October 1980.

Solidarity's brief history as a self-governing and self-limiting institution displays the problems of an independent organization with popular support in a state socialist country. It cannot act as a wholly legitimate opposition and the legitimacy which it does have varies inversely with the legitimacy of the party. Thus the emergence of Solidarity and its official recognition coincided with the lowest point in the history of the party, which was corrupt, internally weak and divided, and without popular support (Lewis, 1985). In spite of this, Solidarity was constrained by the threat of military intervention from the Soviet Union, the depth of the economic crisis which left little room for manoeuvre, and the influence of the Catholic church which took the role of guardian of national identity and survival. The character of the movement was given by the rupture between state and society in Poland and not simply the conflict between workers and the industrial bureaucracy. The composition of the movement was actually quite diverse and sympathy for it extended among a wide cross-section of the population. For a period, the state was forced to concede the right of Solidarity to participate legally in the political process. This was possible, however, because of the weakness of the party's position and not because of significant political reforms. It was a temporary accommodation which came to an abrupt end with the military coup in December 1981 and the restoration of party rule through martial law. Solidarity was driven underground and the issues of economic management and reform were returned to their traditional place within the state bureaucracy. It did not represent a return to the status quo because the party lost any claim it once had to represent the whole of society. The future holds out little prospect that the rift between state and society in Poland will narrow, since the resort to force was a blatant denial of the movement's aims and aspirations. The lasting significance of Solidarity is that it has been the first large-scale national movement to operate more or less freely outside the party and state apparatus in a state socialist society.

The role of the Catholic church in Poland as mediator between the state and society – or at least a significant section of society – helps to explain some of the contrasts between the movements in Hungary in 1956, Czechoslovakia in 1968 and Poland in 1980. The church was not completely identified with the opposition and chose to provide an alternative focus to Solidarity for national feeling and identity. It carefully avoided challenging the legitimacy of the party. The example of the Protestant churches in the GDR provides some interesting comparisons despite important differences in the political cultures of the two countries. The issue is clearly illustrated by the autonomous peace initiatives since 1980. The GDR is widely recognized to be a special case in Eastern Europe because of its economic prosperity, the continuity of its political personnel and policies, and the relative absence of the types of social movement which occurred in Hungary, Czechoslovakia and Poland. According to some observers, the political stability of the country, especially since the closure of the border with West Berlin in 1961, can be attributed to the congruence between the political structure and the values of the political culture (Krisch, 1986). Although the progress of economic growth has not been matched by political liberalization, it is argued that the 'industrial culture' which stresses economic achievement, the national culture, and the comprehensive range of social organizations under party guidance and control amounts to a system of political culture which harmonizes well with the political structure. Since the GDR is better equipped than other Eastern European countries to weather economic crisis and since its party apparatus is under closer scrutiny from the Soviet Union than any other, the patterns of movement and change are unlikely to stem from the economic demands of workers or from internal party conflicts. They are more likely to be expressed in conflicts over the values of the political culture among the intelligentsia and the elite and at the boundary between the 'official' and 'alternative' cultures.

In addition to the well-publicized activities of individual writers and intellectuals in the GDR which illustrate this tendency there is an institutional dimension to the process in which the churches play a significant part. The official view is that religion is a traditional element in society, but both church and state recognize that it has a role within present society. The phrase 'the church within socialism' is used to express this position and in a key announcement, the party leader Erich Honecker referred to the church as 'a self-supporting organization of social significance in socialist society' (see Sandford, 1983, pp. 15–16). This provided some endorsement for the church's role in society but not in relation to politics and the state. However, such a distinction is artificial and does not convey any sense of the bridging role which the church has been drawn into. This can be illustrated by the activities of the peace movement in the GDR.[9] On the one hand, there are the peace activities within the framework of the official political culture: the politically orthodox 'Peace Council of the GDR' and nationally co-ordinated campaigns and petitions involving a very large percentage of the population. On the other, there have been much less extensive 'autonomous peace initiatives' since 1982 which do not have a definite organizational framework and which tend to be politically and culturally non-conformist. The Dresden Peace Forum involving some 5000 young people in 1982 was such an initiative, held under church auspices. Its criticisms of militarist values in the GDR as well as in the West and the wearing of 'Swords into Ploughshares' badges were a test of the church's ability to define issues as 'social' and not 'political'. Recent years have shown that the church has provided a measure of support for alternative cultures without itself becoming identified as an oppositional movement, an 'organizational shelter for the development of an alternative political culture' (Krisch, 1986, p. 52). The issue for the longer term is whether autonomous activities are an expression of a robust political culture or a society which is set on a path towards political crisis and a rupture between the state and society.

There are formidable obstacles to political reform within the state socialist countries even though it is essential for the success of economic reforms. The examples described above illustrate the strict limits on political and cultural emancipation in present circumstances although alternatives can exist and occasionally flourish within the dominant political and ideological framework. The opposition of artists, writers and academics – for instance, in the Charter 77 movement in Czechoslovakia – is symbolically very important, but dissidents from this stratum are distanced from the centres of economic and political power. Liberalization from the 'top downwards' is inhibited by the character of the bureaucratic system and the fact that while professional and technical experts, administrators and party officials may sometimes pursue greater rationality in the running of the economy and society, the pursuit of greater freedom is likely to be construed as disloyalty to the party and state.

There are even greater obstacles to emancipation 'from below'. The examples given of collective protest should not be regarded as equivalent to labour movements within capitalism because the claims of workers cannot be admitted as just one among others in a pluralistic political system. There are no established institutions in the economic sphere for striking compromises between different occupations, strata and interest groups; there is only the party–state itself. Emancipation of subordinate groups, therefore, will require the creation of economic and political conditions for the transformation of structures at every level of society – a 'cultural revolution' (Bahro, 1978). The first requirement in any state socialist society will be some degree of relaxation in the party's monopoly of political power, either as a response to political crisis and the decay of the party apparatus or as a result of deliberate reform policies.

The prospects for change in Eastern Europe have been greatly enhanced by the reformist tone of the political leadership of the Soviet Union under Gorbachev. The themes of *glasnost* and *perestroika* will take time to make inroads into the economic and political institutions of the Soviet Union but the scale and momentum of the changes is without precedent. They appear to mark the early stages of the creation of a public space in which political conflicts will be capable of resolution by more open and democratic means. If this proves to be so, the disjointed patterns of crisis and social conflict described in this chapter will be superseded by another, more continuous, pattern which has yet to take clear shape. In Eastern Europe, the initial response to greater 'openness' in the Soviet Union was muted by the continuing in power of the older generation of party leaders represented by Honecker in the GDR and Kadar in Hungary, whose political fortunes were built on strictly limited economic reforms within the dictatorial party system. However, the leaders

213

of this generation have already been replaced in Hungary with the promise of significant political change. It is likely that the new initiatives for reform in the countries of Eastern Europe will cease to be interpreted as a threat to an immovable orthodoxy because the yardstick of Soviet orthodoxy has itself come to incorporate new measures of flexibility, diversity and participation. Whatever the outcome, the stirrings of reform already present a challenge to social and political science to produce more dynamic models of state socialist development.

Notes

1 This is not to deny that there are serious practical obstacles to the empirical study of movements in state socialist countries. It is easier to describe the history, programmes and style of independent groups than to analyse their relationship to the social and political system as a whole when reliable survey data is lacking.

2 For a discussion of the traditional themes, see Lane, 1976. Lane defines as 'state socialist' those societies modelled on the Soviet Union 'which are distinguished by a state-owned, a more or less centrally controlled, planned economy and a politically dominant Communist Party' (Lane, 1982, p. 1). See also Davis and Scase, 1985, ch. 5.

3 For an account of the workers' councils in Hungary, see Harman, 1983, ch. 7.

4 W. Brus characterizes the period 1953–6 as an interim state between two phases of development, but not a simple repetition. 'By and large, the whole period under consideration may be regarded as one of respite between two development drives, the second of which was not a simple repetition of the first' (in Kaser, 1986, p. 48).

5 See Skilling (1976) for an account of the reform movement. A remark by Gorbachev's spokesman, G. Gersimov, on an official visit to Prague in April 1987 provides an interesting gloss on these events. Asked what was the difference between Dubček and Gorbachev, he answered: 'nineteen years'. (Quoted by Z. Brzezinski in the Seton–Watson Memorial Lecture, 'Cracks in the Soviet Empire', Centre for Policy Studies, 1988.)

6 See, for example, Cliff, 1974; Rakovski, 1978; Littlejohn, 1984; and Davis and Scase, 1985, ch. 5.

7 *Nomenklatura* involves a listing of official positions, the cadres who are eligible for such positions and criteria for appointment. The criteria are political as well as technical. Definition is a problem because details are not published. For a discussion of this see Nove, 1975.

8 For a general account, see Ascherson, 1981. For a sociological analysis of Solidarity, see Touraine, 1983.

9 The most accessible source is Sandford, 1983, which contains a useful bibliography. See also Krisch, 1986.

9

Development and socialism in post-Mao China

JOHN GARDNER

Introduction

Since Mao's death in September 1976, China's leaders have sought to reverse many of the policies associated with the Cultural Revolution of 1966–76. Within a few weeks of his death, the 'Gang of Four' was being accused of 'distorting' many of his principles and policies and, by 1981, it had become established doctrine that Mao himself was responsible, at least in part, for much that had gone wrong not only in the Cultural Revolution but also in the Great Leap Forward.

Criticisms of developments since 1958 included the charge that institutions had been severely damaged. Mao's preference for ongoing mobilization in politics was seen to have resulted in grave instability, violence and injustice on a massive scale. It was further argued that 'Socialist Legality' had been undermined, proper procedures had not been followed, a personality cult on a grotesque scale had been encouraged, and Marxist ideology had been interpreted in an excessively leftist and dogmatic way. The pathological symptoms, as identified by critics, included the rise to power of ignorant and incompetent groups, vicious factionalism, and paralysed and inefficient bureaucracy, and a highly demoralized population.

Despite some real gains, it was alleged that China's economic institutions were singularly unsuited to the goals of modernization. Collectivized agriculture had failed to provide the peasants, still the bulk of the population, with adequate motivation to produce more foodstuffs. The industrial sector was characterized by rigid planning mechanisms, weak management and an undisciplined workforce. Productivity was low, quality was poor, distribution systems were inadequate, and pricing policies were often irrational. 'Self-reliance' often manifested itself as a xenophobic unwillingness to learn from the more advanced economies. Poor education and training had left China with a shortage of skilled labour power, and what it did possess was often underutilized because of deficiencies in job assignment procedures and inadequate incentives.

By the late 1970s, Deng Xiaoping had consolidated his position as China's principal leader and, aided by like-minded groups within the political elite and among various 'constituencies' throughout China, he embarked upon a bold programme of reform and modernization. Although early ambitions to achieve certain targets by the end of the century have since been recognized as unrealistic, the reforms have achieved considerable success in their attempts to shift from the egalitarianism and overly dogmatic prescriptions of the Cultural Revolution, towards more institutionalized structures which give greater prominence to economic growth. Although originally rejecting suggestions that China is losing its revolutionary purity, the reformers' attempts to build 'socialism with Chinese characteristics' contains much that would have been anathema in Mao's last years.

Thus, a vigorous 'open door' policy has transformed relations with the outside world. This has led not only to a proliferation of economic, political and social contacts, but even to the remarkable creation of enclaves in China known as 'Special Economic Zones', which combine Western capital and 'know-how' with cheap Chinese labour. In the urban areas attempts to improve industrial efficiency have included a limited attack on the 'iron rice bowl' idea whereby virtually every employee is guaranteed a job for life. Controversial price reforms have tried to relate the price of goods to their production costs.

Because of space, these particular reforms cannot be considered in this chapter. Instead, it focuses upon three major areas: (1) the political system, and (2) educational and (3) agricultural policies. In contrast with some other changes, reforms in these areas go back to the 1970s and have been particularly dramatic. Thus, a discussion of them offers an indication of what Deng and his colleagues have tried to achieve. Essentially this is to encourage the formation of a social structure which combines relatively authoritarian institutions with a renewed emphasis on education, efficiency and enterprise. In so doing, they have brought about significant changes in political, social and economic relationships.[1]

The political system

Under Deng Xiaoping, the Chinese political system has remained comparatively authoritarian but has, nevertheless, undergone considerable transformation, not least in terms of leadership style and personnel. A major development has been a move to a more collective style of leadership. Although clearly identifiable as the most important of China's leaders since 1979, Deng deliberately chose not to establish himself as *supreme* leader by assuming the chairmanship of the party. That post was given to Hu Yaobang in 1981, and in the following year it was abolished altogether, along with party vice-chairmanships, to prevent such offices being used as the basis on which to build personality cults. Deng remained a member of the Standing Committee of the Politbureau which made him one of the half-dozen most powerful men in China in 'constitutional' terms, but this did not give him significantly more influence that the other principal leaders. Deng also spoke forcefully against the earlier practices of concentrating a multiplicity of offices in a few hands on a 'life-time' basis. He eventually left the Standing Committee in October 1987.[2]

Since 1979 Deng has also attempted to establish new rules and procedures for the purposes of replacing members of the elite. In place of the vicious factionalism of the Mao era, he introduced a system whereby 'redundant' leaders can be eased out of office in a non-violent and dignified manner. Those who fall out of favour are criticized in private, but public debate of their failings is limited and in general they are allowed to 'resign' rather than be 'disgraced'. Often they are permitted to retain somewhat less senior positions as a means of cushioning their shift from power. This process was assisted in 1982 when the new party constitution established a 'Central Advisory Commission' headed by Deng himself. The qualification for membership is to be a party member for at least 40 years and the commission was established in order to encourage veterans to move from positions of power to those in which they have the status of 'elder statesmen', advising top decision-makers.

'Voluntary' resignation is also encouraged. A notable example occurred in September 1985 when over one hundred senior party leaders submitted a collective letter of resignation. Among them were ten members of the Politbureau (with an average age of 80) and sixty-four members of the Central Committee. They claimed they wished to make way for younger and more educated leaders who were better equipped to guide China on the path to modernization. They were publicly praised for their selflessness. Thousands of less senior officials have also been persuaded to step down by various inducements, including generous pension provisions and the retention of official perquisites, such as good housing and the use of cars. Less formally, some have been given assurances that their children will be favoured in the allocation of political positions.

There is, of course, a harsher side to Deng's methods. In 1983 a move to 'rectify' the party was launched to rid it of the more extreme leftist elements who had risen to power during the Cultural Revolution, together with those who were particularly incompetent and corrupt. The scope of this purge has, however, been strictly limited. It is often recognized that many of those involved in leftist excesses had been young and misled; that China could not afford the political and administrative instabilities that would result from massive dismissals; and that a shortage of well-qualified personnel made it impossible to have a 'clean sweep' in the short term. Consequently, rectification has often meant withholding promotion and shunting undesirables 'sideways' rather than dismissing them.

The principal beneficiaries of such reforms have been the younger and better educated officials. Sixty per cent of those elected to the twelfth Central Committee in 1982 were serving on the committee for the first time, two-thirds of them were under 60 years old, and a considerable number were described as 'well-qualified professionals' from various economic ministries. Seventeen per cent were 'professional and technological cadres' as opposed to a mere 2.7 per cent elected to the eleventh Central Committee in 1977, less than a year after Mao's death (*Beijing Review*, 1982, p. 38). Similarly, at the next election for the Central Committee in September 1985, three-quarters of the new members were said to have received higher education. Their average age was 50 (*Beijing Review*, 1985, p. 39). Government appointments have also favoured the relatively young; in September 1985, of the forty-five with ministerial rank, two were in their forties, twenty-two were between 50 and 59, eighteen between 60 and 69, and only three were 70 or more.

Such changes are by no means confined to the central elite. David Goodman (1986) has demonstrated that a feature of provincial political leaders between 1949 and the early 1980s was that, despite frequently large turnovers in party and government personnel, their characteristics scarcely changed. Some 80 per cent of them were born before 1919, they were almost exclusively male, and they had little by way of formal education (except for those who had been to military academies). In the 1980s, official party policy swept away most of this generation so that by 1985 the average age of provincial leaders had fallen to 53 and the proportion of leaders who had held office at this level before the Cultural Revolution was only 1.5 per cent. Indeed, some 20 per cent of them were under 45 years old. More than one-half of the provincial party secretaries were graduates. In other spheres the rise of the qualified has been even more marked. A survey of 3000 key industrial enterprises in 1985 revealed that 89 per cent of factory directors had received higher education, as had 81 per cent of all party secretaries (Goodman, 1986).

These trends are exemplified by reference to two outstanding, but quite typical, members of the elite who first reached the Central Committee in 1982. Li Peng, widely tipped as a future premier, was born in 1929. An engineering graduate, he was partly educated in the Soviet Union, and is a former vice-minister of water conservancy and power. In 1983 he became a vice-premier and, as an energy specialist, he has special competence in a sector of the economy that is crucial to China's economic development. Since 1984 he has headed various key bodies concerned with the construction of nuclear power plants, the development of rural energy, the electronics industry and environmental protection. In 1985 he was placed in charge of the newly established State Education Committee.

Qiao Shi was in his late fifties in 1982 and one of the oldest of what has been described as 'China's group of rising technocrats' (Barnett, 1985). He had a background in the steel industry, having served as a section head in the Anshan Iron and Steel Company, before becoming head of the design institute and later of the research institute of the Jiuquan Iron and Steel Corporation. He also held important party posts dealing with international affairs. His elevation to the Central Committee was followed by a spell in charge of the Central Committee's Organization Department. In 1986 he was appointed to provide fresh stimulus to the party's anti-corruption drive, originally introduced in 1982 to combat the 'less desirable' foreign influences in China.

In addition to promoting the relatively young and well educated, Deng's ascendancy has also been marked by a major reassertion of civilian leadership over the military. Under Mao the People's Liberation Army enjoyed a special political status and in 1969 – admittedly, in very unusual circumstances – gained roughly one-half of the seats on the ninth Central Committee. The 1970s saw some diminution of the army's political power and this has been reduced further in the 1980s. Thus, at the twelfth Party Congress in 1982, army representatives were 20 per cent as against 30 per cent in 1977. Among those members elected for the first time, only 15 per cent had a military background. Of the veterans who resigned in September 1985, roughly one-half were from the military. As of 1987, the Standing Committee of the Politbureau does not contain one single military representative.[3] Its representation in the National People's Congress has also declined, certain defence-oriented ministries have been restored to civilian control, and the army's role as a pressure group in competition for resources has also been dramatically reduced.

There is, of course, a danger in exaggerating the liberal tendencies of the new modernizing elite. Its members remain firmly committed to the concept of party supremacy over the political system and it has moved swiftly to suppress any challenge to it, most notably in the case of the 'Democracy Movement' of 1978–80 and the student demonstrations in favour of 'bourgeois liberalism' in late 1986. Yet its general style has four characteristics which distinguish it from that of the late Mao era. First, there is its attitude towards ideology. Deng and his colleagues have consistently reaffirmed their commitment to Marxism and socialism, but they have insisted that a critical and constructive approach be applied to ideological issues. Thus, in 1985 *Red Flag*, in arguing against dogmatism, asserted that 'it would be a big mistake to say that what the elected authorities are practising is not Marxist simply because it is not what Marx had stated'. It went on to invoke a Chinese proverb, opposing 'trimming the shoe to fit the foot'. In January 1986 it was officially claimed that although the fundamental principles of Marxism still hold true, it has a 'few conclusions that are no longer valid'. Second, there is a new insistence on institutionalism. Party and government bodies have met at the intervals duly prescribed, which is in marked contrast with the wanton flouting of such arrangements in Mao's lifetime. At the same time, there has been an attempt, albeit limited, to separate the functions of the party and the state. Third, and related to this, there have been efforts to create a proper legal system, with the enactment of legislation and rules for procedure. Extensive programmes of legal training have also been introduced. Fourth, the leadership has recognized the need for specialist expert advice, and for a measure of public discussion and criticism. Thus, in the 1980s the National People's Congress is no longer quite the 'rubber stamp' it used to be. Ministers make detailed reports to it and receive criticisms and suggestions. Deputies are more active in articulating the demands of their various 'constituents'. The press has been allowed to play a limited watch-dog role and indulge in a small amount of 'investigative journalism', exposing administrative inefficiency, abuse of power, and corruption. Research institutes, 'think-tanks', professional associations and 'intellectual forums' of every conceivable kind have been established and encouraged to provide expert input into the decision-making process. In short, China is developing a more rational and orderly approach to problem solving than in the past, and showing greater convergence with both Western and socialist models elsewhere.

Educational policies

The development of educational policies illustrates very clearly the contrasting approaches of Mao and Deng. Between 1966 and 1976 what was officially described as a 'revolution in education' was vigorously implemented, and characterized by five major features. First, 'universalization' was emphasized by the provision of primary, secondary and further education. Higher education was cut back and required to assume a more extra-mural role. Second, there were massive reforms in the curricula. Courses at all levels were drastically shortened and given an extremely practical orientation. It was often common for schools to set up their own experimental workshops and farms, for peasants and workers to teach, and for students to spend much of their time in production units. Research institutes and universities were required to give priority to immediate, practical and 'relevant' issues. Third, efforts to 'democratize' the education system involved a deliberate downgrading of those with expertise, and the appointment to positions of authority of those who were alleged to be representatives of 'the masses', but most of whom had little or no professional or technical competence. Fourth, politics permeated the entire curriculum to such an extent that even foreign languages were taught by using Mao's translated works as textbooks. Finally, methods of student selection were changed so that priority was given to those of 'good' class background and with the 'correct' political consciousness. Admission to universities was restricted to those who had worked for at least two years and had been vetted by their work units. In so far as universities were allowed to apply academic criteria, these were restricted by the use of quota systems to favour such

221

disadvantaged groups as women, national minorities and people from poor and backward geographical areas. On graduation, most students were expected to return to their various production units.

Stripped of Marxist ideology, this 'revolution in education' contained elements which were part of the conventional wisdom of educational systems elsewhere: namely, 'learning by doing', 'intermediate technology' and 'positive discrimination'. In *quantitative* terms, the achievements were remarkable. Between 1966 and 1987 the primary school population grew from 103 million to 150 million. Junior middle school enrolments increased from 11 million to 43 million and senior middle from 1,370,000 to 13,830,000. There was also a massive swing in favour of those living in the countryside: in 1965 only 9 per cent of senior middle school students were from rural areas, in 1976 the figure was 62 per cent. By 1976 women filled one-third of all university places and in the same year they made up 45 per cent of the total enrolments at primary school level. National minorities also improved their representation (*Zhongguo Jiaoyu Chengji*, 1985, pp. 22–3, 106, 196–7).[4]

There was, however, a price to be paid for this great exercise in social engineering. The radical ideas advanced by Mao and his followers were seldom implemented with sensitivity or skill and frequently manifested themselves as a crude and corrupt anti-intellectualism. Those who sought to apply high academic standards were branded as 'stinking intellectuals' and practical work often entirely replaced formal classroom instruction. The involvement of laymen placed many educational institutions under the control of those with little or no expertise and who had been selected through no discernible democratic process. They often relied on intimidation and frequently encouraged pupils to rebel against their mentors. University entrance procedures were often corrupted by cadres who used their contacts to ensure that their own children were offered places. At the same time, an emphasis on politics, as well as the general xenophobia of the period stifled intellectual and scientific creativity. Higher education suffered particularly badly. Student enrolments fell from 674,000 in 1965 to a mere 478,000 in 1970 and slowly rose to 564,000 in 1976. On the most conservative estimate, China 'lost' at least 1 million graduates during this period, and the quality of those produced was often poor. Another casualty was the network of specialized secondary schools which provided China with many of its intermediate-level technicians.

It is an indication of the severity of China's educational

difficulties that changes in policy started to be introduced as early as 1977 and well before other economic and political reforms (Gardner, 1977).[5] Deng, himself, assumed special responsibilities for education and science after his own rehabilitation that year. Since then it has been official policy to regard teachers as valued modernizers, whether they be professors of science at celebrated universities or 'engineers of the human soul' in rural primary schools. This policy has been more successful at institutions of higher education than in schools, as the occasional but persistent reports on rowdyism and the demoralization of many teachers indicates. However, attempts to give teachers and lecturers enhanced self-confidence and dignity have been genuine and sustained.

The major break with Maoism has been to restore the quality and standing of universities and other tertiary-sector establishments. The number of universities increased from 404 in 1977 to 704 in 1981 with student numbers rising from 625,000 to 1,279,000 (*Zhongguo Jiaoyu Chengji*, 1985, p. 50). By 1986 China claimed to have over 1000 tertiary institutions. Old scholars have been rehabilitated, courses lengthened, political content pruned, and productive labour has often come to mean nothing more than carrying out laboratory experiments. More importantly, competitive entrance examinations have been restored, testing students' ability across a broad range of academic disciplines. The better universities, designated as 'key points', recruit the most able of China's youth on a nation-wide basis. However, this emphasis upon examinations has given rise to the familiar phenomenon of most educational systems: the children of the better educated perform disproportionately well. Thus, as early as 1978, the party leadership had to admit that 'rather more' children of bourgeois background were being admitted to university at the expense of workers and peasants. They justified this as a regrettable necessity, given China's desperate shortage of skilled people.

A particular feature of university reforms has been the expansion of postgraduate education. In 1977 there were only 226 postgraduates in the whole of China; by 1983 there were over 37,000 (*Zhongguo Jiaoyu Chengji*, 1985, p. 113). Of even greater importance was the decision to send academics and students abroad for study visits. As early as 1980 it was claimed that 5100 students had been sent to 45 countries during the previous two years, and this drive has continued. In 1983 no fewer than 2303 foreign-educated students returned home (*Zhongguo Jiaoyu*

Chengji, 1985, pp. 126, 131). It is impossible to assess the full impact of this group on the development of Chinese society but it appears highly likely that the presence of a rapidly growing and increasingly senior cadre of individuals who have experienced several years of advanced education in the West and in Japan will have consequences which could extend well beyond the confines of science and technology. Indeed, it is increasingly evident that a minority of students and scholars sent abroad are in disciplines relating to management, economics and other social sciences, and this reflects a growing trend within China. In 1975 only 90 undergraduates were enrolled on finance and economics courses; by 1983 this figure had risen to 71,000 (*Zhongguo Jiaoyu Chengji*, 1985, p. 55).

Reforms in higher education have greatly increased the quantity and quality of graduate manpower needed to staff the higher echelons of administrative, managerial and scientific technical structures. Although many university students have grievances over living and working conditions, they can look forward to reasonably satisfying and high-status careers and have the expectation that their job placements will be more sensitive to individual skills and aspirations than in the past. At primary level, too, the educational system has remained committed to the concept of universalism and, indeed, the gradual introduction of compulsory basic education for all children. The most serious problems, in both societal and individual terms, remain at the secondary school level. Reforms in this area have involved the use of 'key point' schools, which are provided with the best-qualified teachers and comparatively good facilities, and which generally recruit on the basis of academic ability within a large catchment area. Some 'key point' schools claim to select their students from only the neighbourhoods in which they are based. However, this apparently 'neutral' policy often disguises the fact that Chinese housing policies reinforce neighbourhood divisions on the basis of socioeconomic characteristics. Thus, many 'key points' tend to be in areas where there are high proportions of university teachers, high-ranking cadres and managers. Some 'key points' are even 'attached' to celebrated universities. Defenders of the system claim that such schools are not so much 'exclusive' training institutions for the very talented as 'models for emulation', to demonstrate to other schools what can be achieved. At one school in Nanning, for example, the principal claimed in an interview with the author in 1986 that 74 per cent of his students went on to university and that this was, by no means, exceptional.

Predictably, the curriculum of 'key point' schools is almost exclusively academic.

Reforms in secondary education also involved the reintroduction of an academic curriculum into ordinary middle schools which cater for the majority. This was, perhaps, an inevitable reaction to the substitution of practical *work* for formal instruction which occurred during the Cultural Revolution, but it has had serious consequences. The major difficulty was that although the massive expansion of secondary schooling during the 1970s had been matched by a corresponding increase in teachers, many of them were unqualified. Some had not even been educated to the level at which they were expected to teach, and many had received no pedagogical training. What appeared to be favourable staff–student ratios disguised the fact that many of the teachers could only be used to teach one subject a few hours a week. Consequently, for many pupils, 'academic' education was a third-rate caricature of what was offered in the 'key point' schools. Most school-leavers had no realistic opportunity for getting into universities and they were equally ill-equipped for obtaining jobs as skilled workers.

When this became particularly apparent in the late 1970s, the leadership's first response was characteristically elitist: the worst schools were closed down. At *junior* middle level, the number of schools fell from 136,000 in 1977 to 87,000 in 1980, with pupil enrolments falling from nearly 50 million to under 45 million. At *senior* middle level, the cuts were even more severe; the number of schools was reduced from 64,900 to only 31,300 and student enrolments almost halved from 18,000,000 to 9,697,000. The burden of these cuts fell most heavily on the rural areas where the number of schools was reduced from 50,900 to 18,475 (*Zhongguo Jiaoyu Chengji*, 1985, pp. 185, 197).

The provision of poor, or at worst no, secondary education not only blighted young lives but also imposed a heavy burden on work units which had to provide its young workers with relevant skills. China has long had an extensive programme of non-formal education involving various forms of in-service, part-time, day-release, evening classes and distance learning. The system could not, however, cope with the failure of the formal institutions, and the expansion of higher education highlighted the problems. Thus, in 1982, it was reported that there was one university graduate for every middle-level technician, whereas a ratio of 1 : 3 would have been more appropriate (World Bank, 1984). However, by the 1980s the difficulties were receiving increasing attention, not least because of surveys carried out by educational research institutes, itself a sign of the new reliance placed on expertise. Research specialists were instrumental in persuading the Ministry of Education that there was a crisis and that it could not be resolved by simply modifying the system; rather, radical transformation was required. Therefore, it was officially decreed in 1982 that senior middle schools were to be reorganized, so that 50 per cent of all pupils would receive technical or vocational rather than general education by the early 1990s. Junior middle schools would also adopt a more vocational curriculum.

Although the correctness of this approach is almost universally accepted by senior educationists and officials, it has proved difficult to implement, for several reasons. Apart from the continuing shortage of good teachers, the provision of equipment remains a problem, and statistics showing the rapid transformation of schools in 'pace-setting' areas conceal a multitude of problems. Accordingly, some 'vocational' schools are relatively sophisticated institutions training business students in basic accountancy, statistics and managerial techniques while others are little more than sweat-shops filled with sewing machines where students are trained for work as machinists for the garment industry. Similarly, the tendency to group 'technical' and 'vocational' schools together obscures the fact that a majority of them are the latter rather than the former; that is, poorly equipped institutions offering rudimentary training to students who will become shop assistants and waiters, rather than skilled workers in modern factories.

A further problem is that many parents and students do not value such education. There is some evidence that the middle schools which are being made more vocational are often those in the poorest districts while the 'good' schools still attempt to cling to their more academic orientation. In May 1985, the Central Committee openly admitted that it had 'failed to make a genuine breakthrough' in its educational reforms although it stressed the need for more technical and vocational training 'for many years'. One of the major reasons, it suggested, was that 'the out-worn concept of belittling vocational and technical education is deeply rooted' (Central Committee, 1985, p. 20). To overcome this, two measures have been implemented. The first is to carry out a massive propaganda campaign to foster the idea that it is an honour to work in any trade or profession. The second is to require labour and personnel departments to introduce regulations based on the principle of 'training before employment'. All work units are to give preference to employing graduates of vocational and technical schools, and to pay them properly. Thus, the guarantee of jobs and decent wages, together with further funding for the vocational schools is likely to stimulate the growth of a technically competent stratum in China. It will also inevitably increase the social divisions between those who have and those who have not acquired modern technical skills.

Agricultural policies

When the Communist Party achieved victory in 1949 its membership was overwhelmingly made up of peasants. It was also led by people who, for the most part, had operated in a rural environment for up to twenty years and even longer. The leadership's concern for the well-being of the peasants, together with their personal knowledge of the countryside, suggested that the development of the agricultural sector would be handled with greater sensitivity and skill and according to strategies quite different from those adopted in the Soviet Union. Indeed, the worst excesses of Stalinist collectivization were avoided and the bulk of the peasantry was officially accorded a high 'status' in the People's Republic. Yet the situation at the time of Mao's death was depressing in many respects. Between 1953 and 1978 the annual average rate of growth for agriculture was about 3.2 per cent. Grain production had increased by only 10 per cent since 1952, cotton output was virtually the same, and oil crops had declined by one-quarter. On average, peasant consumption had risen by only 2 per cent a year (Goodman *et al.*, 1986, p. 35). Reasons for this poor performance include inadequate policies of population control, a shortage of readily cultivable land, and the encroachment of the expanding urban population into areas which could be used for arable farming. Many difficulties, however, were the consequences of agricultural policy *per se*. Between 1949 and 1958 China's peasant population experienced a series of radical reorganizations which concluded with the creation of the communes. These were the principal contributors to the problems of rural China in the aftermath of the Great Leap Forward and, from 1959 onwards, they underwent various reorganizations affecting, *inter alia*, levels of decision making, incentives and the extent to which private plots and free markets were tolerated. The question of what was produced was also important. As Kenneth Walker has observed, from the early 1960s to the late 1970s, an official emphasis on maximizing grain production led regional governments to plough up pasture land, to reduce the area of industrial crops, and to raise the multiple cropping index, with disastrous consequences in many areas:

> For example, the ploughing of grassland in livestock areas produced severe environmental damage so that neither grain nor livestock production prospered. The reduction of industrial crop production affected the growth of light industry and, therefore, foreign trade as well as farm incomes. And although the raising of the multiple cropping index did, at times, increase grain output, marginal costs exceeded marginal revenue and the peasants bore the consequent financial losses.
>
> (Walker, 1984, p. 783)

Following Mao's death, there was great pressure to change the system. From 1978 peasants in a number of areas, with the passive or active approval of many local officials, began to reorganize the system so that it provided them with better incentives and rewards. Many of the districts most affected were poor, and, according to earlier orthodoxy, should have gained most from collectivism. Of the various schemes introduced, the most popular has been the 'responsibility system' whereby peasant households sign a contract with the production team to which they belong. Under this scheme the land technically remains the property of the collective but is assigned to individual households for their own use. Tools are either provided by the team or purchased from it. Each contract stipulates how the household must meet specific obligations to the state by way of production quotas and taxes, and to the collective for investment and welfare services. Thereafter, it is free to dispose of its production and income as it deems appropriate (Walker, 1984, p. 787).

In October 1980 this localized introduction of family farming was endorsed at national level, and by the end of 1982 it had become the well-established norm in China. The introduction of real incentives has been accelerated by measures to increase the size of private plots and to promote the growth of a free market in agricultural produce. Prices for various agricultural products have been raised and the development of rural entrepreneurs are permitted to hire labour but local regulations designed to control this are regularly ignored by both peasants and officials. In 1984 a further stimulus was given to peasant initiative when it was recognized that the assignment of land on a short-term basis was detrimental to good husbandry, and it became permissible for households to have plots assigned to them for 15 years. Thus, in practice, private farming had been reintroduced.

These reforms have been spectacularly successful in raising output. Between 1981 and 1983 total agricultural output rose by an annual average of 8.7 per cent, in 1984 by 17 per cent, and in 1985 by 13 per cent. The official media were replete with accounts describing the transformation of many rural areas where enterprising peasants have achieved a remarkable degree of prosperity, both by farming more efficiently and by developing numerous side-line activities. A typical example of the benefits of reform is provided in a 1987 report on the rural township of Danzhou in Hunan province, where the responsibility system was introduced in 1979. Under the new arrangements some peasants completed within three months work which had previously taken a year. Apart from diversifying crop and livestock production, the township was able to establish 430 collectively owned enterprises such as processing factories, building materials plants, construction teams, transport teams and bamboo-weaving workshops. The value of Danzhou's agricultural and industrial output rose from 9.4 million yuan in 1979 to 26.4 million in 1986. The villagers' average per capita income increased from 112 to 625 yuan per year (*China Reconstructs*, 1987, pp. 32–44). In the most favoured regions, peasant households are able to enjoy incomes which are the envy of the urban professional classes. Indications of this new prosperity are found in the construction of larger and better houses, the purchase of trucks and tractors, the acquisition of much sought-after consumer goods such as televisions, videos and cameras, and the ability of peasant families to travel on sight-seeing holidays.

The reforms, then, are extremely popular with the bulk of the peasantry. Yet they are not without drawbacks. In 1985 Chen Yun, one of China's most eminent statesmen and economists, spoke for many when he expressed disquiet at the 7.5 per cent fall in the grain harvest in that year. One of the major reasons for this was that some peasants, in areas well suited for grain production, have switched to other activities which provide them with better returns. Similarly, in some areas, good arable land has been destroyed to provide ponds for profitable fish farming or housing. There has also been some weakening of political control in the countryside, over and above the diminution of high-level direction implicit in the reforms. In part, this reflects the desire of many local officials to neglect their duties in order to 'get rich first' and, in part, the growing willingness of a more affluent and independent peasantry to resist policies which they dislike. Thus, many families reject official directives on family planning and consider that heavy fines are a small price to pay for increasing their households' labour power. Moreover, peasant willingness to invest in developmentally valuable projects are often accompanied by a strengthening of traditional practices which the leadership regards as frivolous, 'feudal' and socially harmful. These include lavish expenditure on religious ceremonies and weddings. In 1987 an article in *Chinese Women* reported a 1986 survey on 'bride price' in a district of Shanxi province. It showed that this much-condemned custom appears to have continued unabated since 1949. Further, the new prosperity seems to have subjected it to inflationary pressures since, whereas in the 1970s the amount of 'bride price' demanded was of the order of 1000 to 1200 yuan, in the 1980s it has reached 5000 to 10,000 (*Inside China Mainland*, 1987, pp. 34–5).

One of the most common and noticeable consequences of the various agricultural reforms has been the exacerbation of old divisions and the creation of new ones in rural society. These are territorial in that some regions, particularly those in coastal provinces with traditions of relative prosperity and with easy access to major urban centres, have been able to surge forward. Inland provinces, on the other hand, especially in the south-west and north-west, have had fewer opportunities. The gap between the rich and the poor has also widened, even in areas of general prosperity. The principle of 'everybody eating from the same big pot' is now condemned for hindering economic advance in the past, but it did provide a safety net for the weaker members of society. The present reforms favour those who not only possess initiative, but also belong to healthy families with strong sons. It discriminates against not only the incompetent but also families who lack male offspring, or whose children have moved away. In some areas collective welfare systems have deteriorated while the growth of 'privatized' services does not always cater for those who are most in need. As early as 1982 the problems of 'families in difficulty' because of the reforms were being discussed and the rise in the number of beggars, although partly due to a loosening of controls, also testifies to the existence of real poverty in rural areas.

The situation is not so much that the poor are getting poorer as that the rich are getting richer. For example, a survey of three prefectures in Heilongjiang province studied the question of hired labour. It noted that hired labour comprised just over 1 per cent of the labour force in the areas concerned and conceded that the hiring of labour by household enterprises could bring economic benefits to both individuals and society. Most of the households hiring labour employed between one and seven persons. But in rare instances, households hiring over one hundred workers were discovered. In one of the prefectures studied, a typical income differential between employer and employee was 26 : 1 (*Inside China Mainland*, 1987, pp. 26–7). By the beginning of 1986 proponents of reform were claiming that inequalities could be kept within bounds by a combination of progressive taxation and an improvement in welfare services. Clearly, inequalities are increasing and they cannot be radically reduced without undermining many of the underlying principles of reform.

Conclusion

Under Mao, the life chances of China's citizens were partly the product of nature, nurture and luck. They also depended heavily on an officially prescribed 'class status'. In the early years of the People's Republic, 'class status' related to one's socioeconomic position before 1949 and/or one's role in working for or against Communist victory. There was a simple logic which decreed that landlords, bureaucratic capitalists and counter-revolutionaries would suffer; poor peasants, workers and revolutionary cadres and soldiers would benefit; and the 'national bourgeoisie' would occupy an intermediate position because they possessed the 'good' feature of being patriots with the 'bad' of being class exploiters. Subsequently, with the radical restructuring of society, 'class status' could be defined in terms of occupation and political standpoint. In the Cultural Revolution, the latter became almost an independent variable. However, whatever definition or combination was used, 'class status' mattered and was manipulated by those in power. Millions, who were not guilty of any real crime, suffered, including those who were simply the children of people from 'bad' class backgrounds. The system particularly disadvantaged the educated and it often favoured those with 'good' class origin or an 'acceptable' political standpoint. By the end of the 1970s, it became recognized by China's new leaders that a preoccupation with class had largely outlived its usefulness and, in the 1980s the President of the Academy of Social Sciences indicated the new approach when he claimed that one of the central tenets of 'socialism with Chinese characteristics' was a willingness to show respect for 'human resources'. Political criteria have by no means completely disappeared in determining who shall be promoted and, given the insistence on the central role of the party, it could not be otherwise. However, it is now possible for individuals to pursue their careers without constant attention to political issues. Short of a major economic or international crisis, it is difficult to envisage any return to the ultra-leftism of the Cultural Revolution. The reformers are well placed to remain in power in the 1990s, to continue to pursue their present-day efforts to temper the rigidities of central planning with some accommodation for market forces, and to allow a measure of private enterprise to exist alongside socialism and collectivism. As such, the socio-political structures of China are likely to become increasingly complex as it continues to evolve into a more pluralistic society.

Notes

1   Goodman *et al.*, 1986, provide a useful and short guide to recent developments in China.
2   Deng's principal statement on leadership is 'On the Reform of the System of Party and State Leadership' (Deng, 1983).
3   Marshal Ye Jianying had stubbornly held on to his position, but was compelled to resign through very poor health in 1985 at the age of 89.
4   *Zhonggou Jiaoyu Chengji* (*Achievement of Education in China*) is a compilation of over 500 pages, providing the most comprehensive volume of statistics on education ever produced in China.
5   Attempts to repair the damage done to education had been made by the then Minister of Education as early as 1975 but were defeated by the 'Gang of Four'.

Bibliography

Adams, M., Maybury, R., and Smith, W. (1988), 'Trends in the distribution of earnings 1973–1976', *Employment Gazette*, February, 75–82.

Advanced Systems Group Report (1985), *Advanced Manufacturing Technology* (London: NEDO).

Allatt, P. and Yeandle, S. (1986), ' "It's not fair is it?": youth unemployment, family relations and the social contract', in S. Allen, A. Waton, K. Purcell and S. Wood (eds), *The Experience of Unemployment* (London: Macmillan).

Allen, S. (1982), 'Women in local labour markets', in J. Laite (ed.), *Bibliographies on Local Labour Markets and the Informal Economy* (London: Social Science Research Council).

Allen, S. (1983), 'Production and reproduction: the lives of women homeworkers', *Sociological Review*, vol. 31, no. 4.

Allen, S. (1988), 'Gender, race and class in the 1980s', in C. Husband (ed.), *Race in Britain*, 2nd edn (London: Hutchinson).

Allen, S., and Smith, C. R. (1975), 'Minority group experience of the transition from education to work', in P. Brannen (ed.), *Entering the World of Work: Some Sociological Perspectives* (London: Department of Employment, HMSO).

Allen, S., and Wolkowitz, C. (1987), *Homeworking: Myths and Realities* (London: Macmillan).

Allen, S., Saunders, L., and Wallis, J. (eds) (1974), *Conditions of Illusion* (Leeds: Feminist Books).

Almond, G. A., and Verba, S. (1963), *The Civic Culture* (Princeton, NJ: Princeton University Press).

Anthias, F. (1980), 'Women and reserve army of labour: a critique of Veronica Beechey', *Capital and Class* 10.

Anthony, F. D. (1986), *The Foundation of Management* (London: Tavistock).

Ascherson, N. (1981), *The Polish August: The Self-Limiting Revolution* (London: Penguin Books).

Ashton, D. N. (1986), *Unemployment under Capitalism: The Sociology of British and American Labour Markets* (Brighton: Wheatsheaf).

Atkinson, J. (1984), *Flexibility, Uncertainty and Manpower Management* (Sussex: Institute of Manpower Studies, report no. 89).

Baake, E. W. (1933), *The Unemployed Man* (London: Nisbet).

Badham, R. J. (1986), *Theories of Industrial Society* (New York: St Martin's Press).

Bagnesco, A. (1977), *Tre Italie: La Problematica Territoriale dello Sviluppo Italiano* (Bologna: Il Molino).

Bahro, R. (1978), *The Alternative in Eastern Europe* (London: New Left Books).

Bamford, J. (1987), 'The development of small firms, the traditional family and agrarian patterns in Italy', in R. Goffee and R. Scase (eds), *Entrepreneurship in Europe* (London: Croom Helm).

Banton, M. (1967), *Race Relations* (London: Tavistock).

233

Banton, M. (1977), *The Idea of Race* (London: Tavistock).

Barber, A. (1985), 'Ethnic origin and economic status', *Employment Gazette* (Department of Employment, HMSO).

Barker, D. L., and Allen, S. (1976a), *Sexual Divisions and Society: Process and Change* (London: Tavistock).

Barker, D. L., and Allen, S. (1976b), *Dependence and Exploitation in Work and Marriage* (London: Longman).

Barker, M. (1981), *The New Racism* (London: Junction Books).

Barnett, A. D. (1985), *The Making of Chinese Foreign Policy* (London: Taurus).

Barraclough, G. (1974), 'The end of an era', *New York Review of Books*, 27 June, pp. 14–20.

Barraclough, G. (1975), 'The Great World Crisis I', *New York Review of Books*, 23 January, pp. 20–9.

Barraclough, G. (1976), 'The haves and the have nots', *New York Review of Books*, 13 May, pp. 31–41.

Barraclough, G. (1978a), 'Waiting for the new order', *New York Review of Books*, 26 October, pp. 45–53.

Barraclough, G. (1978b), 'The struggle for the Third World', *New York Review of Books*, 9 November, pp. 47–58.

Barnett, M., and McIntosh, M. (1982), *The Anti-Social Family* (London: Verso).

Barron, R. D., and Norris, G. M. (1976), 'Sexual divisions and the dual labour market', in D. L. Barker and S. Allen (eds), *Dependence and Exploitation in Work and Marriage* (London: Longman).

Barthelemy, P. (1982), 'Travail au noir et économie souterraine: un état de la recherche', *Travail et Emploi*, no. 12, 25–33.

Bassett, P. (1986), *Strike Free: New Industrial Relations in Britain* (London: Macmillan).

Batstone, E. (1984), *Working Order* (Oxford: Basil Blackwell).

Bawden, D. L., and Palmer, J. L. (1984), 'Social policy: challenging the welfare state', in J. L. Palmer and I. V. Sawhill (eds), *The Reagan Record: An Assessment of America's Changing Domestic Priorities* (Cambridge, Mass.: Ballinger).

Bechhofer, F., and Elliott, B. (eds) (1981), *The Petite Bourgeoisie: Comparative Studies of the Uneasy Stratum* (London: Macmillan).

Beechey, V. (1978), 'Women and production: a critical analysis of some sociological theories of women's work', in A. Kuhn and A. M. Wolpe (eds), *Feminism and Materialism: Women and Modes of Production* (London: Routledge & Kegan Paul).

Beechey, V. (1983), 'What's so special about women's unemployment?' *Feminist Review*, no. 15.

Beechey, V. (ed.) (1986a), *Women in Britain Today* (Milton Keynes: Open University Press).

Beechey, V. (1986b), 'Women's employment in contemporary Britain', in V. Beechey and E. Whitelegg (eds), *Women in Britain Today* (Milton Keynes: Open University Press), pp. 77–131.

Bell. A. (1986), *Against Racism and Fascism in Europe*, Socialist Group, European Parliament.

Bell, C., and Roberts, H., (eds) (1984), *Social Researching: Politics, Problems and Practice* (London: Routledge & Kegan Paul).

Bell, D. (1974), *The Coming of Post-Industrial Society* (London: Heinemann).

Bell, D. (1976), *The Cultural Contradictions of Capitalism* (London: Heinemann).

Bell, D. (1985), 'The social framework of the information society', in T. Forester (ed.), *The Information Technology Revolution* (Oxford: Basil Blackwell).

Bellis, P. (1979), *Marxism and the USSR* (London: Macmillan).

Ben Tovim, G., Gabriel, J., Law, I., and Stredder, K. (1986), *The Local Politics of Race* (London: Macmillan).

Berg, M. (1988), 'Women's work, mechanization and the early phases of industrialization in England', in R. E. Pahl (ed.), *On Work* (Oxford: Basil Blackwell), ch. 3.

Bethnal Green and Stepney Trades Council (1978), *Blood on the Streets: A Report on Racial Attacks in East London*.

Binns, P., and Haynes, M. (1980), 'New theories of Eastern European class societies', *International Socialism*, series 2, no. 7.

Birch, A. (1984), 'Overload, ungovernability and de-legitimation: the theories and the British case', *British Journal of Political Science*, vol. 14.

Block, F., and Hirschhorn, L. (1979), 'New productive forces and the contradictions of contemporary capitalism', *Theory and Society*, vol. 7, pp. 363–95.

Bonney, N. (1987), *Gender, Household and Social Class* (University of Aberdeen, Department of Sociology, unpublished paper).

Boris, E., and Daniels, C. (eds) (1988), *An Anthology on Homework* (Champaign, Ill.: University of Illinois Press).

Bosanquet, N. (1986), 'Interim report: public spending and the welfare state', in R. Jowell, S. Witherspoon, and L. Brook (eds), *British Social Attitudes: the 1986 Report* (Aldershot: Gower).

Bottomore, T. (1975), *Marxist Sociology* (London: Macmillan).

Bottomore, T. (1984), *Sociology and Socialism* (Brighton: Wheatsheaf).

Bottomore, T. (1985), *Theories of Modern Capitalism* (London: Allen & Unwin).

Bowles, S., and Gintis, H. (1982), 'The crisis of liberal democratic capitalism: the case of the United States', *Politics and Society*, vol. 11, no. 1, pp. 51–93.

Bowles, S., and Gintis, H. (1986), *Democracy and Capitalism: Property, Community, and the Contradictions of Modern Social Thought* (London: Routledge & Kegan Paul).

Bradley, H. K. (1987), 'Degradation and resegmentation: social and technological change in the East Midland hosiery industry 1800–1960', unpublished PhD thesis, University of Durham.

Brah, A. (1986), 'Unemployment and racism: Asian youth on the dole', in S. Allen *et al.* (eds), *The Experience of Unemployment* (London: Macmillan).

Brake, M. (1985), *Comparative Youth Culture* (London: Routledge & Kegan Paul).

Braudel, F. (1970), 'History and the social sciences: the long term', *Social Science Information*, vol. 9, no. 1, pp. 145–74.

Braverman, H. (1974), *Labor and Monopoly Capital: The Degradation of Work in the Twentieth Century* (New York and London: Monthly Review Press).

Brittan, S. (1975), 'The economic contradictions of democracy', *British Journal of Political Science*, vol. 5, pp. 129–59.

Brittan, S. (1977), *The Economic Consequences of Democracy* (London: Temple Smith).

Brittan, S. (1985), '. . . and the same old problems', *Encounter*, April.

Bromley, R., and Gerry, C. (1979), *Casual Work and Poverty in the Third World* (Chichester and New York: Wiley).

Brown, A. H. (ed.) (1985), *Political Culture and Communist Studies* (White Plains, NY: M. E. Sharpe).

Brown, A. H., and Gray, J. (eds) (1979), *Political Culture and Political Change in Communist States*, 2nd edn (London: Macmillan).

Brown, C. (1984), *Black and White in Britain: the Third Policy Studies Institute Survey* (London: Policy Studies Institute).

Brown, C. J. F., and Sheriff, T. D. (1979), 'De-industrialisation: a background paper', in F. Blackaby (ed.), De-Industrialisation (London: Heinemann).

Brown, M. (1974), Sweated Labour: A Study of Homework (London: Low Pay Unit, Pamphlet no. 1).

Brown, W. (ed.) (1981), The Changing Contours of British Industrial Relations (Oxford: Basil Blackwell).

Brown, W. (1986), 'The changing role of trade unions in the management of labour', British Journal of Industrial Relations, vol. 24, no. 2, pp. 159–68.

Brown, W., and Sissons, K. (1984), 'Industrial relations in the next decade', Industrial and Labour Relations Review, pp. 9–21.

Bruegel, I. (1979), 'Women as a reserve army of labour: a note on recent British experience', Feminist Review, no. 1.

Buchanan, D. (1983), 'Technological imperatives and strategic choice', in G. Winch (ed.), Information Technology in Manufacturing Processes (London: Rosendale).

Buchanan, D., and Boddy, D. (1983), Organisations in the Computer Age: Technological Imperatives and Strategic Choice (Aldershot: Gower).

Burawoy, M. (1983), 'Between the labour process and the state', American Sociological Review, vol. 45, pp. 587–605.

Burton, C. (1985), Subordination: Feminism and Social Theory (Sydney: Allen & Unwin).

Carlo, A. (1974), 'The socio-economic nature of the USSR', Telos, no. 21.

Castells, M. (1975), 'Immigrant workers and class struggle in advanced capitalism', Politics and Society, Vol. 5, pp. 33–66.

Castles, S., and Kosack, G. (1973), Immigrant Workers and Class Structure in Western Europe (London, Institute of Race Relations and Oxford: Oxford University Press).

Castles, S., Booth, H., and Wallace, T. (1984), Here for Good (London: Pluto Press).

Central Committee of the Communist Party of China (1985), Decision on the Reform of China's Educational Structure (Beijing: Foreign Press).

Central Statistical Office (1986), Social Trends, no. 16 (London: HMSO).

Central Statistical Office (1987), Social Trends, no. 17 (London: HMSO).

Chadwick, M. (1983), 'The recession and industrial relations', Employee Relations, vol. 5, no. 5.

Child, J. (1985), 'Managerial strategies, new technology and the labour process', in D. Knights, H. Willmot, and D. Collinson (eds), Job Redesign (Aldershot: Gower).

China Reconstructs (1987), August.

Churches Committee on Migrant Workers (1987), Migrant Women Speak (London and Geneva: Search Press and World Council of Churches).

Churchward, L. (1973), The Soviet Intelligentsia (London: Routledge & Kegan Paul).

Clegg, S., Boreham, P., and Dow, G. (1986), Class, Politics and the Economy (London: Routledge & Kegan Paul).

Cliff, T. (1963), Russia: A Marxist Analysis (London: Socialist Review).

Cliff, T. (1974), State Capitalism in Russia (London: Pluto Press).

Cockburn, C. (1986), 'Women and technology: opportunity is not enough', in K. Purcell, S. Wood, A. Waton and S. Allen (eds), The Changing Experience of Employment (London: Macmillan).

Cohen, G. A. (1978), Karl Marx's Theory of History: A Defence (Princeton, NJ: Princeton University Press).

Coles, R. (1986), 'School leaver, job seeker, dole reaper: young and unemployed in rural England', in S. Allen, A. Waton, K. Purcell and S. Wood, The Experience of Unemployment (London: Macmillan).

Comer, L. (1974), *Wedlocked Women* (Leeds: Feminist Books).

Cooke, P. (1982), 'Class relations and uneven development in Wales', in G. Day *et al.*, *Diversity and Decomposition in the Labour Market* (Aldershot: Gower).

Coombs, R. (1985), 'Automation, management strategies and labour-process change', in D. Knights, H. Willmot and D. Collinson (eds), *Job Redesign* (Aldershot: Gower), pp. 142–70.

Coulson, M., Branka, M., and Wainwright, H. (1975), 'The housewife and her labour under capitalism – a critique', *New Left Review*, Jan.–Feb.

Coyle, A. (1982), 'Sex and skill in the organisation of the clothing industry', in J. West (ed.), *Work, Women and the Labour Market* (London: Routledge & Kegan Paul).

Coyle, A. (1984), *Redundant Women* (London: The Women's Press).

Crouch, C. (1979), 'The state, capital and liberal democracy', in C. Crouch (ed.), *State and Economy in Contemporary Capitalism* (London: Croom Helm).

Crozier, B. (1979), *The Minimum State* (London: Hutchinson).

Cunnison, S. (1986), 'Gender, consent and exploitation among sheltered housing wardens', in K. Purcell, S. Wood, A. Waton and S. Allen (eds), *The Changing Experience of Employment* (London: Macmillan).

Curran, J. (ed.) (1984), *The Future of the Left* (Cambridge: Polity Press).

Current Digest of the Soviet Press (1986), vol. 38, no. 46, pp. 6–8.

Current Digest of the Soviet Press (1987), vol. 39, no. 18, pp. 5–6.

Dalla Costa, M. (1972), *The Power of Women and the Subversion of the Community* (Bristol: Falling Wall Press).

Davis, A. (1982), *Women, Race and Class* (London: The Women's Press).

Davis, H. (1980), *Beyond Class Images* (London: Croom Helm).

Davis, H. (ed.) (1986), *Ethics and Defence* (Oxford: Basil Blackwell).

Davis, H. (1987), 'Independent economic activity under state socialism', in R. Goffee and R. Scase (eds), *Entrepreneurship in Europe: the Social Processes* (London: Croom Helm).

Davis, H., and Scase, R. (1985), *Western Capitalism and State Socialism* (Oxford: Basil Blackwell).

Davis, J. (1972), 'Gifts and the UK economy', *Man*, vol. 7, no. 3, pp. 408–29.

Davis, M. (1986), *Prisoners of the American Dream: Politics and Economy in the History of the US Working Class* (London: New Left Books).

Delphy, C. (1984), *Close to Home* (London: Hutchinson).

Deng, Xiaoping (1983), 'On the reform of the system of party and state leadership', in *Selected Works of Deng Xiaoping* (Beijing).

Dennis, M. (1986), 'Degradation or humanisation? Work and scientific–technical progress in the GDR', in M. Gerber (ed.), *Studies in GDR Culture and Society 6* (Lanham, Md: University Press of America).

Department of Employment (1987a), '1984 Census of Employment and Revised Employment Estimates', *Employment Gazette*, January, pp. 31–7.

Department of Employment (1987b), 'Membership of Trade Unions in 1985', *Employment Gazette*, vol. 95, no. 2 (February), pp. 84–6.

Dex, S. (1985), *The Sexual Division of Work* (Brighton: Wheatsheaf).

Dex, S., and Shaw, L. B. (1986), *British and American Women at Work: Do Equal Opportunities Policies Matter?* (London: Macmillan).

Ditton, J. (1977), 'Perks, pilferage and the fiddle', *Theory and Society*, vol. 4, pp. 1–38.

Djilas, M. (1966), *The New Class: An Analysis of the Communist System* (London: Allen & Unwin).

Doeringer, P. B., and Bosanquet, N. (1973), 'Is there a dual labour market in Great Britain?' *Economic Journal*, June.

Drewnowski, J. (ed.) (1982), *Crisis in the East European Economy: the Spread of the Polish Disease* (London: Croom Helm).

Duffield, M. (1985), in *Race and Labour in Twentieth Century Britain* (London: Frank Cass).

Economic Commission for Europe (1985), *The Economic Role of Women in the ECE Region* (New York: United Nations).

Economist (1983), 4 June.

Economist Intelligence Unit (1982), *Coping with Unemployment: The Effects on the Unemployed Themselves* (London: EIU).

Edmonds, J., and Reilly, J. M. (1985), *Global Energy: Assessing the Future* (New York: Oxford University Press).

Edwards, P. K. (1985a), 'Managing labour relations through the recession', *Employee Relations*, vol. 7, no. 2, pp. 3–7.

Edwards, P. K. (1985b), 'Managing through the recession: the plant and the company', *Employee Relations*, vol. 7, no. 3, pp. 4–8.

Edwards, P. K., and Scullion, H. (1982), *The Social Organisation of Industrial Conflict* (Oxford: Basil Blackwell).

Edwards, R. C. (1979), *The Contested Terrain* (London: Heinemann).

Edwards, R. C., Reich, M., and Gordon, D. M. (eds) (1975), *Labour Market Segmentation* (Lexington: D. C. Heath).

Eisenberg, P., and Lazarsfeld, P. F. (1938), 'The psychological effects of unemployment', *Psychological Bulletin*, vol. 35.

Eisenstein, H. (1984), *Contemporary Feminist Thought* (London: Allen & Unwin).

Elliott, B. (1984), 'Cities in the eighties: the growth of inequality', in P. Abrams and R. Brown (eds), *UK Society; Work, Urbanism and Inequality* (London: Weidenfeld & Nicolson).

Elliott, B., and McCrone, D. (1987), 'Class, culture and morality: a sociological analysis of the new conservatism', *The Sociological Review*, vol. 35.

Elliott, B., Bechhofer, F., McCrone, D., and Black, S. (1982), 'Bourgeois social movements in Britain: repertoires and responses', *The Sociological Review*, vol. 30.

Elliott, B., *et al.* (1988), 'Anxieties and ambitions: the petite bourgeoisie and the new right in Britain', in D. Rose (ed.), *Social Stratification and Economic Decline* (London: Hutchinson).

European Trade Union Institute (1985), *Flexibility and Jobs – Myths and Realities* (Brussels: ETUI).

Feher, F., Heller, A., and Markus, G. (1983), *Dictatorship over Needs* (Oxford: Basil Blackwell).

Feige, E. L. (1979), 'How big is the irregular economy?' *Challenge*, Nov.–Dec., pp. 5–13.

Fermman, L. A., Berndt, L., and Selo, E. (1978), *Analysis of the Irregular Economy: Cash Flow in the Informal Sector* (University of Michigan/Wayne State University).

Fevre, R. (1984), *Cheap Labour and Racial Discrimination* (Aldershot: Gower).

Fevre, R. (1986), 'Contract work in the recession', in K. Purcell, S. Wood, A. Waton and S. Allen (eds), *The Changing Experience of Employment* (London: Macmillan).

Filippov, F. R. (1985), 'Nauchno-tekhnicheski progress i sovershenstvovanie sotsial'noy struktury sovetskogo obshchestva', *Sotsiologicheskie issledovaniya*, no. 4.

Fine, B., and Harris, L. (1985), *The Peculiarities of the British Economy* (London: Lawrence & Wishart).

Foudi, R., Stankiewicz, F., and Vaneecloo, N. (1982), Les chomeurs et l'économie informelle, in *Travail Noir, Productions Domestiques et Entraide*. (Lille: Laboratoire d'Analyse des Systèmes et du Travail, University of Lille), pp. 11–24.

Fox, A. (1974), *Beyond Contract: Work, Power, and Trust Relations* (London: Faber).

Fox, A. (1985), *History and Heritage* (London: Allen & Unwin).

Francis, A. (1986), *New Technology at Work* (Oxford: Clarendon Press).

Francis, A., Snell, M., William, P., and Winch, G. (1982), 'The impact of information technology at work', in L. Bannon, U. Barry and O. Holst (eds), *Information Technology: Impact on the Way of Life* (Dublin: Tycooly International), pp. 182–94.

The Free Nation (1978), 'Quangos "the outriders of the corporatist state" ', August, pp. 4–17.

Freeman, D., Clark, J., and Soete, L. (1982), *Unemployment and Technical Innovation* (London: Frances Pinter).

Friedman, M. (1962), *Capitalism and Freedom* (Chicago: University of Chicago Press).

Frobel, H., Heinrichs, J., and Kreye, O. (1980), *The New International Division of Labour* (Cambridge: Cambridge University Press).

Furedi, F. (1986), *The Soviet Union Demystified: A Materialist Analysis* (London: Junius).

Gabor, I. R. (1985), 'Second economy: general lessons of the Hungarian experience' (in Hungarian), *Valosag*, vol. 2, 2, 19–37. (Reprinted in a modified form in a forthcoming volume edited by Paul Hare, London: Allen & Unwin).

Gaertner, W., and Wenig, A. (1985), *The Economics of the Shadow Economy* (New York and Heidelberg: Springer).

Galasi, P. (1985), 'Extra income and labour market position', in P. Galasi and G. Sziráczki (eds), *Labour Market and Second Economy* (Frankfurt and New York: Campus Verlag).

Galasi, P., and Sziráczki, G. (eds) (1985), *Labour Market and Second Economy in Hungary* (Frankfurt and New York: Campus Verlag).

Galbraith, J. (1968), *The New Industrial State* (London: Penguin).

Galtung, J. (1973), *The European Community: A Superpower in the Making* (Oslo and London: Universitetsforlaget/Allen & Unwin).

Gamarnikow, E., Morgan, D., Purvis, J., and Taylorson, D. (eds) (1983), *Gender, Class and Work* (London: Heinemann).

Gamble, A. (1986), 'The political economy of freedom', in R. Levitas (ed.), *Ideology and the New Right* (Oxford: Basil Blackwell).

Game, A., and Pringle, R. (1983), *Gender at Work* (Sydney: Allen & Unwin).

Gardiner, J. (1976), 'Political economy of domestic labour in capitalist society', in D. L. Barker and S. Allen (eds), *Dependence and Exploitation in Work and Marriage* (London: Longman).

Gardner, J. (1977), 'Chou Jung-hsin and Chinese education', *Current Scene*, November–December.

Gardner, J. (1982), *Chinese Politics and the Succession to Mao* (London: Macmillan).

Garnsey, E., Rubery, J., and Williamson, F. (1985), 'Labour market structure and work-force divisions', in R. Deem and G. Salaman (eds), *Work, Culture and Society* (Milton Keynes: Open University Press), pp. 40–76.

Gerry, C. (1985), 'The working class and small enterprises in the UK recession', in N. Redclift and E. Mingione (eds), *Beyond Employment* (Oxford: Basil Blackwell).

Gershuny, J. I. (1979), 'The informal economy: its role in industrial society', *Futures*, pp. 3–15.

Gershuny, J. I. (1983), *Social Innovation and the Division of Labour* (Oxford: Oxford University Press).

Gershuny, J. (1987), 'The leisure principle', *New Society*, 13 February, pp. 10–13.

Gershuny, J., and Pahl, R. E. (1979/80), 'Work outside employment: some preliminary speculations', *New Universities Quarterly*, vol. 34, Winter.

Gilbert, M. (1981), ' A sociological model of inflation', *Sociology*, vol. 15, no. 2, pp. 185–209.

Gill, C. (1985), *Work, Employment and the New Technology* (Cambridge: Polity Press).

Gill, T., and Whitty, L. (1983), *Women's Rights in the Workplace* (London: Penguin).

Gilroy, P. (1987), *There Ain't No Black in the Union Jack* (London: Hutchinson).

Glatzer, W., and Berger, R. (1988), 'Household composition, social network and household production in Germany', in R. E. Pahl (ed.), *On Work* (Oxford: Basil Blackwell), ch. 23.

Glucksman, M. (1986), 'In a class of their own? Women workers in the new industries in inter-war Britain', *Feminist Review*, no. 24.

Glyn, A., and Harrison, J. (1980), *The British Economic Disaster* (London: Pluto Press).

Goffee, R., and Scase, R. (1985), *Women in Charge: The Experiences of Female Entrepreneurs* (London: Allen & Unwin).

Goffee, R., and Scase, R. (1987), *Entrepreneurship in Europe* (London: Croom Helm).

Goldring, M. (1987), 'The Thatcher effect: two nations on the same street', *The Listener*, 2 April, pp. 12–13.

Goldthorpe, J. H. (1978), 'The current inflation: towards a sociological account', in F. Hirsch and J. H. Goldthorpe (eds), *The Political Economy of Inflation* (London: Martin Robertson), pp. 186–216.

Goldthorpe, J. H. (1983), 'Women and class analysis: in defence of the conventional view', *Sociology*, vol. 17, no. 4.

Goldthorpe, J. H. (1984), 'Women and class analysis: a reply to replies', *Sociology*, vol. 18, no. 4.

Goldthorpe, J. H. (1985), 'The end of convergence: corporatist and dualist tendencies in modern western societies', in *Order and Conflict in Contemporary Capitalism* (Oxford: Oxford University Press).

Goldthorpe, J. H., Lockwood, D., Bechhofer, F., and Platt, J. (1969), *The Affluent Worker in the Class Structure* (Cambridge: Cambridge University Press).

Goodman, D. (1986), 'The National CCP Conference of September 1985 and China's leadership changes', *China Quarterly*, March.

Goodman, D., Lockett, M., and Segal, G. (1986), *The China Challenge* (London: Routledge & Kegan Paul).

Gorbachev, M. S. (1986), 'Report to 27th Party Congress, 25 February', *Pravda*, 26 February.

Gordon, D. M., Edwards, R., and Reich, M. (1982), *Segmented Work: Divided Workers* (Cambridge: Cambridge University Press).

Gordon, P. (1983), *White Law: Racism in the Police, Courts and Prison* (London: Pluto Press).

Gordon, P. (1985), *Policing Immigration: Britain's Internal Controls* (London: Pluto Press).

Gorz, A. (1982), *Farewell to the Working Class* (London: Pluto Press).

Gough, I. (1979), *The Political Economy of the Welfare State* (London: Macmillan).

Gough, I. (1983), 'Thatcherism and the welfare state', in S. Hall and M. Jacques (eds), *The Politics of Thatcherism* (London: Lawrence & Wishart).

Gouldner, A. (1979), *The Future of Intellectuals and the Rise of the New Class* (Macmillan).

Grossman, G. (1977), 'The "second economy" of the USSR', *Problems of Communism*, vol. 26, no. 5, pp. 25–40.

Grossman, G. (1982), 'The "shadow economy" in the socialist sector of the USSR', in NATO Economics Directorate – Proceedings of an Annual Colloquium 1982, *The CMEA Five-Year Plan (1981–1985) in a New Perspective* (Brussels: NATO).

Grunberg, L. (1986), 'Workplace relations in the economic crisis', *Sociology*, vol. 20, no. 4, pp. 503–31.

Guardian (1987), 'Battle looms over NEDO', 13 July.

Gutmann, P. M. (1977), 'The subterranean economy', *Financial Analyst's Journal*, Nov.–Dec.

Habermas, J. (1976), *Legitimation Crisis*, trans. T. McCarthy (London: Heinemann).

Hailsham, Lord (1978), *The Dilemma of Democracy* (London: Collins).

Hakim, C. (1987a), 'Homeworking in Britain, *Employment Gazette*, vol. 95, no. 2. Reprinted in R. E. Pahl (ed.) (1988), *On Work* (Oxford: Basil Blackwell).

Hakim, C. (1987b), *Home-based work in Britain*, Research Paper no. 60 (London: Department of Employment).

Hamilton, M., and Hirszowicz, M. (1987), *Class and Inequality in Pre-Industrial Capitalist and Communist Societies* (Brighton: Wheatsheaf).

Hall, S. (1983), 'The great moving right show', in S. Hall and M. Jacques (eds), *The Politics of Thatcherism* (London: Lawrence & Wishart).

Hall, S. (1986), 'No light at the end of the tunnel', *Marxism Today*, December.

Halsey, A. H. (1987), 'Britain's class society', Guardian, 13 July.

Harman, C. (1983), *Class Struggles in Eastern Europe* (London: Pluto Press).

Harris, C. C. (1987), *Redundancy and Recession* (Oxford: Basil Blackwell).

Harrison, P. (1985), *Inside the Inner City* (London: Penguin).

Harvey, D. (1982), *The Limits to Capital* (Oxford: Basil Blackwell).

Hayek, F. (1976a), *The Road to Serfdom* (London: Routledge & Kegan Paul).

Hayek, F. (1976b), *The Constitution of Liberty* (London: Routledge & Kegan Paul).

Heilbroner, R. (1977), *Business Civilization in Decline* (London: Penguin).

Heilbroner, R. (1985), *The Nature and Logic of Capitalism* (New York and London: W. W. Norton).

Heinze, R. G., and Olk, T. (1982), 'Development of the informal economy: a strategy for resolving the crisis of the welfare state, *Futures*, June, pp. 189–204.

HMSO (1987), *The Government's Expenditure Plans 1987–88 to 1989–90* (London: HMSO).

Heseltine, M. (1987), *Where There's a Will* (London: Hutchinson).

Hesselman, L. (1983), 'Trends in European industrial intervention', *Cambridge Journal of Economics*, June.

Hewitt, P. (1975), *Rights for Women* (London: National Council for Civil Liberties).

INDUSTRIAL SOCIETIES

Hilferding, R. (1981), *Finance Capital: A Study of the Latest Phase of Capitalist Development*, trans. M. Watnick and S. Gordon (London: Routledge & Kegan Paul). First published in 1910.

Hill, I. H. (1975), 'The end of the Russian peasantry?', *Soviet Studies*, vol. 27, no. 1.

Hirsch, F. (1977), *Social Limits to Growth* (London: Routledge & Kegan Paul).

Hirschman, A. O. (1982), *Shifting Involvements: Private Interest and Public Action* (Princeton, NJ: Princeton University Press).

Hirszowicz, M. (1980), *The Bureaucratic Leviathan: A Study in the Sociology of Communism* (London: Martin Robertson).

Hobsbawm, E. (1968), *Labouring Men* (London: Weidenfeld).

Hobsbawm, E (1981), 'The forward march of labour halted?', in E. Hobsbawm, M. Jacques and F. Mulhern, *The Forward March of Labour Halted?* (London: Verso/NLB).

Hobsbawm, E. (1984), 'Marx and history', *New Left Review*, no. 143 (Jan.–Feb.), pp. 39–50.

Hodgson, P. E. (1983), *Our Nuclear Future?* (Belfast and Ottawa: Christian Journals).

Hogan, J. J. (1987), 'President Reagan's fiscal policies: the record of his first term', *Politics*, vol. 7, no. 1, pp. 14–20.

Hogg, S. (1985), 'Making sense of the jobless numbers', The Times, 24 June.

Hope, E., Kennedy, M., and de Winter, A. (1976), 'Homeworkers in north London', in D. L. Barker and S. Allen (eds), *Dependence and Exploitation in Work and Marriage* (London: Longman).

Hough, J. F., and Fainsod, M. (1979), *How the Soviet Union is governed* (Cambridge, Mass.: Harvard University Press).

Hunt, A. (1980), 'Some gaps and problems arising from government statistics on women at work', *Women and Government Statistics*, EOC Research Bulletin, no. 4, Autumn.

Hunt, J. (1982), 'A woman's place is in her union', in J. West (ed.), *Work, Women and the Labour Market* (London: Routledge & Kegan Paul).

Hurstfield, J. (1986), 'Women's unemployment in the 1930s: some comparisons with the 1980s' in S. Allen, S. Waton, K. Purcell and S. Wood (eds), *The Experience of Unemployment* (London: Macmillan).

Huws, U. (1982), *Your Job in the Eighties* (London: Pluto).

Huws, U. (1984), *The New Homeworkers: New Technology and the Changing Location of White Collar Work*, Pamphlet no. 28 (London: Low Pay Unit).

Hyman, R. (1985), 'Managerial strategies in industrial relations and the control of labour', in K. Lilja, K. Rasenen and R. Tainio (eds), *Problems in the Redescription of Business Enterprises*, Helskinki School of Economics, pp. 9–41.

Hyman, R. (1985), 'Managerial strategies in industrial relations and the control of labour', in K. Lilja, K. Rasenen and R. Tainio (eds), *Problems in the Redescription of Business Enterprises*, Helsinki School of Economics, pp. 9–41. alternative strategies', *Capital and Class*, vol. 15, pp. 115–49.

Hyman, R., and Price, R. (1979), 'Labour statistics', in J. Irvine, I. Miles and J. Evans (eds), *Demystifying Social Statistics* (London: Pluto Press).

Ignatieff, M. (1984), *The Needs of Strangers* (London: Chatto & Windus).

ICHIESTA (1986), Special symposium: *Economia Informale, Strategie familiari e Mezzogiorno*, no. 74 (October–December).

Inside China Mainland (1987), (Taipeh).

Institute of Race Relations (1979), *Police against Black People*, Evidence submitted to the Royal Commission on Criminal Procedure.

242

Itogi vsesoyuznoy perepisi naseleniya 1970g (1972), vol. 5.

Jahoda, M. (1982), *Employment and Unemployment: A Social Psychological Analysis* (Cambridge: Cambridge University Press).

Jahoda, M., Lazarsfeld, P. F., and Zeisal, H. (1933), *Marienthal* (London: Tavistock).

James, S. (1975), *Sex, Race and Class* (Bristol: Falling Wall Press).

Jenkins, C., and Sherman, B. (1979), *The Collapse of Work* (London: Eyre Methuen).

Jessop, B., Bonnett, B., Bromley, S., and Ling, T. (1984), 'Authoritarian populism, two nations, and Thatcherism', *New Left Review*, no. 147 (Sept.–Oct.), pp. 32–60.

Jones, B. (1982), 'Destruction or redistribution of engineering skills', in S. Wood (ed.), *The Degradation of Work?* (London: Hutchinson), pp. 179–200.

Jones, B., and Rose, M. (1986), 'Re-dividing labour: factory politics and work reorganization in the current industrial transition', in K. Purcell, S. Wood, S. Allen and A. Waton (eds), *The Changing Experience of Work* (London: Macmillan), pp. 35–57.

Jones, Caradog, D. (ed.) (1934), *The Social Survey of Merseyside* (Liverpool: Liverpool University Press).

Joseph, G. I., and Lewis, J. (1981), *Common Differences* (New York: Anchor Books).

Joshua, H., and Wallace, T. (1983), *To Ride the Storm: the 1980 Bristol 'Riot' and the State* (London: Heinemann).

Karklins, R. (1986), *Ethnic Relations in the USSR* (Winchester, Mass.: Allen & Unwin).

Kaser, M. C. (ed.) (1986), *The Economic History of Eastern Europe 1919–1975. Vol III Institutional Change within a Planned Economy* (Oxford: Clarendon Press).

Katz, H., and Sabel, C. (1985), 'Industrial relations and industrial adjustment in the car industry', *Industrial Relations*, vol. 24, no. 3, pp. 295–315.

Kautsky, K. (1971), *The Class Struggle*, trans. W. E. Bohn (New York: W. W. Norton). First published in 1892.

Kavanagh, D. (1987), *Thatcherism and British Politics: The End of Consensus?* (Oxford: Oxford University Press).

Kelly, J. (1985), 'Management's redesign of work: labour process, labour markets and product markets', in D. Knights, H. Willmot and D. Collinson (eds), *Job Redesign* (Aldershot: Gower), pp. 30–52.

Kerr, C., Dunlop, T., Harbison, F., and Mayers, C. A. (1973), *Industrialism and Industrial Man* (London: Penguin).

Keynes, J. M. (1972), 'Economic possibilities for our grandchildren' (1930), in *The Collected Writings of John Maynard Keynes*, Vol. IX: *Essays in Persuasion* (London: Macmillan).

Kilpatrick, A., and Lawson, T. (1980), 'On the nature of industrial decline in the UK', *Cambridge Journal of Economics*, March.

King, A. (1976), 'The problem of overload', in *Why is Britain Becoming Harder to Govern?* (London: BBC).

King, D. (1987), *The New Right* (London: Macmillan).

King, R., and Nugent, M. (1979), *Respectable Rebels* (London: Hodder & Stoughton).

Kitwood, T. (1984), 'A farewell wave to the theory of long waves', *Universities Quarterly*, vol. 38, no. 2, pp. 158–78.

INDUSTRIAL SOCIETIES

Klein, T., Merz, J., and Wolff, K. (1986), *Poverty, Secondary Occupation and Household Production*, Working Paper no. 214, Sonderforschungbereich 3 Mikroanalytische Grundlagen der Gesellschatspolitik, J. W. Goethe-Universität Frankfurt and Universität Mannheim, September.

Kohn, M. L. (in press), 'Cross-national research as an analytic strategy', *American Sociological Review*.

Konrad, G., and Szelenyi, I. (1979), *Intellectuals on the Road to Class Power* (Brighton: Harvester).

Korpi, W. (1983), *The Democratic Class Struggle* (London: Routledge & Kegan Paul).

'KPSS v tsifrakh' (1986), *Partiynaya zhizn*, no. 14.

Krieger, J. (1986), *Reagan, Thatcher, and the Politics of Decline* (Cambridge: Polity Press).

Krisch, H. (1985), *The German Democratic Republic: The Search for Identity* (Boulder, Colo.: Westview).

Krisch, H. (1986), 'Changing political culture and political stability in the German Democratic Republic', *Studies in Comparative Communism*, vol. 19, no. 1, Spring, pp. 42–53.

Kristol, I. (1979), *Two Cheers for Capitalism* (New York: Mentor Books).

Kudat, A., and Sabuncuoglu, M. (1980), 'The changing composition of Europe's guest-worker population', *Monthly Labor Review*, vol. 103, no. 10, pp. 10–17.

Kumar, K. (ed.) (1971), *Revolution: The Theory and Practice of a European Idea* (London: Weidenfeld & Nicolson).

Kumar, K. (1977), 'Continuities and discontinuities in the development of industrial societies', in R. Scase (ed.), *Industrial Society: Class, Cleavage and Control* (London: Allen & Unwin).

Kumar, K. (1978), *Prophecy and Progress: The Sociology of Industrial and Post-Industrial Society* (London: Penguin).

Kumar, K. (1983), 'Pre-capitalist and non-capitalist factors in the development of capitalism: Fred Hirsch and Joseph Schumpeter', in A. Ellis and K. Kumar (eds), *Dilemmas of Liberal Democracies: Studies in Fred Hirsch's Social Limits to Growth* (London: Tavistock).

Kumar, K. (1987), *Utopia and Anti-Utopia in Modern Times* (Oxford: Basil Blackwell).

Kumar, K., and Ellis, A. (eds) (1983), *Dilemmas of Liberal Democracies* (London: Tavistock).

Labour Research Department (1986), *Part-Time Workers*.

Lambeth, London Borough of (1981), *Final Report of the Working Party into Community/Police Relations in Lambeth* (Lambeth Borough).

Lampert, N. (1985), *Whistleblowing in the Soviet Union: Complaints and Abuses under State Socialism* (London: Macmillan).

Land, H. (1976), 'Women: supporters or supported?' in D. L. Barker and S. Allen (eds), *Sexual Divisions and Society* (London: Tavistock).

Lane, C. (1987), 'The impact of the economic and political system on social stratification and social mobility: Soviet lower white-collar workers in comparative perspective', *Sociology*, vol. 21, no. 2, May, pp. 171–98.

Lane, D. (1976), *The Socialist Industrial State* (London: Allen & Unwin).

Lane, D. (1982), *The End of Social Inequality? Class, Status and Power under State Socialism* (London: Allen & Unwin).

Lane, D. (1985), *Soviet Economy and Society* (Oxford: Basil Blackwell).

Lane, D. (1987), *Soviet Labour and the Ethic of Communism* (Brighton: Wheatsheaf).

244

Lane, D. (ed.) (1988), *Elites and Political Power in the USSR* (London: Allen & Unwin).

Lane, D., and O'Dell, F. (1978), *The Soviet Industrial Worker* (Oxford: Martin Robertson).

Lefort, C. (1986), *The Political Forms of Modern Society: Bureaucracy, Democracy, Totalitarianism* (Oxford: Basil Blackwell).

Leiss, W. (1978), *The Limits to Satisfaction: On Needs and Commodities* (London: Marion Boyars).

Lenin, V. I. (1960), 'The state and revolution', in *Selected Works in Three Volumes* (Moscow: Foreign Languages Publishing House), Vol. 2, pp. 301–420. First published in 1917.

Lenski, G. (1978), 'Marxist experiments in destratification: an appraisal', *Social Forces*, vol. 57, no. 2, December.

Leonard, D., and Speakman, M. A. (1986), 'Women in the family: companions or caretakers?' in V. Beechey and E. Whitelegg (eds), *Women in Britain Today* (Milton Keynes: Open University Press).

Levykin, I. T. (1984), 'K voprosu ob integral 'nykh pokazatelyakh sotsialisticheskogo obraza zhizhi', *Sotsiologicheskie issledovaniya*, no. 2.

Lewis, P. G. (1985), 'Political legitimacy in communist Poland', in D. Held, J. Anderson, B. Gieben, S. Hall, L. Harris, P. Lewis, N. Parker and B. Turok (eds), *States and Societies* (Oxford: Basil Blackwell).

Leys, C. (1985), 'Thatcherism and British manufacturing: a question of hegemony', *New Left Review*, no. 151 (May–June), pp. 5–25.

Lipset, S. M. (1981), 'Whatever happened to the proletariat?', *Encounter*, vol. 56, June, pp. 18–34.

Littlejohn, G. (1984), *A Sociology of the Soviet Union* (London: Macmillan).

Littler, C., and Salaman, G. (1984), 'The social organisation of work', in K. Thompson (ed.), *Work, Employment and Unemployment* (Milton Keynes: Open University Press).

Liverpool Black Caucus (1986), *The Racial Politics of Militant in Liverpool* (Liverpool and London: Merseyside Area Profile Group and Runnymede Trust).

Lockwood, D. (1986), 'Class, status and gender', in R. Crompton and M. Mann (eds), *Gender and Stratification* (Cambridge: Polity Press).

Low Pay Unit (1988).

Luxemburg, R. (1972), *The Accumulations of Capital – An Anti-Critique*, trans. R. Wichman (New York and London: Monthly Review Press). First published in 1921.

Lyon, D. (1986), 'From "post-industrialism" to "information society": a new social transformation?' *Sociology*, vol. 20, no. 4, pp. 577–88.

McCrone, D., and Elliott, B. (1982), *The City: Patterns of Domination and Conflict* (London: Macmillan).

McInnes, J. (1987), *Thatcherism at Work* (Milton Keynes: Open University Press).

McKee, L., and Bell, C. (1986), 'His unemployment, her problem: the domestic and marital consequences of male unemployment', in S. Allen, A. Waton, K. Purcell and S. Wood (eds), *The Experience of Unemployment* (London: Macmillan).

McLennan, G. (1984), 'Contours of British politics', G. McLennan, D. Held and S. Hall (eds), in *State and Society in Modern Britain* (Cambridge: Polity Press).

Macmillan, H. (1938), *The Middle Way* (London: Macmillan).

Maddison, A. (1982), *Phases of Capitalist Development* (Oxford and New York: Oxford University Press).

Maier, C. (1978), 'The politics of inflation in the twentieth century', in F. Hirsch and J. H. Goldthorpe (eds), *The Political Economy of Inflation* (London: Martin Robertson), pp. 37–72.

Malcolmson, R. W. (1988), 'Ways of getting a living in eighteenth century England'. Reprinted in R. E. Pahl (ed.), *On Work* (Oxford: Basil Blackwell), ch. 2.

Malthus, T. (1985), *An Essay on the Principles of Population* (London: Penguin). First published in 1798.

Manchester Guardian Weekly (1987), 29 March.

Mandel, E. (1974), 'Ten theses on the social and economic laws governing the society between capitalism and socialism', *Critique*, no. 3.

Manwaring, T., and Wood, S. (1985), 'The ghost in the labour process', in D. Knights, H. Willmot and D. Collinson (eds), *Job Redesign* (Aldershot: Gower), pp. 171–96.

Marsden, D., Morris, T., Willman, P., and Wood, S. (1985), *The Car Industry* (London: Tavistock).

Marshall, G. (1983), 'Some remarks on the study of working-class consciousness', *Politics and Society*, vol. 12, no. 5, pp. 263–301.

Marshall, G., Rose, D., Vogler, C., and Newby, H. (1985), 'Class, citizenship, and distributional conflict in modern Britain', *British Journal of Sociology*, vol. 36, no. 2, pp. 259–84.

Martin, J., and Roberts, C. (1984), 'Women and employment', *A Lifetime Perspective* (London: Department of Employment/Office of Population Censuses and Surveys, HMSO).

Martin, R. (1987), 'The quiet triumph of the new realism', *Times Higher Education Supplement*.

Martin, R., and Wallace, J. (1984), *Working Women in Recession* (Oxford: Oxford University Press).

Marx, K. (1954), *Capital*, Vol. I, trans. S. Moore and E. Aveling (Moscow: Foreign Languages Publishing House).

Marx, K. (1959), *Capital* (Foreign Languages Publishing House).

Marx, K. (1959), *Capital*, Vol. III (Moscow: Foreign Languages Publishing House).

Marx, K. (1968), *Theories of Surplus Value* (Moscow: Foreign Languages Publishing House).

Marx, K. (1973), *Grundrisse*, trans. M. Nicolaus (London: Allen Lane).

Marx, K., and Engels, F. (1962), *Selected Works in Two Volumes* (Moscow: Foreign Languages Publishing House).

Massey, D. (1983), 'The shape of things to come', *Marxism Today*, no. 27.

Massey, D. (1984), *Spatial Divisions of Labour* (London: Macmillan).

Mattera, P. (1985), *Off the Books* (London and Sydney: Pluto Press).

Matthews, J. (1984), *Good and Mad Women* (Sydney: Allen & Unwin).

Matthews, M. (1978), *Privilege in the Soviet Union* (London: Allen & Unwin).

Matthews, S. H. (1982), 'Re-thinking sociology through a feminist perspective', *American Sociologists*, vol. 17, no. 1.

Mayer, A. J. (1981), *The Persistence of the Old Regime: Europe to the Great War* (New York: Pantheon Books).

Megert, W. van (1972), *Stranger in our Community* (Amsterdam: Keesings).

Melotti, U. (1977), *Marx and the Third World* (Macmillan).

Merritt, G. (1982), *World out of Work* (London: Collins).

Middlemas, K. (1979), *Politics in Industrial Society: The Experience of the British System* (London: Andre Deutsch).

Middlemas, K. (1986), *Power, Competition and the State Vol. 1. Britain in Search of Balance, 1940–1961* (London: Macmillan).

Middlemas, K. (1987), 'The life in death of the corporate state', New Statesman, 26 June.

Mies, M. (1986), Patriarchy and Accumulation on a World Scale (London: Zed Books).

Miles, R. (1982), Racism and Migrant Labour (London: Routledge & Kegan Paul).

Miles, R., and Phizacklea, A. (1980), Labour and Racism (London: Routledge & Kegan Paul).

Mill, J. S. (1986), On Liberty (London: Penguin).

Miller, S. M. (1986), 'New welfare state models and mixes', Social Policy, vol. 17, no. 2, pp. 10–18.

Millett, K. (1971), Sexual Politics (London: Sphere).

Mills, G. B. (1984), 'The budget: a failure of discipline', in J. L. Palmer and I. V. Sawhill (eds), The Reagan Record: An Assessment of America's Changing Domestic Priorities (Cambridge, Mass.: Ballinger).

Millward, N., and Stevens, M. (1987), British Workplace Industrial Relations 1980–84 (Aldershot: Gower).

Mingione, E. (1983), 'Informalization, restructuring and the survival strategies of the working class', International Journal of Urban and Regional Research, vol. 7, no. 3, pp. 311–39.

Mingione, E. (1985), 'Social reproduction of the surplus labour forces: the case of Italy', in N. Redclift and E. Mingione, Beyond Employment: Household, Gender and Subsistence (Oxford: Basil Blackwell).

Mingione, E. (1988);, Work and informal activities in urban southern Italy in R. E. Pahl (ed.), On Work (Oxford: Basil Blackwell), ch. 25.

Mitchell, J., and Oakley, A. (eds) (1986), What is Feminism? (Oxford: Basil Blackwell).

Mitter, S. (1986), 'Industrial restructuring and manufacturing homework: immigrant women in the UK clothing industry', Capital and Class, no. 27.

Moe, T. M. (1985), 'The politicized presidency', in J. E. Chubb and P. E. Peterson (eds), The New Direction in American Politics (Washington, DC: The Brookings Institution).

Moore, R. S. (1977a), 'Migrants and the class structure of Western Europe', in R. Scase (ed.), Industrial Society: Class, Cleavage and Control (London: Allen & Unwin).

Moore, R. S. (1977b), Racism and Black Resistance in Britain (London: Pluto Press).

Moore, R. S. (1982), The Social Impact of Oil (London: Routledge & Kegan Paul).

Moore, R. S. (1986), 'Immigration and racism' in R. Burgess (ed.), Exploring Society (London: Longman).

Moore, R. (1988), 'Afterword' in J. Lewis, M. Porter and M. Shrimpton, Women, Work and the Family in the British, Canadian and Norwegian Offshore Oilfields (London: Macmillan).

Moore, R. S., and Wallace, T. (1975), Slamming the Door (London: Martin Robertson).

Morgan, D. H. J. (1986), 'Gender' in R. G. Burgess (ed.), Key Variables in Social Investigation (London: Routledge & Kegan Paul).

Morokvasic, M., et al. (1986), 'Small firms and minority groups', International Sociology, vol. 1, no. 4, pp. 397–419.

Moser, C. (1978), 'Informal sector or petty commodity production: dualism or dependence in urban development', World Development, vol. 6, no. 9.

Moss, R. (1977), The Collapse of Democracy (London: Sphere).

Murray, F. (1983), 'The decentralisation of production – The decline of the mass-collective worker', Capital and Class, vol. 22.

Myrdal, A., and Klein, V. (1968), *Women's Two Roles: Home and Work* (London: Routledge & Kegan Paul).

Narkhoz SSSR v 1984g (1985), *Narodnoe khozyaystvo v SSSR v 1984g* (Moscow).
Narkhoz SSSR v 1985g (1986), *Narodnoe khozyaystvo v SSSR v 1985g* (Moscow).
Navarro, V. (1985), 'The 1984 election and the new deal: an alternative explanation' (in two parts), *Social Policy*, vol. 15, no. 4, pp. 3–10, and vol. 16, no. 1, pp. 7–17.
Nettl, J. P. (1981), quoted in M. Wiener, *English Culture and the Decline of the Industrial Spirit, 1850–1980* (London: Penguin).
Newby, H., Vogler, C., Rose, D., and Marshall, G. (1985), 'From class structure to class action: British working class politics in the 1980s', in B. Roberts, R. Finnegan and D. Gallie (eds), *New Approaches to Economic Life* (Manchester: Manchester University Press).
Nichols, T. (1986), *The British Worker Question* (London: Routledge & Kegan Paul).
Northcott, J., and Rogers, P. (1984), *Micro-electronics in British Industry* (London: Policy Studies Institute).
Northcott, J., Forgarty, M., and Trevor, M. (1985a), *Chips and Jobs* (London: Policy Studies Institute).
Northcott, J., Knetsch, W., and De Lestapis, B. (1985b), *Microelectronics in Industry, An International Comparison* (London: Policy Studies Institute).
Nove, A. (1975), 'Is there a ruling class in the USSR?', *Soviet Studies*, vol. 27, no. 4.
Nowak, S. (1976), 'Meaning and measurement in comparative studies', in S. Nowak (ed.), *Understanding and Prediction: Essays in the Methodology of Social and Behavioural Theories* (Dordrecht, Holland: Reidel), pp. 104–32.

Oakley, A. (1981), *Subject Women* (Oxford: Martin Robertson).
Oakley, A., and Oakley, R. (1979), 'Sexism in official statistics', in J. Irvine, I. Miles and J. Evans, *Demystifying Social Statistics* (London: Pluto Press).
Oberdorfer, D. (1987), in *Manchester Guardian Weekly*, 5 April.
OCIPE/CCP (Office Catholique sur les problèmes européens), (1979), 'Sur les droits de l'homme en Europe', pp. 22–44 and 'Les droits des immigrés', *Objectif Europe*, no. 5, June.
O'Connor, J. (1973), *The Fiscal Crisis of the State* (New York: St Martin's Press).
O'Connor, J. (1984), *Accumulation Crisis* (New York and Oxford: Basil Blackwell).
O'Connor, J. (1987), *The Meaning of Crisis: A Theoretical Introduction* (New York and Oxford: Basil Blackwell).
OECD (1980), *Women and Employment Policies for Equal Opportunities* (Paris).
OECD (1985), *The Integration of Women into the Economy* (Paris).
OECD (1986a), *Flexibility in the Labour Market: the Current Debate* (Paris).
OECD (1986b), *Employment Outlook* (Paris).
Offe, C. (1985), *Disorganized Capitalism: Contemporary Transformations of Work and Politics* (Cambridge: Polity Press).
Offe, C., and Keane, J. (1984), *Contradictions of the Welfare State* (London: Hutchinson).
O'Higgins, M. (1980), *Measuring the Hidden Economy: A Review of Evidence and Methodologies* (London: Outer Circle Policy Unit).
O'Higgins, M. (1985), 'The relationship between the formal and hidden economies: an exploratory analysis for four countries', in W. Gaertner and A. Wenig (eds), *The Economics of the Shadow Economy* (New York and Heidelberg: Springer), pp. 127–43.

Pahl, R. E. (1984), *Divisions of Labour* (Oxford and New York: Basil Blackwell).

Pahl, R. E. (1987), 'Does jobless mean workless? Unemployment and informal work', *Annals AAPSS*, 493 (September), pp. 34–46.

Pahl, R. E. (ed.) (1988a), *On Work: Historical, Comparative and Theoretical Approaches* (Oxford and New York: Basil Blackwell).

Pahl, R. E. (1988b), 'Some remarks on informal work, social polarisation and the social structure', *International Journal of Urban and Regional Research*, June.

Pahl, R. E., and Wallace, C. (1985), 'Household work strategies in economic recession', in N. Redclift and E. Mingione (eds), *Beyond Employment* (Oxford: Basil Blackwell), ch. 6.

Pahl, R. E., and Wallace, C. (1987), 'Neither angels in marble nor rebels in red: privatisation and working-class consciousness', in D. Rose (ed.), *Social Stratification and Economic Decline* (London: Hutchinson).

Panitch, L. (1980), 'Recent theorisations of corporatism: reflections on a growth industry', *British Journal of Sociology*, vol. 31, no. 2.

Parker, G. (1988), 'Who cares? A review of empirical evidence from Britain', in R. E. Pahl (ed.), *On Work* (Oxford: Basil Blackwell), pp. 496–512.

Parkin, F. (1972), *Class, Inequality and Political Order* (London: Paladin).

Parkin, F. (1979), *Marxism and Class Theory: A Bourgeois Critique* (London: Tavistock).

Parry, R. (1986), 'Social policy', in H. Drucker, P. Dunleavy, A. Gamble and G. Peele (eds), *Developments in British Politics 2* (London(Macmillan).

Parsons, T. (1943), 'The kinship system of the contemporary United States', *American Anthropologist*, vol. 45.

Paukert, L. (1984), *The Employment and Unemployment of Women in OECD Countries* (Paris: OECD).

Pearson, R. (1986), 'Female workers in the First and Third Worlds: the "greening' of women's labour', in K. Purcell, S. Wood, A. Waton, and S. Allen (eds), *The Changing Experience of Employment* (London: Macmillan).

Phillips, A., and Taylor, B. (1980), 'Sex and skill: notes towards a feminist economics', *Feminist Review*, no. 6.

Phillips, K. (1982), 'Post-conservative America', *New York Review of Books*, 13 May, pp. 27–32.

Phizacklea, A. (ed.) (1983), *One Way Ticket* (London: Routledge & Kegan Paul).

Phizacklea, A., and Miles, R. (1980), *Labour and Racism* (London: Routledge & Kegan Paul).

Pickvance, G. (1986), 'Comparative urban analysis and assumptions about causality', *International Journal of Urban and Regional Research*, vol. 10, no. 2, pp. 162–84.

Piore, M. J. (1975), 'Notes for a theory of labour market stratification', in R. C. Edwards, M. Reich and D. M. Gordon (eds), *Labour Market Segmentation* (Lexington, Mass.: D. C. Heath).

Piore, M., and Sabel, C. F. (1984), *The Second Industrial Divide: Possibilities for Prosperity* (New York: Basic Books).

Platt, S. (1986), 'Recent trends in parasuicide ("attempted suicide") and unemployment among men in Edinburgh', in S. Allen, A. Waton, K. Purcell and S. Wood (eds), *The Experience of Unemployment* (London: Macmillan).

Polanyi, K. (1957), *The Great Transformation* (Boston: Beacon Press).

Poole, M. (1986), *Industrial Relations* (London: Routledge & Kegan Paul).

Poole, M., Mansfield, R., Blyton, P., and Frost, P. (1982), 'Managerial attitudes and behaviour in industrial relations', *British Journal of Industrial Relations*, vol. 20, no. 3, pp. 285–307.

Poole, M., Brown, W., Rubery, J., Sisson, K., Tarling, R., and Wilkinson, F. (eds) (1984), *Industrial Relations in the Future* (London: Routledge & Kegan Paul).

Portes, A., and Sassen-Koob, S. (1987), 'Making it underground: comparative material on the informal sector in Western market economies', *American Journal of Sociology*, vol. 93, no. 1, pp. 30–61.

Price, R. (ed.) 'Information, consultation and control of new technologies'.

Przeworski, A. (1977), 'Proletariat into a class: the process of class formation from Karl Kautsky's *The Class Struggle* to recent controversies', *Politics and Society*, vol. 7, no. 4, pp. 343–401.

Pugh, H. S. (1984), *Estimating the Extent of Homeworking*, Report no. 15, (London: City University Social Statistics Research Unit).

Purcell, J. (1983), 'The management of industrial relations in the modern corporation', *British Journal of Industrial Relations*, vol. 21, pp. 1–16.

Purcell, J., and Sissons, K. (1983), 'Strategies and practice in the management of industrial relations', in G. S. Bain (ed.) *Industrial Relations in Britain* (Oxford: Basil Blackwell), pp. 95–119.

Purcell, K., Wood, S., Waton, A., and Allen, S. (eds) (1986), *The Changing Experience of Employment* (London: Macmillan).

Rakovski, M. (1978), *Towards an East European Marxism* (London: Allison & Busby).

Rau, Z. (1987), 'Some thoughts on civil society in Eastern Europe and the Lockean contractarian approach', *Political Studies*, vol. 35, pp. 573–92.

Redclift, N., and Mingione, E. (1985), *Beyond Employment* (Oxford and New York: Basil Blackwell).

Renooy, P. H. (1984), *Twilight Economy: A Survey of the Informal Economy in the Netherlands* (Amsterdam: The University, Faculty of Economic Sciences).

Reports by the Experience and Future Discussion Group (DIP) Warsaw (1981), *Poland: The State of the Republic* (London: Pluto Press).

Roberts, B. R. (1987), *Labor Markets and Class Organization: Britain, Spain and Mexico*. Paper presented to a Thematic Session at the Annual Meeting of the American Sociological Association in Chicago (University of Texas at Austin: mimeo).

Roberts, H. (ed.) (1981), *Doing Feminist Research* (London: Routledge & Kegan Paul).

Roberts, B., Finnegan, R., and Gallie, D. (eds) (1985), *New Approaches to Economic Life* (Manchester: Manchester University Press).

Robertson, J. (1985), *Future Work: Jobs, Self-employment, and Leisure after the Industrial Age* (Aldershot: Gower).

Robins, K., and Webster, F. (1982), 'New technology: a survey of trade union response in Britain', *Industrial Relations Journal*, vol. 13, no. 1, pp. 7–25.

Roemer, J. (1982), *A General Theory of Exploitation and Class* (Cambridge, Mass.: Harvard University Press).

Rose, M., and Jones, B. (1985), 'Managerial strategy and trade union responses in work reorganization schemes at establishment level', in D. Knights, H. Willmot and D. Collinson (eds), *Job Redesign* (Aldershot: Gower), pp. 81–106.

Rose, R. (1980), *Changes in Public Employment: A Multi-Dimensional Comparative Analysis* (Glasgow: Centre for the Study of Public Policy, University of Strathclyde).

Rose, S., Kamin, L. J., and Lewontin, R. C. (1984), *Not in our Genes* (London: Penguin).

Rousseas, S. (1979), *Capitalism and Catastrophe: A Critical Appraisal of the Limits to Capitalism* (Cambridge: Cambridge University Press).

Rowbotham, S. (1979), 'The trouble with patriarchy', *New Statesman*, 21–8 December.

Sabel, C. F. (1982), *Work and Politics* (Cambridge: Cambridge UniversityPress).

Salaman, G. (1984), *Class at Work* (London: Batsford).

Salaman, G. (1986), *Working* (London: Tavistock).

Sandford, J. (1983), *The Sword and the Ploughshare: Autonomous Peace Initiatives in East Germany* (London: Merlin Press/END).

Scase, R. (1977a), *Social Democracy in Capitalist Society* (London: Croom Helm).

Scase, R. (ed.) (1977b), *Industrial Society: Class, Cleavage and Control* (London: Allen & Unwin).

Scase, R., and Goffee, R. (1982), *The Entrepreneurial Middle Class* (London: Croom Helm).

Scase, R., and Goffee, R. (1987), *The Real World of the Small Business Owner*, 2nd edn (London: Croom Helm).

Schmitter, P. (1985), 'Neo-Corporatism and the state', in W. Grant (ed.), *The Political Economy of Corporatism* (London: Macmillan).

Schumpeter, J. (1976), *Capitalism, Socialism, and Democracy*, 5th edn (London: Allen & Unwin).

Schutt, J., and Wittington, R. (1984), 'Large firms and the rise of small units', Small Firms Research Conference (Nottingham: mimeo).

Scitovsky, T. (1977), *The Joyless Economy: An Inquiry into Human Satisfaction and Consumer Dissatisfaction* (New York: Oxford University Press).

Searchlight (1985), 'Hiding in London – four more Italian terrorists?', No. 117, March, p. 6.

Searchlight (1986), 'Bologna accused linked to London terrorist cell', No. 127, January, pp. 2–3.

Searchlight (1987), 'Wanted German Nazi safe in London', No. 143, May, p. 3.

Searchlight (1987), 'Arrest spotlight on London fugitives', No. 143, May, p. 5.

Seccombe, W. (1974), 'The housewife and her labour under capitalism', *New Left Review*, Jan.–Feb.

Seidel, G. (1986), *The Holocaust Denial* (Leeds), *Beyond the Pale Collective* (Leeds).

Serpieri, R., and Spano, A. (1986), *Scelte Informale Nell'Agire di Consumo* (Messina, Sicily: University of Messina).

Shaikh, A. (1985), 'Economic crises', in T. Bottomore (ed.), *A Dictionary of Marxist Thought* (Oxford: Basil Blackwell), pp. 138–43.

Sen, A. K. (1983), 'The profit motive', *Lloyd's Bank Review*, no. 147, pp. 1–20.

Senker, P. (ed.) (1985), *Planning for Microelectronics in the Workplace* (Aldershot: Gower).

Sik, E. (1988), 'Reciprocal exchange of labour in Hungary', in R. E. Pahl (ed.), *On Work* (Oxford: Basil Blackwell), ch. 24.

Sinfield, A. (1981), *What Unemployment Means* (Oxford: Martin Robertson).

Skilling, H. G. (1976), *Czechoslovakia – The Interrupted Revolution* (Princeton, NJ).

Skilling, H. G. (1981), *Charter 77 and Human Rights in Czechoslovakia* (London: Allen & Unwin).

Skocpol, T. (1979), *States and Social Revolutions* (Cambridge: Cambridge University Press).

Skolka, J. V. (1976), 'Long-term effects of unbalanced labour productivity growth: on the way to a self-service society', in L. Solari and J.-N. du Pasquier (eds), *Private and Enlarged Consumption: Essays in Methodology and Empirical Analysis* (Amsterdam: North-Holland), pp. 280–301.

Smith, S. (1986), *Britain's Shadow Economy* (Oxford: Clarendon Press).

Smith, S., and Wield, D. (1987), 'New technology and bank work: banking on IT as an "organizational technology" ', in R. Finnegan, G. Salaman and K. Thompson (eds), *Information Technology: Social Issues* (Sevenoaks: Hodder & Stoughton), pp. 98–113.

Sorge, A., Hartmann, G., Warner, M. E., and Nicholas, I. (1983), *Microelectronics and Manpower in Manufacturing* (Aldershot: Gower).

Spender, D. (1987), 'Journal on a journal', *Women's Studies International Forum*, vol. 10, no. 1.

Stark, D. (1986), 'Rethinking internal labour markets: new insights from a comparative perspective', *American Sociological Review*, vol. 51, pp. 492–504. Reprinted in R. E. Pahl (ed.), (1988), *On Work* (Oxford: Basil Blackwell).

Stark, D. (1988), 'Towards a polyphonic economy: the diversification of organisational forms in Hungary', in V. Nee and D. Stark (eds), *Remaking the Economic Institutions of Socialism: China and Eastern Europe* (Stanford, Calif.: Stanford University Press).

Streek, W. (1987), 'The uncertainties of management in the management of uncertainty', *Work, Employment and Society*, vol. 3, pp. 281–308.

Sweezy, P. M. (1972), *Modern Capitalism, and other Essays* (New York and London: Monthly Review Press).

Sweezy, P., and Bettelheim, C. (1971), *On the Transition to Socialism* (New York and London: Monthly Review Press).

Taylor-Gooby, P. (1987), 'Citizenship and welfare', in R. Jowell and S. Witherspoon (eds), *British Social Attitudes: The 1987 Report* (Aldershot: Gower).

Terry, M. (1983), 'Shop steward developments and management strategies', in G. S. Bain (ed.), *Industrial Relations in Britain* (Oxford: Basil Blackwell), pp. 69–91.

Terry, M. (1986), 'How do we know if shop stewards are getting weaker?', *British Journal of Industrial Relations*, vol. 24, no. 2, pp. 169–79.

Therborn, G. (1977), 'The rule of capital and the rise of democracy', *New Left Review*, no. 103 (May–June), pp. 3–41.

Therborn, G. (1984), 'The prospects of labour and the transformation of advanced capitalism', *New Left Review*, no. 145 (May–June), pp. 5–38.

Thomas, J. J. (1988), 'The politics of the black economy', *Work, Employment and Society*, June.

Thurow, L. C. (1981), *The Zero-Sum Society: Distribution and the Possibilities for Economic Change* (London: Penguin).

Tokes, R. L. (ed.) (1979), *Opposition in Eastern Europe* (London: Macmillan).

Top Pay Unit (1988), *Income Survey* (London: Income Services Data).

Touraine, A. (1971), *The Post-Industrial Society* (New York: Random House).

Touraine, A. (1983), *Solidarity: The Analysis of a Social Movement, Poland 1980–81* (Cambridge: Cambridge University Press).

Toynbee, A. (1962), *A Study of History*, Vol. 4: *The Breakdown of Civilizations* (Oxford: Oxford University Press).

Trehub, A. (1986), Radio Liberty Report, RL 399/86 (23 October) (Munich).

Turner, H. A., Roberts, G., and Roberts, D. (1977), *Management Characteristics and Labour Conflict* (Cambridge: Cambridge University Press).

Ungerson, C. (1987), *Policy Is Personal: Sex, Gender and Informal Care* (London: Tavistock).

United Nations (1987), *Our Common Future: Report of the World Commission on Environment and Development* (Oxford and New York: Oxford University Press).

Useem, M. (1983), 'Business and politics in the US and the UK', *Theory and Society*, vol. 12, no. 3.

Van Ginneken, W., and Garzuel, M. (1983), *Unemployment in France, The Federal Republic of Germany and the Netherlands,* (Geneva: International Labour Office).
Vestnik statistiki (1981), no. 2.
Vestnik statistiki (1982a), no. 10.
Vestnik statistiki (1982b), no. 11.

Walby, S. (1983), 'Patriarchal structures: the case of unemployment', in E. Gamarnikow, D. Morgan, J. Purvis and D. Taylorson (eds), *Gender, Class and Work* (London: Heinemann).
Walker, K. R. (1984), 'Chinese agriculture during the period of readjustment', *China Quarterly*, December.
Wallace, C., and Pahl, R. E. (1986), 'Polarisation, unemployment and all forms of work', in S. Allen, A. Waton, K. Purcell and S. Wood (eds), *The Experience of Unemployment* (London: Macmillan).
Wallerstein, I. (1979), *The Capitalist World-Economy* (Cambridge: Cambridge University Press).
Webb, S., and Webb, B. (1938), *Soviet Communism: A New Civilisation*, vol. 2 (New York: Scribners).
Weber, M. (1968), *Economy and Society* (New York: Bedmister Press).
Weber, M. (1976), *The Agrarian Sociology of Ancient Civilizations*, trans. R. I. Frank (London: New Left Books).
Webster, J. (1986), 'Word processing and the secretarial labour process', in K. Purcell, S. Wood, A. Waton and S. Allen (eds), *The Changing Experience of Employment* (London: Macmillan).
Wedderburn, Lord (1985), 'The new policies in industrial relations law', in P. Fosh and C. Littler (eds), *Industrial Relations and the Law in the 1980s* (Aldershot: Gower), pp. 22–6.
West, J. (ed.) (1982), *Work, Women and the Labour Market* (London: Routledge & Kegan Paul).
Westergaard, J. (1965), 'The withering away of class', in P. Anderson and R. Blackburn (eds), *Towards Socialism* (London: Penguin).
White, S. (1986), 'Economic performance and communist legitimacy', *World Politics*, vol. 38, no. 3. Original source: (1984), *Statisticheski ezhegodnik stranchlenov SEV* (Moscow).
Wiener, M. (1981), *English Culture and the Decline of the Industrial Spirit, 1850–1980* (London: Penguin).
Wilkinson, F. (ed.) (1981), *The Dynamics of Labour Market Segmentation* (London: Academic Press).
Williams, R. (1983), *The Year 2000* (New York: Pantheon Books) (published in Britain as *Towards 2000*).
Williamson, P. J. (1985), *Varieties of Corporatism* (Cambridge: Cambridge University Press).
Wilson, A. (1978), *Finding a Voice* (London: Virago).
Wilson, D., Butler, R., Cray, D., Hickson, D., and Mallory, G. (1982), 'The limits of trade union power in organizational decision-making', *British Journal of Industrial Relations*, vol. 20, no. 3, pp. 322–41.
Winckler, J. (1977), 'The corporatist economy: theory and administration', in R. Scase (ed.), *Industrial Society: Class, Cleavage and Control* (London: Allen & Unwin).

Woodall, J. (1982), *The Socialist Corporation and Technocratic Power: The Polish United Workers' Party, Industrial Organisation and Workforce Control 1958–80* (Cambridge: Cambridge University Press).

Wolfe, A. (1977), *The Limits of Legitimacy: Political Contradictions of Contemporary Capitalism* (New York: The Free Press).

Wood, E. M. (1984), 'Marxism and the course of history', *New Left Review*, no. 147 (Sept.–Oct.), pp. 95–107.

World Bank (1984), *China: Long-term Issues and Options: Annex A – Issues and Prospects in Education* (Washington, DC: World Bank).

Wray, K. (1986), 'The demand for labour in a textile local labour market', unpublished PhD thesis, University of Loughborough.

Wright, E. O. (1980), 'Varieties of Marxist conceptions of class structure', *Politics and Society*, vol. 9, no. 3.

Zaslavskaya, T. (1985), (Discussion) *Izvestiya*, 1 June.

Zhongguo Jiaoyu Chengji (*Achievement of Education in China*) (1985) (Beijing).

INDEX